## More praise for *My Life as a Jew*

'I thought I understood everything there was to understand about my own life as a Jew. But Michael Gawenda's fearless, magisterial book, tracing an arc from Hannah Arendt's "banality of evil" to the casual dinner-party anti-Semitism of contemporary leftists, cracked me open, and nothing has been the same for me since.'

**JULIE SZEGO,** writer and journalist

'Michael Gawenda has gifted us a book of rare honesty that lays bare a social democrat's personal and intellectual life journey. It stands as a challenge to those open to difficult conversations — about heritage and identity, empathy and its erasure, and the point where friendship ends.'

**Emeritus Professor ANDREW MARKUS**

'Michael Gwenda's book is searingly candid and a very good read, though it's pretty confronting for Gentiles to grasp fully the divisions that characterise Jewish communities. He has neither spared himself nor others in examining what it means to celebrate being a modern Jew in Australia.'

**GERALDINE DOOGUE,** journalist and broadcaster

T0349450

# My Life as a Jew

Michael Gawenda is one of Australia's best-known journalists and authors. In a career spanning four decades, he was a political reporter, a foreign correspondent based in London and in Washington, a columnist, a feature writer, and a senior editor at *Time* magazine. He was editor and editor-in-chief of *The Age* from 1997 to 2004.

Michael Gawenda has won numerous journalism awards, including three Walkley Awards. He was the inaugural director of the Centre for Advancing Journalism at the University of Melbourne and is the author of four books.

# My Life
# as a Jew

Michael Gawenda

SCRIBE

*Melbourne • London*

Scribe Publications
18–20 Edward St, Brunswick, Victoria 3056, Australia
2 John St, Clerkenwell, London, WC1N 2ES, United Kingdom
3754 Pleasant Ave, Suite 100, Minneapolis, Minnesota 55409, USA

Published by Scribe 2023

Typeset in Caslon 12.5/17pt by the publishers

Printed and bound in the UK by CPI Group (UK) Ltd, Croydon CR0 4YY

Scribe is committed to the sustainable use of natural resources and the
use of paper products made responsibly from those resources.

978 1 761380 47 1 (Australian edition)
978 1 957363 70 7 (US/UK edition)
978 1 761385 32 2 (ebook)

A catalogue record for this book is available from
the National Library of Australia.

scribepublications.com.au
scribepublications.co.uk
scribepublications.com

*For my sisters, Hinda, Cesia, and Rita.*
*I hope I have honoured them.*

# CONTENTS

# CHAPTER ONE

# The end of a friendship

Over the years, some of my friendships have withered and died, natural deaths caused by change and a narrowing of time, but I am thankful for those that have survived my growing old. These friendships—childhood ones that are still alive, friendships with fellow journalists, and some more recent ones, miraculously recent because I thought new friendships would no longer happen to me, given my age—are no less a part of me than is my family. Not like family, because family is unchosen and the connections are unbreakable, whatever happens. But my friends, as much as family, are central to who I am, how I see myself.

My friendship with Louise Adler did not wither with time. It ended suddenly and fiercely. Until now, I have been unable to write about this ending. I was afraid, and fear is a cancer for writers. I was afraid of publicly revealing a part of me that I have not revealed before, and I feared that perhaps I would be betraying Louise, or rather betraying things between us that were and should remain private. But here I am, finally writing about it, the end of our friendship. I feel the fear, but I am sure that if I were writing about someone else, and Louise and I were still friends, she would urge me to write it, and she would find a way to get it published. And she would cry, 'Damn the consequences!'

Our friendship was decades long, and it ended abruptly, but, looking back, I see that it had been unravelling for years. I remember the date it ended. It was Saturday 9 October 2021, when I wrote to Louise and said I felt betrayed by her. It was Shabbes, the Sabbath, meant to be a day of rest, but we secular Jews do not follow every divine rule of Shabbes observance.

From the start of our friendship, the fact that we were Jews was important to both of us. Ours was a friendship that had started more than 30 years before, slowly at first, both of us taking small steps at a time, when Louise was arts editor of *The Age* and I was deputy editor. I think it was a difficult time for Louise, and I hope I was there for her, and not just because that was my role on the paper. Part of my job was to listen, and try to smooth over — never fix, because fixing was impossible — the internecine conflicts between journalists and editors, and journalists and journalists, that are part of the fabric of most newsrooms.

Louise had a particularly hard time because she was not a journalist, and the editor, Alan Kohler, who loved left-field appointments, had brought her in as arts editor. She was not made welcome, to say the least. Some of the hostility towards her was because she was regarded as a pushy, loud woman. This was and remains a common anti-Semitic stereotype, and is also a way of characterising a woman's behaviour in terms that are never used to describe men.

When did we become friends? In my memory, it was some time in 1993, when Helen Demidenko won the Miles Franklin Award for *The Hand That Signed the Paper*. Demidenko presented herself as a child of Ukrainian parents, and the main character in her book, she suggested at various times, was based on her grandfather, who was accused of being a Nazi during the war, a murderer of Jews. The book tried to explain — if not quite justify—why this man had become a Nazi murderer. When it turned out that Demidenko was really Helen Darville, the daughter of English migrants, Louise was outraged; indeed, beside herself with rage. We spent hours and hours talking about this hoax, about its meaning—not just, or even primarily, for Australian literature, but for Holocaust memory and the distortion of Holocaust history, even for Holocaust denial. How could a hoax like this be perpetrated, and how could a book like this win the Miles Franklin, our major literary prize?

We were furious together, over many cups of coffee. We were two outraged Jews—secular left-wing Jews, for whom the Holocaust and its remembrance and its lessons for humanity were to a large extent what being Jewish meant for us. Louise is ten years younger than me, but our parents were Holocaust survivors—not of the camps, but survivors nevertheless, who had managed to flee or hide when the Nazis came after the Jews. Our parents, the sort of parents they were to us, were shaped by the Holocaust. It sat there, this dark thing, in our families, among the survivors and us children.

This is when our friendship started, when we read that phony novel about the Holocaust. We were passionately angry about this book, and that's how our friendship continued for the next 30 years, two Jews in often wildly animated conversation. It continued after Louise left *The Age* and became a publisher, and I was appointed *The Age*'s editor. It went into hibernation after I stepped down as editor and went to Washington, although we were in contact occasionally during those Washington years. Our friendship needed physical presence, eye contact, and talk, talk, talk. When I returned to Melbourne, we took up where we left off.

Louise did a lot for me. She encouraged me to write my first book and, what's more, she published it. She encouraged me to write other books, some of which I did write and she published. But there was one book that she constantly urged me to write and that I did not write. It was a book about us, really, about our pasts. We called it *Jews and the Left*—although, really, it was never going to be a dispassionate historical survey and contemporary analysis of the Jews and the left. For me, it was going to be about whether I had changed, drifted right, or whether the left had changed so that I no longer could easily say that I remained, without qualification, a Jew of the left. Did we ever talk about my conception of this book? I think we did not. I do not think that is the book she had in mind.

We never talked about what our Jewish lives had become, even though that question sat there, like a serving of *cholent* on the table as we talked about our mothers and fathers and our children, and Holocaust literature, and films and Jewish food, and all the other easy stuff about being Jewish. We did talk about harder things, too, personal things that I raise with some trepidation and will explore later. Both of us have close family members—Louise's husband and my daughter's partner—who are not Jewish. According to the Orthodox religious definition of who is a Jew, both her husband and my son-in-law are fathers of Jewish children because the children's mothers are Jewish. But if her son and my son married non-Jews, their children would not be considered Jews, no matter how Jewish their upbringing and no matter whether they identified as Jews. What does this mean for secular Jews like us? What does it mean if, like me, Louise believes in Jewish peoplehood and in Jewish continuity?

We did talk about this from time to time, but with Jewish jokes about our non-Jewish loved ones, warm and loving jokes, but jokes that circled around this question: if we reject—as we both do—the religious definition of Jewishness, based as it is on blood and matrilineal blood specifically, what then? Do we even need a definition of Jewishness to believe in Jewish peoplehood and Jewish continuity? I cannot answer these questions for Louise, and I am not sure I can answer them for myself, but I will have to try.

Occasionally we did talk about Israel, and I told her that the increasing anti-Zionism in parts of the left made me feel that Jews like me were being cast out of our political home. I had not changed. I was—and remain—a social democrat, a person of the left. But more and more of the left would banish me from the ranks of the comrades, because, in their view, anyone who does not support the dismantling of Israel, either by force or by international pressure, is a Zionist. This is a wildly ahistorical, and destructive, definition of Zionism, because it reduces complex issues of Jewish identity to 'You're either a Zionist Jew or an anti-Zionist Jew.' That is the book I would have written—and perhaps I am writing it now.

We enjoyed ourselves when we were together. Although ours was not a transactional friendship, Louise did good things for me, and I hope I did good things for her, too. I hope my support mattered to her when she was angry and sometimes despairing when she felt that some senior university bureaucrats, who had an oversight role of Melbourne University Publishing when she was its publisher, were treating her—as happened at *The Age*—like a pushy Jewish woman. I defended her when other publishers said they would never deal with her again after some controversy or other, and when some writers said they would not publish with her because they found her difficult. I thought they were wrong at the time, and I still do. When she left Melbourne University Publishing in very trying circumstances, I abandoned a contract I had for a book with MUP because of the way she had been treated.

We remained two Jews drinking coffee and talking, talking, talking. I never talked as much as I talked when I was with her. How is it, then, that we did not talk about those things that would end our friendship? About the sort of Jews we had become, she and I, how each of us had changed, and what the changes might do to our friendship? About Israel—yes, it was about the way each of us thought and felt and worried about Israel, but it was about much more than that, because our feelings about Israel were, and remain, a sort of metaphor for the sort of Jew each of us had become.

Our friendship ended on Shabbes, on Saturday 9 October 2021, when I wrote to tell her that it was over.

Several months earlier, in the middle of 2021, Louise had commissioned and published a booklet by the then ABC senior news executive John Lyons. *Dateline Jerusalem: journalism's toughest assignment* was the title. At first, I thought it was meant to be a slightly humorous, wildly exaggerated title. It was not. Lyons meant it literally. His thesis was simple: the Israel Lobby in Australia had succeeded, through threats and accusations of anti-Semitism, in making cowards of Australian journalists and editors, who regularly self-censored their coverage of Israel's treatment of the Palestinians. Journalists and editors were too afraid, too cowed by threats, to reveal the true horrors of Palestinian suffering at the hands of Israel.

The Lyons booklet was part of a public-policy series that Louise commissioned for Monash University Publishing. Just how the media coverage of the Israel–Palestinian conflict was a public-policy issue is hard to fathom. The rest of the series were written by former politicians, or public-policy wonks. Good and worthy—and, it must be said, coming from the left—but these mostly sank without trace. Not so the Lyons booklet, which had nothing to do with public policy, but which Louise knew would get decent coverage—a journalist writing about the failings of fellow journalists and editors.

Although I was not named, and Lyons had not spoken to me, I felt counted among those cowardly, intimidated editors. How could I not? I had been editor of *The Age* for seven years. I was editor when Bill Clinton's failed peace initiative signalled the end of the Oslo process, which had provided a road map to a two-state solution to the conflict between Israel and the Palestinians. I had been editor during the Second Intifada that followed Clinton's failed peace initiative, when many hundreds of Israeli men, women, and children died in suicide bombings of buses and restaurants and community centres. Many hundreds of Palestinians also died in the Israeli Defense Force's miliary response in the West Bank to the suicide bombings. What's more, I was the only Jewish editor, back then and subsequently, of a major metropolitan paper in Australia. Why would Lyons not have spoken to me? Perhaps he thought he might have discovered that I was not a fellow traveller of the Israel Lobby.

Louise knew all this, because we talked about it after she had commissioned the booklet but before it was published. She and I both knew what Lyons was going to argue. I was not named in the booklet and nor were the majority of the twenty-three editors and senior journalists that Lyons said he had interviewed on the record. They were anonymous. I do not know how many of the anonymous editors that Lyons said he had spoken to confirm his thesis. In his booklet, he asks that he be taken at his word. Frankly, I am not prepared to do that. And nor should any journalist. This is what happens when your work is full of anonymous sources. Anonymous editors—how would any journalist agree to write a story like that? How many editors would publish such a story?

Oddly, the four editors he does name and quote in the booklet do not support his thesis. Two reject it outright, and one neither confirms nor denies it. Lyons quotes him as saying only that the Israel Lobby can be very aggressive and hard to deal with. The editor refers to a particular meeting with a delegation from the lobby. The lobbyists had been rude and aggressive, and he had come close to throwing them out. Poor bloke. An editor being subjected to rude and aggressive behaviour! By a bunch of middle-aged Jews! The fourth editor is Chris Mitchell, who was editor-in-chief of *The Australian* when Lyons was based in Jerusalem. Lyons does not ask Mitchell whether he was cowed by the Israel Lobby. He clearly felt no need to. After all, Lyons was one of the few Australian journalists, it seems, who resisted the brutal pressure of the lobby.

Lyons does name one journalist who was a correspondent based in Jerusalem, who, he wrote, confirmed that the pro-Israel Lobby was abusive and threatening. This journalist was the only one he interviewed, it seems, who had reported on the Israeli-Palestinian conflict. The named journalist, Jodi Rudoren, was not just Jewish, but religiously observant. She is now editor-in-chief of the *Forward*, a left-leaning and storied New York–based Jewish newspaper. Rudoren was Jerusalem correspondent for *The New York Times* back when Lyons was *The Australian*'s correspondent. This is what he writes about her:

> Most journalists based in Jerusalem who report exactly what they see in front of them are trolled and abused. As an indication of how far right much of the pro-Israel lobby has leant, correspondents of the *New York Times* ... have been systematically targeted. Jodi Rudoren, who was from an observant American Jewish family, was attacked even before she landed in Israel. Her crime? After she was announced

as the new *NYT* correspondent, an Arab-American sent her a note of congratulations. She replied with a thank you in Arabic: Shukran. For that, she became a target. Later, a prominent US-based pro-Israel lobby group branded her a 'Nazi bitch'.

For anyone to describe a female journalist as a Nazi bitch is shocking, unacceptable, reprehensible. For a pro-Israel lobby to brand (brand!) a Jewish female journalist a Nazi bitch is beyond disgusting, and that was my immediate reaction when I read this in Lyons' booklet. Then I read it again. Then I went to the endnotes, where Lyons cited his source for the 'Nazi bitch' slur: an article in *The Jerusalem Post*. I read the article. Nowhere in it does Rudoren even hint at her ever being called a Nazi bitch by anyone, let alone by a pro-Israel lobby. In fact, it's a humdrum piece. She is quoted as saying that she greeted people who spoke Arabic with '*Shukran*' ('Thank you'), and that some people had tweeted that this showed she was biased. She pointed out to them that she responded to Hebrew speakers with '*Todah*', a way of saying 'Thank you' in Hebrew. There was nothing in the article about her having been slurred by a pro-Israel lobby.

So where had this 'Nazi bitch' abuse come from? Rudoren must have told Lyons about this terrible attack on her by a pro-Israel lobby.

After the Lyons booklet was published, Rudoren was asked about the 'Nazi bitch' slur. She said she had no memory of anyone saying that to her. And she implied that this was something she would remember, had it happened. She said she would contact Lyons to ask him whether he had a note of her telling him about this terrible thing that had happened to her that she had somehow forgotten. As far as I know, Lyons did not respond, and Rudoren did not pursue it any further.

What does this mean? It illustrates some of the journalistic flaws in the booklet, and it illustrates the deep personal bias that Lyons brought to this ostensibly thoroughly reported piece that purports to nail the way the Israel Lobby operates to make cowards of editors and journalists.

Let me go back to the first sentence of that paragraph about Rudoren's experience with the Israel Lobby. 'Most journalists based in Jerusalem who report exactly what they see in front of them are trolled and abused,' he writes.

Put aside the self-serving suggestion that journalists like him are abused when all they are doing is *accurately* reporting what they see; it is nevertheless probably true that many journalists based in Jerusalem are trolled and abused. But this is probably true for journalists covering virtually any conflict in the world, for journalists reporting any issue or event anywhere. It is true for Jewish journalists reporting from Jerusalem. It is also true that Jewish journalists in America and elsewhere are subjected to organised trolling and abuse—whatever issue they are covering—simply because they are Jews. The trollers even have a symbol for this Twitter abuse that identifies the journalist as a Jew.

But Lyons is making a particular case: the trolls and abusers of the Jerusalem-based journalists—like Rudoren and Lyons—are targeted by pro-Israel lobbyists. Lyons employs a journalistic trick that any experienced reporter should immediately recognise. He goes from writing that Jerusalem-based journalists are trolled and abused to writing that Rudoren was singled out by a far-right Israel Lobby, which called her a Nazi bitch. The abusers, it follows, are organised members of the far-right Israel Lobby.

But Lyons does not name the lobby. Why not? Name and shame! I have been a journalist long enough to know that he does not name the lobby because he does not actually know which alleged lobby it was that did this terrible thing, and he didn't bother to find out. He did not bother to do this fundamental work that journalists are trained to do from when they are cub reporters: check whether what he had been told was true by contacting his source and asking them to confirm the story.

What Lyons does—over and over again in the booklet—is transform every lone Jew who sends nasty messages to editors and journalists, and tweets accusations of anti-Semitism to journalists and editors, and sends messages to editors like me, calling them self-hating Jews. He transforms them into members of this vast pro-Israel lobby. This means he can accuse the lobby of shouting anti-Semitism every time some poor journalist writes something critical, but accurate, about Israel.

It's bullshit. Lyons cannot point to a single instance where an Israeli lobbyist—Mark Leibler, Colin Rubenstein, anyone—has accused editors or journalists of anti-Semitism in their coverage of the conflict between Israel and the Palestinians. He can't, because they don't. It is a straw man. Every sad and crazy Jew who sees anti-Semitism everywhere and in everything becomes a voice of the lobby. Even an aggressive and stupid sub-editor at *The Australian*, who was loud and angry with a young Palestinian-Australian journalist for using the term Palestine, is really a secret agent for the Israel Lobby. It's terrible journalism. And I told Louise it would be.

Did Louise ever wonder why Lyons did not speak to me, why I was not among those 23 editors and senior journalists he said he had spoken to? I have known Lyons for many years. Just before *The Australian* posted him to Jerusalem, we had a cup of coffee, at his request, and we discussed what might be the challenges of covering the conflict between Israel and the Palestinians. I think I told Louise about this, but even if I did not, when she read his manuscript, did she not think it was strange that Lyons had not spoken to me, the only Jewish editor of an Australian metropolitan newspaper, who had had many interactions with the Israel Lobby, both as an editor and a foreign correspondent? Did she not think it strange that he did not talk to me, given I had recently published a biography of Mark Leibler, one of the Israel Lobby's senior people? In *The Powerbroker*, I look at Leibler's role as a leading player in the Israel Lobby. I examine in detail how the lobby operates, how it is financed, how it does its lobbying work. *The Powerbroker* was published by Monash University Publishing. This was the book I had taken away from MUP when Louise resigned after pressure from the board. It had been a tough time for her, and I believed the board had behaved badly. She then acquired the book for Monash, where she was commissioning editor for the special series of booklets on public-policy issues, which included the Lyons booklet.

If Louise had thought it strange and perplexing that Lyons had not spoken to me, she would have done her job as an editor on his manuscript. She commissioned the booklet, and I assume she read the draft. But had she read it, surely she would have asked Lyons why he had not interviewed me. After all, as commissioning editor of the Leibler biography for MUP, she said often to me how fair she thought it was, how I had thoroughly analysed the way the Israel Lobby works, and how I had been forthright about its influence. Did she read the Lyons manuscript, or the Leibler one? She told me she had. Was she telling me the truth when she told me that my book had been forthright about how Leibler used his power in a myriad of ways in his advocacy for Israel?

I wrote an article for *The Age* pointing out that Lyons had not spoken to me, nor named most of the editors who had spoken to him on the record, nor explained just why Jerusalem was the toughest gig in journalism — and, okay, I had a bit of fun with that. In response, Louise wrote an angry piece for *The Guardian* accusing people who criticised Lyons — people like me, I assume — of cynically playing the anti-Semitism card. That clichéd straw man. Lyons' straw man. And the straw man of virtually every anti-Zionist who is challenged by a Jew, Zionist or not.

Who called Lyons an anti-Semite? Who accused Louise of anti-Semitism? Why this response from her? Why did she commission Lyons to write about journalists and the Israel Lobby when she well knew what he was going to argue?

What he was going to argue was there in the letter Louise signed in May 2021 — before she commissioned his booklet — during the conflict between Israel and Gaza. The letter was signed by 400 journalists and 'media workers' and replicated similar letters by journalists and media workers in other countries, including the United States.

It begins with a preamble that sets out the supposed facts — the truth about the Gaza war and about contemporary Israel, as well as its history. The facts, which the Australian journalists and media workers who signed the letter knew to be true, are these:

- Israel's government, led by Benjamin Netanyahu, had unleashed an unprovoked, brutal war against the besieged population of Gaza.
- Seventy-five years after the Nakba — the expulsion by Israel of 750,000 Palestinians — Israel was maintaining an apartheid regime against Palestinians, both in the West Bank and Gaza and inside Israel.

- The only way to deal with this apartheid regime was 'targeted sanctions against complicit Israeli individuals'.

The preamble ends with this:

We believe that the coverage of Palestine must be improved, that it should no longer prioritise the same discredited spokespeople and tired narratives, and that new voices are urgently needed.

Why wasn't this just a little troubling to Louise, let alone to the journalists calling for the targeting with sanctions of 'complicit Israeli individuals'? Who are these individuals that should be targeted? All Israelis who vote? Only those who voted for Netanyahu? What about Israelis on the left who agree that Israel operates an apartheid system in the West Bank but who reject the label when it comes to the treatment and rights of Israeli Palestinians? Perhaps all supporters of Israel—Zionists, Jews, and non-Jews alike—are complicit and should be targeted? Why only Israeli individuals? And what sort of sanctions exactly did Louise sign on to? Did she ask before she signed?

The journalists who signed these letters of course have every right to hold these views. But they do not have the right to state them as facts, as incontestable truths. Each one of their facts—their 'truths'—is contestable and contested. And not only by dreaded Zionists. It is disgraceful for journalists to state as facts or truths what is open to debate and contradiction. This is the road to fake news.

The letter then lists the actions that are needed to address the self-evident facts and truths of the preamble:

- Consciously and deliberately make space for Palestinian perspectives, prioritising the voices of those most affected by the violence.
- Avoid the 'both siderism' that equates the victims of a military occupation with its instigators.
- […] Respect the rights of journalists and media workers to publicly and openly express personal solidarity with the Palestinian cause without penalty in their professional lives.

What this letter calls for, what it urges editors and executive producers to do, is refuse space and a voice to journalists and others who do not accept the black-and-white position of the signatories to this letter — that Israel is the villain that launches savage and unprovoked attacks on the Palestinian people in Gaza, on the powerless and the helpless victims of Israeli villainy.

And who exactly are 'the same discredited spokespeople' and peddlers of 'tired narratives', according to the signatories to this letter? I think both Louise and I know who they are. They are the 'instigators of the occupation' and their supporters, the Israel Lobbyists and their fellow travellers, the Zionists, most of whom happen to be Jews. And, I guess, those 'both siderism' journalists, like me, who practise a form of journalism that does not see the world, and in particular the conflict between Israel and the Palestinians, in Manichean terms.

And who should be heard? Editors and publishers should 'consciously and deliberately make space for Palestinian perspectives prioritising the voices of those most affected by the violence'.

The letter does not say which Palestinian perspectives should be prioritised, as if all Palestinian perspectives — including that of the Palestinians in the West Bank and Gaza, and Palestinian

Israelis — are the same. That is a nonsense, unless you believe, for instance, that the views of Hamas — which advocates the violent elimination of Israel — are no different from the position of the Palestinian Authority, Hamas's sworn enemy.

Can I sum up what this all adds up to? Among the signatories, Louise and these hundreds of journalists want editors and publishers to banish from public debate 'discredited spokespeople' (Jewish leaders), and deny space or time to people who peddle 'tired narratives'. I bet they wanted to say 'false' narratives', but thought better of it and went with 'tired' ones instead.

But why — and by whom, apart from the journalists themselves — are these spokespeople discredited? And what exactly — or even approximately — is a 'tired' narrative?

I found disheartening the demand that journalists be allowed to be partisans for the Palestinian cause. What is this Palestinian cause for which journalists can be partisan? Would it include, for instance, advocating the elimination of Israel with violence? Or attacks on civilians?

But what most troubled me about that last paragraph was this. These journalists and media workers were demanding a wholesale abandonment of one of the central principles of journalism in a liberal democracy: the need for journalists to be independent, open, fair, and not agenda-driven in their work. That's why they have the privilege and the freedom to report the world to us, why they play such a critical role in a liberal democracy.

How is it okay to be a journalist and an advocate for a cause? Is it any cause, or is the Palestinian cause an exception? Does it include other good causes, and if it does, who will distinguish good causes from bad ones? Clearly, it cannot include journalists who advocate for Israel.

What does it mean that journalists and media workers who work for the ABC and SBS signed the letter? What do they think is the role of publicly funded journalism? Can it be partisan? What does it mean that the letter was signed by journalism academics, people who train journalists?

According to these journalists and media workers, what is the role of journalism itself? They do not say. Nor does Louise. Nor does the journalists' union, the Media, Entertainment & Arts Alliance, although it released a statement supporting the right of its members to be advocates for the Palestinian cause.

Louise's signing of this letter was the beginning of the end of our friendship. We arranged to meet so that we could discuss the letter face to face. If I am not mistaken, she did not much defend it when I pointed out why I believed it was so problematic, so wrong. She listened, and I thought she agreed with some of what I had to say. I think she respected the fact that I had spent a lifetime in journalism. There was no anger between us. I was upset, and I told her so, and I explained why the letter was so upsetting. There was, I admit, some exasperation on my part, because I thought she had not thought deeply about what she was signing, and because I believed—and still believe—that she understands little about journalism and its challenges.

Then we laughed together for a while and told each other family stories, how we had all coped with the pandemic and how great it was to meet in person. At one stage, her daughter called. She was working at the ABC. I heard her ask why Louise was talking to me about the letter—me, a supporter of Zionism!—and Louise laughed in response. I think her daughter thought the letter did not go far enough. Then we hugged goodbye, and she paid for the coffee. She always paid for the coffee.

We did see each other one more time, when she told me she had commissioned John Lyons to write a booklet about the media and the Israel Lobby as part of the public-policy series she was commissioning. I was shocked. Stunned. Nothing I had said about the letter she signed had had any effect. Indeed, the letter had prompted her to get Lyons to write a booklet that would explain why journalists and editors had for so long promoted 'tired narratives and discredited spokespeople'. And she knew what the explanation would be: editors and executive producers had been cowed by the bullying and the threats of the 'discredited' spokespeople, the Israel Lobby and their fellow travellers.

When I think about it now, as I write, something wells inside me, a mixture of anger and regret and incomprehension. How could Louise sign that letter and then commission Lyons to describe how powerful Jews have corrupted and intimidated editors into pulling their punches in their coverage of the evils of Israel's treatment of the Palestinians? Presumably, including me. I must have done that in response, censoring *The Age*'s coverage of Israel's evil.

We were both Jews of the left who had been friends for a long time, and it was the fact that we were Jews that made it all so painful. It was not just that I felt accused of being a cowardly editor—is there a worse sort?—in a booklet she had commissioned, but that I was a Jewish editor who, for whatever reason, made sure my paper did not tell the truth of Palestinian suffering. I am not saying Lyons consciously thought about all this, but I think he would have known that, if he had talked to me, I would have told him that his thesis about powerful Jews making cowards of virtually every editor and executive producer in the country was a conspiracy theory that did not stand up to any real scrutiny. I cannot believe that Louise did not see what was so troubling for me about the Lyons booklet that she commissioned and edited.

Yet, on reflection, I can believe it. This idea that powerful Jews, through various means, but mostly involving wealth, have corrupted editors and journalists to stifle coverage of Israel's appalling sins has been a staple of left-wing anti-Zionism for half a century or longer. These powerful Jews do this mostly by offering editors and journalists all-expenses-paid trips to Israel, where they stay—according to Lyons, who has gone on one of these trips—in the most luxurious hotels and drink the most expensive wines. Expensive booze! Devilishly smart, these Israel lobbyists.

That's the soft power these Israel lobbyists employ to shut down coverage of Israel's treatment of powerless Palestinians. How many editors or senior journalists, having stayed at superb hotels and having drunk gorgeous wine, could bring themselves to cover how Israel treats Palestinians? The hard power that the Israel Lobby employs consists of bullying and complaining, and more bullying and more whining, and more complaining. And threatening, of course, but threatening what—violence? damnation? cancellation?—is never clear.

There is nothing new in the Lyons thesis about the power of the Israel lobby. Academics such as Stuart Rees, who set up the Centre for Peace and Conflict Studies at Sydney University, have argued for many years—if argued is the right word—that the Zionist Lobby (he does not call it the Israel Lobby, because Zionism is the foundational source of the evil that is Israel) has the financial power to corrupt, intimidate, and silence politicians, academics, bureaucrats, and journalists when it comes to Israel. Did Louise ever find this sort of stuff troubling? I thought she did, but perhaps I just assumed she did, because, really, it's a full-blown conspiracy theory, isn't it? Involving Jews.

The letter she signed and the booklet she commissioned by Lyons, what did that say about her and me, two secular Jews of the left? I think it said there was no longer the basis for any friendship between us.

When I started writing about all this, I had planned to finish it, and that would be the end. But it turns out not to be the end. I have more to explore about the Jew I was, the Jew I am, and the Jew I am becoming. And what this means about my lifelong connection to the left. I hope that I have the strength and the skill to be honest about the journey I am on. It no longer has anything directly to do with the lost friendship between Louise and me—except that the moment I saw that our friendship was finished was the moment I realised that my journey had begun.

# CHAPTER TWO

# My Zionist sisters

'To be a Jew is not a choice. It is, first of all, a fate.'

— Albert Memmi, Jewish Tunisian novelist, poet, and essayist, 1962 (quoted in *The Lions' Den: Zionism and the left from Hannah Arendt to Noam Chomsky* by Susie Linfield)

I have photographs of my two eldest sisters that were taken during the three-and-a-half years, from May 1946 to November 1949, that my family spent in the displaced persons' camp in an outer suburb of Linz, in Austria. In the black-and-white photographs, my sisters are wearing long-sleeved, dark-coloured shirts, a light-coloured scout-like scarf under the shirt collar, and khaki pants. My oldest sister, who was nineteen when the photograph was taken, is solidly built and looks well fed. Having spent six years in Siberia, where there was never enough to eat, she had eaten non-stop for the first six months of their sojourn in the camp. My middle sister, at seventeen, is less sturdy-looking, though she has struck a sort of defiant, don't-mess-with-me pose. The youngest of my three sisters, who was six years old, is not in the photograph.

I was born in the camp at the beginning of 1947. My parents

and my two eldest sisters had fled Lodz in August 1939, just before the German invasion of Poland and the arrival of not just the Wehrmacht, but also the SS and the Gestapo. Lodz, not very far from the German border, was the second major Polish city to be conquered by the invading German army. Left behind to perish from hunger and disease in the Lodz ghetto, or in the death camp at Chelmno, where they were gassed in mobile gas trucks, were two of my mother's brothers and their families, and my father's only sister, her husband, and their eight-year-old daughter, Chavele, whose name we gave my newborn daughter forty years later, in Melbourne.

The uniforms my sisters are wearing in these photographs were given to them by one of the young people who had travelled to the camp from Palestine to encourage the Jews, especially young Jews like my sisters, to go to Palestine — they called it Eretz Yisrael — and help build the Jewish homeland. These *shlichim* — emissaries — were in most of the DP camps in Germany and Austria.

More than 250,000 Jews passed through DP camps in Allied-occupied Germany, Austria, and Italy after the war. Perhaps half had escaped from Poland to the Soviet Union before the German army invaded Poland. The rest had somehow managed to survive the concentration camps and ghettos. Unlike so many of their family members, they had not been sent to one of the six extermination camps in Poland — Chelmno, Belzec, Sobibor, Treblinka, Majdanek, and the extermination camp that was part of the vast Auschwitz-Birkenau concentration camp complex — where the vast majority of the millions of Jews transported to these camps were gassed, often within hours of their arrival. Instead, they had been lucky enough to be sent to concentration camps, where they were put to work in quarries and factories run by major German industrial firms. In these camps, many Jews died of starvation and disease, and some were shot by guards for infractions of the rules, although what these rules were, the boundaries they were not to transgress, was never clear.

In the DP camp, my oldest sister fell in love with a young man who had survived several concentration camps. His whole family had perished. He was alone. They met at the vegetable garden that they had helped the *shlichim* plant and nurture, which became a sort of training ground for life on the kibbutzim in Eretz Yisrael. I do not know whether my sister and the young man met while they were working in the garden or on one of the nights when the young men and women of the camp sat around a campfire, and danced to and sang the Hebrew songs of a Zionist dreaming. But they fell in love, and within months they were married, not long after I was born.

My sisters often told me stories of 'the kibbutz', as they called the vegetable garden in the DP camp, and of how they desperately wanted to go to Eretz Yisrael—but would never have left my parents and me and their younger sister behind. Instead, after three years in the camp, they came to Australia with the rest of the family. We managed to get to Australia because my father had a cousin in Melbourne who sponsored us. We arrived in Melbourne on board the *Continental* in November 1949.

For my sisters, those times in the camp, the work in the vegetable garden, and the campfires and the dancing and the songs made them life-long Zionists, lovers of Israel, and despisers of all who belittled it or wished it harm. We were in the camp when the United Nations voted to partition Palestine in 1947, and we were there in 1948 when David Ben-Gurion declared Israel's independence, and we were still there during the 1948 war between Israel and the surrounding Arab states that followed the independence declaration.

My mother also wanted to go to Palestine. Two of her sisters had survived the war, having escaped to Russia. They, too, had left Poland before the German invasion. The younger of the two was married to my father's best friend from Lodz, from 'home'. They had three children: two daughters the same age as my two older sisters, and a son who was my younger sister's age. The older of my mother's sisters had also been married—that was the rumour—but apparently her husband had died in Russia. Illiterate, emotionally disturbed, often furious, she had somehow made her way from Russia to Poland, and then on to a different DP camp from ours in Austria, where she was reunited with her sister and brother-in-law, and their children.

The whole group were still there when my mother learnt they had survived. She did not manage to visit them from our camp, and never saw the younger of her sisters and her family again. Her older sister, alone and traumatised, ended up in Palestine, where she was reunited with her sister and her sister's family. In 1955, my mother sponsored her, and she migrated to Australia from Israel. She lived with my family for the rest of her life. Unlike my family, my mother's family had no one to sponsor them in Australia or the US, or anywhere else in the world. All countries had severely restricted the number of Jewish refugees, most of them Holocaust survivors, that they were prepared to take. And so, hundreds of thousands of shattered Jews lived in camps, waiting to be rescued. The *Yishuv*—the Jewish community in Palestine—sent *shlichim* to rescue Jews and smuggle them into British Mandate Palestine.

Despite the best efforts of the mandatory regime in Palestine to keep them out, thousands of Jews made it to Eretz Yisrael—my mother's sisters and their families among them. Many of these Holocaust survivors, the younger ones like my mother's brother-in-law, fought in the war of independence within months, even weeks, of landing in Palestine. Tens of thousands more of the stateless, traumatised Jews in the DP camps later sailed for Israel after independence, legally, to be greeted at the docks in Haifa by cheering crowds. In all, over 150,000 Holocaust survivors had been settled in Israel by 1952.

My mother failed to convince my father to take the family to Palestine; he refused to even consider it. He was close to fifty and had been imprisoned in Siberia for making anti-Stalin statements. He was desperate to get away from Europe, but not to another place where there was likely to be a war, and he had his cousin in Australia who could get visas for the family. He knew nothing about the place, except that it was a long way away and peaceful.

By the time we arrived in Australia, my mother had resigned herself to never again seeing her family in Israel. A few years later, she received a letter from the Jewish Agency in Poland telling her that a third sibling, a brother who she thought had disappeared somewhere in Russia, was alive, and was soon to leave Poland for Israel. He and his wife had two sons and two daughters. My mother apparently cried for days after my father read her the letter. She was illiterate. My father taught her to read and even to write a bit in Yiddish, but until she died, she signed forms with a neat and rather small cross.

These are not memories, but rather stories told me, mainly by my sisters. My first memory of having a family in Israel is of the cardboard box of tinned foods that my mother packed every month to send to her family there. I still have photographs somewhere of us standing in front of a box of food, my younger sister and me waving and smiling. And I have photographs of my Israeli family, a horde of them, standing in front of the cardboard box we had sent them, all waving to the camera. They are vivid, these memories. I was perhaps five or six years old, but I remember how my mother looked as she stared at the photographs from Israel and listened as my father read the letter in Yiddish written by my mother's lost and found brother.

Neither my mother nor my father ever went to Israel, and it was not until my sisters were middle-aged that they went there and met the family my mother felt she had abandoned. Given that they were such fervent Zionists, I do not know why my sisters waited so long before going to Eretz Yisrael. Perhaps they thought it would be traumatic, would bring back memories of what they had hoped to do — and in the end did not do — in that DP camp, which was to go and be pioneers, to help build the Jewish state.

As a boy, I knew none of this. They were my sisters, but they were really of another, earlier generation. What they believed and felt about Israel was rooted in their experience — the war years of exile, the years in the DP camp when no country wanted them, when only Israel offered them hope of a Jewish future after the Nazi genocide.

I was three years old when my family arrived in Melbourne, and I have no memories of the DP camp. My memories are all Australian. Even so, they are Jewish memories. And in those photographs of my sisters in the DP camp, and of the cardboard boxes of tinned food we sent to Israel, and the photographs of these Israelis, and of my family standing in front of those boxes waving in delight, these memories are somehow connected to Israel, to its vitality, and to the threats to its existence.

# CHAPTER THREE

# An unorthodox Jew

I was eleven years old when my mother died. I mention it here because I was not a secular left-wing Jew while she was alive. My mother believed in the God of the Jews, and tried as hard as she could—given that she was married to a man committed to Jewish secularism—to be observant. From the time I started school, she sent me to after-school religious instruction classes two nights a week at the Caulfield *shul* (synagogue), near where we lived at the time and where I had gone to kindergarten. There I learnt to recite Hebrew prayers—the ones for Shabbes, the Sabbath, I'm sure, and other prayers in the Hebrew prayer book for various Jewish festivals, such as the prayers for the holy days of Rosh Hashanah and Yom Kippur. I did not learn the Kaddish, the prayer for the dead, until the day I first recited it by my mother's grave at her funeral, the day after she died.

To be observant is to be committed to demanding daily rituals, to a life as a Jew—a life, in part at least, of separation from non-Jews. For instance, every year before Pesach, Passover, my mother would clean every place in the house that had contained leavened bread—*chametz* in Hebrew. She would check every cupboard in the kitchen, and my three older sisters and I would help her store the contents in boxes in my parents'

bedroom. She would scrub the stove. She would take some of
our pots and pans, and some crockery and cutlery, out to the
backyard. She would dig a hole and pour several buckets of
water into it.

Then, with our help, she would put the all the things that
needed to be made kosher for Passover into the hole, and we
would cover everything in mud, and scrub vigorously until
my mother told us it was done. Like many families back then,
we could not afford to have separate utensils and crockery for
Pesach, and this was the way my mother had always made the
kitchen kosher for Pesach from when she was a young girl.

My mother was illiterate, as I've said, but this didn't matter
much because women did not recite the prayers in shul, and
they did not read the Passover *Haggadah*—the book that tells
the story of the Jews' flight from slavery in Egypt. What the
women did do on Seder night (the first night of Passover),
while the father of the family read the Haggadah, was prepare
the festive meal, serve it, and bring a bowl of water three times
to my father so he could wash his hands at the appropriate
times. All the while, he sat in a big armchair with big feather
cushions behind his back, as was the tradition, dressed
immaculately in his best suit. It felt like it took an eternity
for him to read the Haggadah and to get us to ask the ritual
Four Questions and answer them. He did try every year to
leave bits out, to speed things up, but while my mother was
illiterate, she knew—always knew—when he was trying to
pull a swifty, and she would tell him quite firmly not to try to
fool her.

After my mother died, my two eldest sisters insisted that
my father continue to recite the whole Haggadah every Pesach,
but there was no more washing dishes and pots and cutlery in
mud. My sisters took me to shul each year on Rosh Hashanah

and on Yom Kippur, where I could attend *Yizkor*, the session on Yom Kippur morning that was devoted to prayers for the dead. I could attend only because I was an orphan: people whose parents were still alive were not allowed to recite the *Yizkor* prayers.

The youngest of my three sisters, who was six years older than me, had gone to Mount Scopus College because my mother was determined that she go to a Jewish secondary school, and it was the only such school back then. To pay the fees, my mother worked two shifts: a day shift, and an evening shift in a sock factory. At Mount Scopus, my sister learnt to say the Shabbes prayers and the prayers for the high holidays, and she learnt Hebrew. Although she could have led a Seder, she never did, because she accepted the Orthodox position that girls or women do not conduct Seders. Later, my wife and my children often had Shabbes dinner at her place. She taught my daughter and my son to say the Shabbes prayers. By then, she had rejected the Orthodox restrictions on women.

My mother could not afford to send me to Mount Scopus. A year and a bit after she died, I had my bar mitzvah at the Caulfield shul. But shortly after my mother died, my father said I no longer had to go to those after-school classes at the shul, and that it would be enough for me to go to the Sholem Aleichem Yiddish school on Sunday mornings and on Wednesdays after school for a short session. Until then, I had been going to Yiddish classes on top of those at the shul.

It took a decade after my mother died for me to become a secular left-wing Jew, the sort of Jew I thought my father was. What I realised later was that he had had a far greater grounding in Judaism than I had, and a love for some aspects of Judaism that, in my ignorance, I could not have. His whole education had consisted of his years at a *cheder*—a religious school that the vast majority of Jewish boys of his generation in Eastern Europe went to from the age of five until their bar mitzvah at thirteen. After his bar mitzvah, my father became an apprentice weaver in Lodz. Like many working-class Jewish men of his generation, having discarded what he considered the obscurantism of the rabbis who were his cheder teachers, he became an autodidact who read widely in Yiddish, Polish, and, later, Russian literature.

He also became a socialist, though he was always a fierce anti-communist. From the time he arrived in Australia, my father was a supporter of the Labor Party, a working man most of his life whose Jewishness was culture- and history-based. He was a great lover of the Yiddish language and literature, and a keen student of Jewish history—though, paradoxically for a secularist, he had a spot in his heart for the religious rituals and practices of his childhood. Every early Sunday evening, he would sit me down, and together we would read from the *Tanach*, the Hebrew Bible, though we would, of course, read it in translation, in Yiddish.

My father did not regard Israel as central to his sense of himself as a Jew, but Israel mattered to him. Close family had gone there after the war, along with people he had known in the DP camp. He was tied to his family and to these Jews.

When we arrived in Australia, we lived in a rented house in Caulfield. As far as I know, my father never considered sending me to a Jewish school. Instead, I went to a state primary school in a nearby suburb at which there were many Jewish children. My parents also enrolled me at the Sholem Aleichem Sunday school, a secular school where we learnt Yiddish and some Hebrew. When I was in grade three, we moved from Caulfield to the inner-city working-class suburb of Fitzroy because my parents had bought a milk bar and grocery shop. At my new school, I was the only Jewish child in my class. During religious instruction classes, I was allowed to go outside and play handball against the red-brick wall of the school building in the asphalt-covered quadrangle. So I could continue to learn to read and write Yiddish, my father sent me to the nearby I.L. Peretz Sunday school — the northern suburbs' sister school to Sholem Aleichem.

A year after my mother died, we moved back to Caulfield, and I went back to Sholem Aleichem, from which I graduated when I was 16 years old. Apart from Yiddish Sunday schools, where I spent every Sunday morning for ten years, my father sent me to Skif, the youth movement of the Bund. Before the war, the Bund had been the major Jewish working-class, anti-Zionist movement in Eastern Europe, with hundreds of thousands of supporters. My father had been a Bundist in Lodz. Most Bundists were murdered during the war, and a tiny remnant of the movement — perhaps, at first, a couple of thousand people among the post-war refugees allowed to settle in Australia — set up shop in Melbourne.

Bundists were socialists, anti-Zionists, and committed to Yiddish and Yiddish culture. We were militantly secular. Yet, for all its secularism and internationalism, its belief in a socialist brotherhood of man, the Bund nevertheless believed in Jewish peoplehood, which was about a shared history and, it must be said, a shared fate over many centuries. Bundists suffered for this belief from the early days of Russian revolutionary politics in the 1900s, when the Bund refused to support the Bolsheviks against the Mensheviks because the Bolsheviks denied Jewish peoplehood.

Some Bundists left the Bund in protest and joined the Bolsheviks — and no doubt disappeared into the gulag during Stalin's purges, where, I often imagined, they found former

Bundist colleagues who had refused to forcibly join the Bolsheviks after the Russian Revolution, instead escaping to Poland. They had been sent to the gulag after the pact between Nazi Germany and the Soviet Union in August 1939, and the subsequent Soviet takeover of eastern Poland and the Baltic states, because they were deemed bourgeois nationalists — labelled as Zionists — because they insisted that the Jews were a people. But the Bund was not a nationalist movement. Bundists — unlike Zionists — did not believe the Jews were a nation. They were a people of the world.

By the time my father died, when I was in my early twenties, I was not the sort of Jew my father had been or that he had hoped I would be. I was no longer active in the Bund, and went to no meetings, although I remained a sort of non-committed fellow traveller. I am not sure what sort of Jew I was. I had nothing much to do with the Jewish community. I attended no Jewish functions or events. I stopped going to Holocaust commemorations after my father died. And I rarely went to shul — never for services, and only every now and then, reluctantly, for a bar mitzvah or a wedding.

What sort of Jew was I in my twenties? Two years after I finally managed to secure a journalism cadetship and was working at *The Age*, I read Philip Roth's *Portnoy's Complaint*. I was so taken by this book that I resolved to write a review of it. It was not going to be a straightforward review written in a bland and anonymous reviewer's voice, but a piece by a young Jewish man about a fictional Jewish man around the same age who spent a lot of time masturbating in strange and often off-putting ways, and who had a very Freudian relationship with his mother. I was not much interested in Alexander Portnoy's masturbation, though not too much should be read into that. There was also a lot in the book about Portnoy's obsession with *shikses*, non-Jewish women, and his horror at the thought of a relationship with a Jewish woman.

It took me many days, perhaps weeks, to write the review, because I was a police reporter stationed at the then police headquarters in Russell Street, working afternoon and night shifts, and no news editor was going to give me time away from Russell Street to write ... what, exactly?

What I wrote was that Sophie Portnoy, Alexander's mother, was every Jewish mother. She was a woman who examined her son's stool when he was a boy. She persecuted and suffocated him the way Jewish mothers do. She was a sort of Nazi substitute, I wrote, because the Holocaust was long ago and Jews were no longer persecuted, and anti-Semitism was no longer kosher or widespread. The reason why Sophie Portnoy was a substitute for Nazis was that Jews needed to be persecuted for the sake of Jewish continuity. Jewish mothers were great persecutors.

The piece was published prominently in *The Saturday Age*. Beforehand, the deputy editor called me into his office and told me he would publish the piece because it was well written and a bit like the 'New Journalism stuff' he had read about, and he wanted more young voices in the paper — but, really, seeing Sophie Portnoy as a Nazi? Was that what the book was about? Post the Holocaust, could Jewish mothers really be seen as the new Nazis? I could see that he wanted to ask me about my mother, and whether I had a problem, but he did not ask these questions.

Here's what I think it meant about the Jew I was when I wrote that article for *The Age*. I was the sort of Jew who thought he understood Portnoy's troubled relationship with his mother — particularly the way she persecuted him, even though my mother had died when I was a child and, as far as I know, never persecuted me — as analogous to the way the Nazis had persecuted the Jews. And Jews needed persecution to remain Jews. If the Nazis were gone, why not Jewish mothers like Sophie Portnoy?

I know — crazy. I still sometimes wonder why the deputy editor published my fantasy-filled, self-exposing piece.

And yet, and yet.

What does it mean, for instance, that in the days leading up to the Six-Day War in June 1967, when it seemed that Israel was on the brink of being annihilated by the Arab armies massed and ready to invade, I lined up at Beth Weizmann — which was the home for a number of Jewish organisations, including the Melbourne Zionist organisation headquarters — along with some of my fellow former anti-Zionist *Skifistn* (members of Skif), to volunteer my services to Israel in any way the Israeli authorities thought could help?

Perhaps I was looking for an adventure. Yet that can't be all of it. I never volunteered to go to any other country where I might have been able to help — even in a minuscule way — people in dire straits. I was a socialist back then, an internationalist, and, I thought, not much of a Jew at all.

I later realised that this was not true. I was a Jew, tied — in a way that could never be untied — to my Jewish forebears, and to my family in Australia and in Israel. Whether I liked it or not, I was connected to Israel, the Jewish state. I never believed that the establishment of Israel would 'solve the 'Jewish problem', normalise Jews, make them a nation among nations, as the founder of Zionism, Theodor Herzl, had argued. But I was invested in Israel's survival in part because it was full of Jews. I was unbreakably part of the Jewish people. But I was not a Zionist. I was not a nationalist.

Among Jews of the left—communists, Marxists, and social democrats alike—there were Jews who felt no connection to Judaism, which, in many ways, they despised. Nor did they feel connected to Jewish history and Jewish culture. I knew such Jews. They were fervent anti-Zionists, internationalists—they believed that only a worldwide socialist revolution could free Jews from their tortured history and their persecutors, and allow them to entirely assimilate into a socialist paradise, a brotherhood of man. But some of these Jews also lined up with me at Beth Weizmann, ready to go and die for the threatened Jews in Israel. It was not so easy to reject wholesale the notion of Jewish peoplehood—the feeling of belonging, even if it was a belonging against your will.

But this epiphany that I was part of the Jewish people was fleeting. It did not change my Jewish life. I was mostly a shallow Jew, unconcerned with and uninterested in Jewish issues. Yet when Israel was threatened—in 1967, and again during the Yom Kippur War in 1973—I became an anxious, fretful Jew, and lay awake wondering whether, only decades after the Nazi genocide, another genocide of the Jews was looming.

I talked to a friend, a woman who had been friends with one of my sisters in the DP camp in Austria, about my fears for the Jews in Israel. She understood. She was older than me, and she knew about such fears. But, mostly, we did not talk about Jews or Israel. She was an artist and a weaver. Often, when we talked, she would sit by her spinning wheel and spin the wool she would use in her wall hangings. She encouraged me to write.

She made *aliyah*—the Hebrew word meaning 'going up', emigrating to Israel—in 1972, less than a year before the Yom Kippur War, with her ten-year-old son. Although her decision had been a long time coming, I was surprised, shocked, when she told me she was going to live in Israel. She was dear to me.

She had spent the war years either in concentration camps or in Russia—I don't know which, because we never talked about it. Sometimes, she would say that I should also come live in Israel, but no more than that, so I never took this to be a serious suggestion.

Shortly before she left, I went to see her. I was about to take a motorbike trip around Australia with a friend, both of us inspired by the film *Easy Rider*. My weaver friend who was about to leave for Israel looked at me—dressed in my jeans and leather jacket and black boots, and at my Aquarius silver medallion that hung by a leather cord around my neck—for what seemed a long time. She hugged me, and said she had thought about it, but had decided not to give me a portrait she had painted of me some time before. She would give it to me when I came to visit her in Israel.

It was not until I was thirty-three, eight years after my friend had moved there, that I made that visit. I was based in London for the Herald and Weekly Times media organisation in pre-Murdoch days. One day, the Melbourne *Herald*'s foreign editor suggested I go to Israel and write a few pieces for the paper. It would be good, he said, to have the Jerusalem dateline, and he was sure that the pieces—perhaps a series—could be well promoted to celebrate the paper's foreign correspondents. He liked my work, and I think he made this suggestion partly because he knew I had family in Israel, and he thought I should go see them and, of course, do some writing for the paper. And I was coming to the end of my posting in London.

For the first time, along with my wife and children, I met my cousins, the children of my mother's younger sister. I also met her brother's children, the brother she thought had been lost somewhere in Russia. By this time, my aunt and uncle had died. My daughter—my son was still a baby—loved her cousins from the start. They were so boisterous, loud, and physical, and they looked exotic—not at all like us—and they babbled away in a strange language, and they were constantly hugging my children, my wife, and me. One cousin, a wild young man who liked to drink and fight, told my daughter stories of his exploits in the Israeli army, most of which were probably untrue. He promised to show her the rifle he kept at home as an army reservist. I don't remember whether he did that, but my daughter remembers him and his exuberant affection for her, and she still talks about him every now and then. He died young, in his early fifties.

In 1981, when I made that first trip to Israel, I wrote the series the foreign editor had envisaged. I think there were four pieces, but I remember only one headline: 'Fifty Years From Now, Will Israel Still Exist?' This caused a stir in the Jewish community back in Melbourne. The foreign editor met a concerned delegation of Jewish leaders, and I reckon he apologised to them, because he called me to say the headline should have been changed, but that he was glad I had gone to Israel.

He did ask me why I had not written a personal piece about visiting Israel for the first time, and seeing family and describing what their lives were like. I no longer remember what I said, but back then, journalists did not write 'I' stories. It had not crossed my mind to write anything personal.

And yet in those weeks in Israel with my wife and small children—the time spent with my Israeli family, the way they took time off work to act as guides on our adventure—I went from an attitude of indifference to something approaching affection for Israel. Tentatively, and only over time, I embraced what the Tunisian Jewish writer Albert Memmi once said: being a Jew was not a choice, but a fate.

I learnt at Skif that my fate was to be part of the Jewish people. I still believe that is my fate. But I have come to believe that the Bund was catastrophically mistaken in its unshakeable belief that internationalism, socialism, secularism, and democracy were the ways to vanquish anti-Semitism and to free the Jewish people to thrive. The extermination by the Nazis of the majority of Eastern European Jews—and the vast majority of Bundists—destroyed these dreams at an unbearable cost, even though the Bundist remnants in Australia somehow remained internationalists, true believers in a better world in which socialism would triumph and Jewish life could flourish, without the fear of anti-Semitic annihilation.

I no longer believe that socialism will ever be an answer to the 'Jewish Question', which is to say the persistence of anti-Semitism in ever-mutating forms across different cultures and political systems. But I remain a person of the left.

I am a social democrat. I support a large role for government in regulating capitalism: in taming its excesses, its rapaciousness, and its tendency to work against human solidarity and our natural desire to form ourselves into mutually supporting communities. I believe that governments must tackle inequality—a growing cancer in liberal democracies—in part through a tax system that is truly progressive and redistributive, and in part by creating genuine equality of opportunity that rests, above all, on two foundations of a good society.

The first is universal health care combined with a social safety net, including proper funding for low-income housing, which provides a secure floor for people who, for any number of reasons, are struggling to live decent and productive lives. The second is a publicly funded education system—with no taxpayer funding for private schools—that gives students from all families, but especially those suffering the consequences of unemployment and dysfunction, an education that will enable them to pursue a life of meaning and fulfilment. I believe trade unions have a vital role to play in tackling growing inequality. It is a tragedy that fewer and fewer workers are members of trade unions, and it is a major failure of the trade union movement that it has been unable to find a way to unionise the swelling number of casual workers who are badly paid, exploited, and, at best, treated shoddily by their employers.

The Polish writer and philosopher Leszjek Kolakowski brilliantly summed up the strengths, weaknesses, and challenges of social democracy in an article published in *Encounter* magazine in 1982:

> The trouble with the social democratic idea is that it does not stock and does not sell any of the exciting ideological commodities which various totalitarian movements—Communists, Fascist, or Leftist—offer dream-hungry youth. It has no prescription for the total salvation of mankind ... Democratic Socialism requires, in addition to commitment to a number of basic values, hard knowledge and rational calculation ... it is an obstinate will to erode by inches the conditions which produce avoidable suffering, oppression, hunger, wars, racial and national hatred, insatiable greed and vindictive envy.

Bundists are, in the main, social democrats. They support the sort of social democracy that Kolakowski so memorably described. But I am not a Bundist anymore. There is a word we were taught at Skif that summed up the way the Bund saw the Jewish people. That word was *doikeyt*, 'hereness'. The Jews were a people of the world and not a nation. At the same time, the Bund's work was to help create thriving and culturally rich

Jewish communities wherever Jews lived. That was the future for the Jews, a people of the world, working for a better world for the Jews and for all people. But for me, that dream world had largely been annihilated by the Nazis. And by the reality of Israel. I have come to believe that the seventy-five-year life of Israel, with its almost miraculous achievements and its serious flaws, is the most profound development in the history of the Jews since the destruction of the Second Temple and the creation of the Jewish diaspora. For most Jews, Israel has transformed what it means to be a Jew.

# CHAPTER FOUR
# Falling for Israel

I have been to Israel three times as a foreign correspondent and several times to visit my family, to be a tourist, and to see my old friend who made aliyah with her ten-year-old son in 1972. But as a journalist I never wrote about my family or the times I spent with my old friend. I thought that if I wrote about my family and my friend, my journalism would be compromised — it would be judged through the lens of my being a Jew. I spent a lifetime determined not to be a Jewish journalist. I now think that was a mistake. It was as if I were hiding the fact that I was a Jew. Perhaps this explains why my editor in 2006, when I was the Fairfax correspondent in Washington, could ask whether it was a good idea for me to cover an Israeli election, given the fact that I was Jewish.

I was furious. He backed down, and I flew from Washington in March 2006 to cover the Israeli elections. I went to the West Bank city of Ramallah, and interviewed Palestinian Authority (PA) politicians and senior Hamas officials. I spoke to Israeli politicians and analysts. It was a tumultuous election. Ariel Sharon had resigned from Likud to form the Kadima Party, taking several senior Likud politicians with him, including Ehud Olmert, who was to become prime minister when Sharon had a stroke from which he never regained consciousness.

Likud suffered major losses in the election. Many commentators thought Benjamin Netanyahu was finished. Of course, he wasn't. The war between Hezbollah and Israel in July and August that year was the beginning of Netanyahu's path back to power.

Olmert, meanwhile, before his 2008 resignation as prime minister, and well before his later convictions for corruption and subsequent jailing, offered the PA a peace deal. It would have seen the establishment of a Palestinian state in the West Bank, with its capital in East Jerusalem and a transit corridor connecting the West Bank with Gaza. There was no official response from the PA to the offer. For many Israelis and many diaspora Jews, the PA's rejection of Olmert's two-state plan was the beginning of the end of any hope for a two-state solution to the conflict between Israelis and Palestinians.

I wrote several pieces for the paper about the election. I think most were published prominently. I have not re-read these pieces, and I am not interested in whether I 'got the election and its aftermath right'. Chances are I did not, that I was no more prescient and prophetic about the future of the conflict than the hundreds of journalists and foreign correspondents who also covered the 2006 election.

What remains most memorable about that assignment was, firstly, my interview with Dr Aziz Dweik, the newly elected Speaker of the Palestinian Legislative Council in his office in Ramallah. He was a member of Hamas—at that time, Hamas and the PA had temporarily patched up their differences and shared offices in Ramallah.

He was a small man, his beard neatly trimmed, and he greeted me formally as he rose from behind his large antique-looking desk. Leaning on the wall behind him was a Palestinian flag, and on the wall was a map of Palestine from the river to the sea. He spoke with great precision. When I asked him how he could justify terrorism aimed at civilians, killing women and children, he answered that it was Israel that targeted women and children, and civilians. The Palestinian people had no army, no tanks, and no fighter jets. He said that they had no alternative to armed resistance—against all Israelis. We talked back and forth about this, about terrorism, suicide bombings, Israel's air attacks on Gaza, and the deaths of Palestinian men, women, and children. And about Hamas fighters and suicide bombers. We talked about the Hamas charter and its hostility to Jews, its eliminationist ideology. He said, 'You are Jewish. Do you feel hostility from me?'

The other thing I remember well is a lunch in a busy café on the main square in Ramallah. I was with two PA officials and my 'fixer'. The food was delicious—the café was known for its hummus. It was crowded and noisy, and I thought, *This is like the cafés in Jerusalem or Haifa, or even in parts of Tel Aviv. The people look the same. The hum of conversation is the same.* Israel, it struck me then, was a Middle Eastern country. Even some Ashkenazi Jews—European Jews—like the younger members of my family who were born and raised in Israel, looked Middle Eastern.

Like most journalists at the time, I did not write about any of this. I think this was a major failing of the coverage of the Israel–Palestinian conflict: that Israel and Palestine were hardly ever much more than abstractions in the coverage, with no sense of the lives of Israelis and Palestinians—their food and their literature, their societies. I wondered why we did not let our readers in on the limitations of our reporting. Without a fixer to organise interviews and translate—few of us spoke Arabic—Western journalists like me could not go to the West Bank or Gaza and confront PA or Hamas politicians. We could not just approach Palestinians on the street and talk to them, certainly not in Gaza, and mostly not in the West Bank. Interviews with Palestinians were organised by the fixer, and those 'ordinary' Palestinians were chosen by Hamas officials. It was easier organising interviews with PA officials in the West Bank, but a fixer was still required.

I was too busy being a journalist in the three weeks I spent in Israel covering the 2006 elections to spend much time with my family there. They were very disappointed that I did not stay with them or allow any of them to act as my guide and driver while I was working. I now regret that I did not spend more time with them.

I visited my friend, the weaver and painter, several times in Jerusalem. I had not seen her for several years. She was ill with Parkinson's disease, but she was determined to take me to a small restaurant cut into a sandstone hill that led down to the Western Wall. After lunch, we walked over to the Western Wall Plaza. She wanted me to put on *tefillin*, prayer boxes, or phylacteries. She approached a young man wearing the characteristic garb of the Lubavitcher Hasidim, and he came up to me and took the straps and the little boxes of the *tefillin* from a velvet sack and strapped them on my arm. I stood with him by the ancient stones of the outer wall of the Second Temple while he said the prayer that men say each weekday morning when they put on *tefillin*.

Then we went back to my friend's apartment, which she had bought not long after arriving in Israel with her son. It was in the Old City, in the Jewish quarter, in a sandstone building beside a courtyard of ancient cobblestones at the centre of four buildings where other artists and writers lived. Her apartment was also her studio, where she painted and where she wove her wall hangings. She had become a well-known and in-demand artist in Israel and the US. Her son had become observant. He had done his military service and had then furthered his studies in Judaism at a Jerusalem yeshivah before studying computer engineering at Tel Aviv University.

Over the years, each time I visited them, and especially after the Second Intifada, I found that my friend and her son had moved more to the right. They were religious Zionists, and not of the moderate kind — these were disappearing in Israel even then. They leaned towards the messianism of the settler movement, which was increasingly displacing the secular left-wing Zionism of Israel's founding political class.

In some ways, they had become strangers to me. And I to them. They were now Israelis. I was Australian. Had I lived in Israel, I thought I would have voted for either the Labour Party or perhaps even Meretz, the party to the left of Labour. We did talk about these things, but I could feel that my friend, and even more so her son, thought that I did not and could not understand what it was like to be an Israeli, and what it felt like to be surrounded by people who hated you. But the bonds that had bound us when I was young remained, and we were Jews. We shared a collective fate. We knew each other in a visceral way that I cannot easily explain.

Many non-Jews have explained this kind of mutual identification as an example of Jewish 'separateness', or even as a Jewish sense of superiority.

It is not that; it is not that at all. The isolation of the Jews throughout history was partly self-inflicted, but in the main was forced on them by the non-Jews among whom they lived. It is true that Judaism is a faith of separation: the rituals of daily life, the laying on of *tefillin* each morning, the command to eat only kosher food, the holiness, and the rituals of Shabbes all distinguish Jews from non-Jews. But, mostly, the isolation of the Jews from their larger host societies—in Europe and in the Middle East—was imposed rather than chosen. The Jews were a powerless and threatened minority. Even when they burned with a desire to assimilate, to rid themselves of the curse of being chosen and despised for it, even when they renounced their Jewishness, even when they took on the faiths and ideologies of those who disliked them and even hated them, they remained trapped by their fate, the fate of being Jews.

It is a fate I now accept.

Every time I visited Israel, it became less and less of an idea, and more and more real. I felt connected to my friend and her son, and not just because of our shared past. I felt connected to this place full of Jews, a kaleidoscope of Jews of every colour and belief. I felt immersed in a bewildering variety of Jews, and I felt more connected than ever with the Jewish people.

I have been a journalist all my adult life, and through those decades I thought the fact that I was a Jew was immaterial, neither an advantage nor an impediment. Times change. I wonder, if I were starting out now, would it be possible for a Jew like me—the Jew I have become—to have the sort of career that I have had?

The Jew I have become is one who has grown to care deeply about Israel. I suppose it is a kind of love. That is a bald and startling statement, even to me. Perhaps love is the wrong word, but I do not know what the right word might be. I think it is the sort of love you have for family. I am not an Israeli. I am not an Israeli patriot. I am an Australian patriot, although I believe that Israel's existence is one of the most remarkable, even miraculous, things in Jewish history, and that it would be a catastrophe for the Jewish people if it ceased to exist. This love I feel is familial. Family is mainly not chosen, but it can be chosen, the way Ruth in the Hebrew bible chose to be part of the Jewish family. The love I am talking about is not exclusionary. To have a familial love for the Jewish people, I do not need a rigid, blood-related definition of who is a Jew.

Israel, for me, is not the fulfilment of an ideology or of a religious, millennium-long yearning. Its existence is not a God-given miracle, the fulfilment of God's promise to the Jews, although, as I've said, its founding so soon after the greatest catastrophe to befall the Jews feels miraculous. It's a place where half the world's Jews live. More than that, it's a place where Jews have agency, have won for themselves the right—yes, at a great cost to the Palestinians—to self-determination. This is a right that Jews had not had or exercised for millennia. The result of this powerlessness was pogroms over many centuries, expulsions from many countries, including England and Spain, and, after the creation of Israel, some Arab countries in Africa and the Middle East, and the attempted, almost successful, genocide by the Nazis of the Jews of Europe.

I don't think I have ever talked about any of this to my old Bundist friends or family members—or with my former friends like Louise Adler, people of the left like me. Why, I wonder? One reason is that, unlike me, these Jews—Bundists, and disillusioned former Zionists alike—feel unfairly burdened by Israel. They feel they are being held responsible for its appalling failings, its shocking, even racist, treatment of the Palestinians, its ugly settler-movement messianism. What my Bundist friends see in Israel is confirmation of what Bundists warned would happen before the state was created. We told you so, they say: Zionism, the state of Israel, and Jewish nationalism would exacerbate, not solve, the 'Jewish problem'. Anti-Semitism, far from diminishing, would increase. The sins of Israel would be visited on the heads of innocent diaspora Jews. Bundists did not become disillusioned by the reality of Israel, because they never believed the myths about the place and its history in the first place.

By contrast, many former Zionists who once believed in an Israel where pioneers in khaki shirts and shorts worked in the fields all day, and at night came together in the communal halls of the kibbutzim and danced the hora around a roaring campfire, have given up on Israel. Israel is now a pain, always there to be dealt with, always doing terrible things that Jews have to condemn repeatedly, feeling obliged to say again and again that they are Jews, not Zionists, and have no responsibility for what the Jews in Israel are doing.

Strangely enough, it is Jews who were once Zionists who most strongly and publicly express these views. They are among the signatories of letters like the one signed by the 400 or more journalists and media workers—the one my friend Louise signed—calling for the silencing of Jewish leaders and the suppression of tired (Zionist) narratives. They are like the former communists for whom it was a lasting trauma to discover that they had believed in *The God that Failed*—the title of a book of six self-excoriating essays by former communists, including Arthur Koestler, who wrote *Darkness at Noon*.

A few years ago, I was at lunch at Louise's place. Around the table sat lawyers and writers and journalists and theatre people. Louise was a great publisher and an even greater networker. Some of the guests, perhaps even most, were Jews. At one stage, one of the people at the table looked up from his food and said, 'Zionism is evil—surely that is undeniable.' We were talking about the latest war between Israel and Hamas. This statement felt like a challenge to the Jews at the table, but there was silence for what seemed a long time. Then we moved on to some book or other, or a film. No one said, 'Hang on a minute, "evil"? What, like Nazism is evil? In that ballpark? Are you saying that half the world's Jews, much more than half, who say they are Zionists and who feel a deep and unshakeable sense of connection to Israel—not to mention, of course, the seven million Israeli Jews—all these Jews are evil, like the Nazis?'

I did not say anything either. It felt to me that, in this gathering, to say that Zionism was evil was, for many people at the table, to state the obvious, even though there were a couple of people at the table who I know were appalled by this characterisation of Zionism. But we were silent—I think because it was clear that most of the people at this lunch shared the view that Zionism was a racist, colonialist, ultra-nationalist movement that had driven Palestinians from their homes and had subjected them to more than half a century of brutal occupation. At a lunch like this, I was shocked into silence.

Twenty years before, at a lunch in London in 2001, the then French ambassador to Britain said something similar when he turned to one of the lunch guests and said: 'All the current troubles in the world are because of that shitty little country, Israel. Why should the world be in danger of World War III because of those people?'

I do not think Zionism is evil. I never have, not when I was a Bundist, even when I was an anti-Zionist Bundist. Neither did the left-wing Zionists I knew when I was young. Nor did they—as many now do—consider being called a Zionist an insult. They believed that Zionism was the Jewish people's national liberation movement. They believed that making aliyah and going to live in Israel, becoming an Israeli citizen, was central to the Zionist project.

Many of them went to Jewish day schools, and were members and even leaders of youth groups. We anti-Zionists often met with these young left-wing Zionists, and sometimes even with members of extreme right-wing groups. Most memorable were the games of footy we played, the Zionists against the *Skifistn*, games we often won despite the Zionists having vastly more members than us—we, the remnants of a once great movement and, in the main, unloved by most Jews. We all knew what Zionism meant, and we understood the Bund's history, its long and often vicious ideological struggle with Zionism. But Zionist was not a hateful label for us budding Bundists.

Zionist, anti-Zionist, non-Zionist—these labels no longer mean what they once meant to us left-wing, anti-Zionist Jews and to most of the young, left-wing, secular Jews in the Zionist youth movement. These labels are now freighted with new, dark meanings, and every diaspora Jew is forced to choose which label fits best. And we have learnt that making that forced choice, publicly, has consequences.

What did I believe back then? The world was revealed to me through my education in the Bund and Skif. My teachers and mentors were Bundists, and some remained my mentors well into my adulthood, right up to their deaths.

What they taught me was that peoplehood was not about an attachment to a piece of land. Peoplehood was not nationalism. Jewish peoplehood had nothing to do with the Holy Land, with biblical prophecy, or with messianic dreams. Jews were a people, not a nation. Just as nationalism had brought catastrophe to Europe, Jewish nationalism, we were taught, could only bring catastrophe to the Jews. Our dream was a post-nationalist world, a globalised world, although not the globalised world we are living in today.

We believed that such a world was possible and desirable, and good for the Jewish people. We believed in such a world even after the Holocaust and the establishment of the state of Israel. We believed in it even when, after the war, European states, and Canada and the US and Australia — countries that had done so little to rescue Jews threatened by the Nazis before the war — severely restricted the number of Jewish refugees, mainly Holocaust survivors, they would admit. This, at a time when these countries had mass-migration programs that brought in millions of European refugees and migrants to their shores. In the end, those survivors of the Nazi genocide who were refused entry — numbering close to 200,000 people — ended up in Palestine and, after 1948, in Israel.

How was it, then, that we Jews of the left who had never been Zionists held on to the ideology of internationalism after the Holocaust and the abject misery and traumas of the Holocaust survivors waiting for resettlement? I think it was because ideology and a commitment to an ideology are blinding. And because in the two decades after the Holocaust, in Australia, the US, and Canada, and in Europe, too, we believed that anti-Semitism had finally died, along with its millions of Jewish victims.

Yet it was a paradox. Anti-Semitism seemed to have died after the Holocaust because the world had seen where Jew-hatred leads. At the same time, many of we post-war young Jews lived with parents who were survivors. In a sense, we lived with the millions who had been murdered in the Holocaust. And so anti-Semitism was both absent and overwhelmingly present in our lives. Its absence allowed us our internationalist dreams: the presence in our lives of living, breathing victims of Jew-hatred meant it was near impossible for anyone on the left, especially the Jewish left in the 1950s and into the 1960s, to regard Zionism as evil, or to regard Israel as a colonial state. Who were the colonisers, after all? The shattered Jews who came to Palestine because many had nowhere else to go. And unspoken most of the time, but always there, was guilt and the expiation of it, by the nations who had voted for the partition of Palestine, in the 'gift' to the Jews of Israel.

But the Holocaust did not gift the Jews Israel. That is an obscenity. At the core of Zionism, from the time it became a mass movement among Eastern European, mainly secular, Jews in the last decade of the nineteenth century, was Theodor Hertzl's central proposition: only when Jews became a nation like any other would Jews be 'normalised', and only then would Jews, in their own state, cease to be history's victims and become actors in their own history. After centuries of persecution and powerlessness, the ingathering of the Jews, the end of the Jewish diaspora — of Jewish exile, the Zionists argued — would save the Jewish people.

Far away, in Melbourne after the war, the Zionist youth movements and the Bundists' youth wing, Skif, sometimes met on the Mornington Peninsula beaches where we had our summer camps — the Bundist kids in Dromana, the Zionist kids either in Frankston or in one of the more salubrious suburbs further down the peninsula. We and the Zionist boys and girls would sometimes debate Zionism, and internationalism, and our commitment to hereness. But all of us shared an understanding of Zionism and what it meant to be a Zionist. We never debated whether Israel should exist. We never debated whether Israel was or was not a racist, colonialist state.

The debate about Zionism was a wholly Jewish one, between Jews like us who believed Zionism would not solve the Jewish problems of powerlessness and victimhood and would end up being a catastrophe for the Jews, and the Zionists who believed the Jews must return to their own land, their ancient homeland, where they would live in a nation-state like other people.

As far as I can remember, the plight of the Palestinian people was not the main concern, neither of the anti-Zionist internationalists nor of the Zionist youth movements. Nor can I remember ever debating whether Israel had a right to exist, or whether it should be dismantled and replaced by either a bi-national or a majority Arab state. We thought the UN partition plan and the establishment of the state of Israel had answered these questions. This could not be undone.

We were wrong. The question of whether Israel should exist, whether it should be a nation-state like all nation-states, was not resolved by the UN vote for partition or by the birth of the state. On the left, especially the pro-Soviet left — the Soviet Union promoted the UN 1975 resolution that Zionism was a form of racism — and in the so-called New Left, which grew out of the anti–Vietnam War movement, at least, the question was never settled. It was not just about the question of whether Israel should have been created, but whether, one way or another, it should be dismantled. Because Zionism was and always had been a colonialist, racist enterprise — an evil enterprise, as that person at Louise's lunch table so pithily put it.

What was new about the New Left of the 1960s was its concentration on anti-colonialism and anti-imperialism. Zionism, according to it, was a colonialist-settler ideology, and all such ideologies were racist. I knew some New Leftists when I was at Monash University. While they were mainly focused on the obscenity of the war in Vietnam, from time to time Zionism would be called out as another manifestation of the evils of imperialism. Israel, in particular, was seen to be part of the American imperialist enterprise. For the New Left, it was anti-colonialism and anti-imperialism, reactions to unrestrained capitalism, that defined their leftism. The Vietnam War profoundly influenced this shift from the focus on the exploitation—and liberation—of the working class under capitalism to the exploitation and colonial enslavement of subject peoples across the third world by the imperial West. In time, this would become a mainstream view on the left. Who, nowadays—apart from unreconstructed Marxists—talks about the need to liberate the working class from the yoke of the capitalist exploiters?

But I do not think these were the views of the broad, social-democratic, non-communist, or anti-communist left—who called themselves democratic socialists back then. These leftists, too, had fantasies about Israel. For most of them, Israel had realised the dream of democratic socialists. The kibbutzim were paradisiacal places where voluntary collectivism—unlike the Soviet variety—showed that the dreams of democratic socialism were not pipe dreams. The early Zionist settlers in Palestine were mostly secular socialists, and some were communists. The Israeli Labour Party, in power since Israel's birth in 1948, was like Australia's Labor Party, grounded in a powerful union movement. The Israeli Labour Party and its trade union allies had close ties to the social-democratic parties of the West, in Europe, Canada, and Australia.

One day in July 1982, I sat beside the driver of a car ferrying Bob Hawke, a prominent Australian Labor Party politician. Hawke, who was immensely popular, and who had been the leader of the country's peak union body, the Australian Council of Trade Unions, sat in the back. I was spending the week with him in the lead-up to his first, unsuccessful challenge to Bill Hayden's leadership of the parliamentary Labor Party. I wrote a long piece about the week I spent with Hawke, but I did not write about what happened in the car. We were talking about his mentors. He talked of the transport magnate Peter Abeles, who was a post-war Jewish refugee. Tears welled in Hawke's eyes, and he sobbed for the Jews murdered in the Holocaust and cried tears of joy as well for the survivors who had helped build the Israeli miracle. He had many friends in the Israeli trade union movement. He was close friends with many Israeli Labour politicians. Israel, he said, was the standard-bearer of hope in the post-Holocaust world.

In 1988, in Melbourne, prime minister Hawke was the main speaker at a Jewish community function to celebrate the success of the Soviet Jewry movement with its slogan 'Let My People Go'. A group of refuseniks — Soviet Jews who had originally been denied permission to emigrate, primarily to Israel, whose remaining brethren were known as Prisoners of Zion — had come from Israel to take part in the celebrations. Hawke was considered a hero of the refuseniks, and a leading advocate for the Prisoners of Zion.

In his speech, he welcomed the refuseniks and said they had been an inspiration for people everywhere who were prepared to risk their lives for freedom. Then he went on to say that the refuseniks were like the black South Africans fighting for their freedom, and like the Palestinians fighting for their right to self-determination. This speech caused a rupture with some leaders of the Jewish community with whom Hawke had been particularly close — a rupture that was never mended.

The Israel in which Hawke was emotionally as well as politically invested, the Israel that had taken in all those Holocaust survivors and had then gone on to become a democratic socialist country, no longer existed. In Israel, the right was on the ascendant. The Labour Party no longer had a vice-like grip on government. And the Palestinians were an occupied people, many of them in refugee camps, and the occupation was by then, in 1988, twenty-one years long.

Towards the end of his life, Hawke was not only a trenchant

critic of Benjamin Netanyahu, Israel's longest-serving prime minister, but he was disappointed in Israel, critical of the sort of country it had become.

Bob Carr, a former Australian Labor Party state premier and foreign minister, had once shared Hawke's fantasies about Israel. Like Hawke, Carr fell out of love with Israel. He was like many people in the international working-class movement who had once imbued Israel with a mythical significance, who came to understand, painfully, with regret, and, in Carr's case, with hostility and bitterness, that Israel was not, and could never be, the nation that embodied their socialist dreams.

In the first two decades after the Holocaust, the democratic left in the West believed in the main that Zionism was a national liberation movement, and liberation movements were favoured because they were at the heart of the anti-imperialist project.

I think the disillusionment started with the 1967 Arab–Israeli War, and the subsequent Israeli occupation of the West Bank and Gaza, which had previously been occupied by Jordan and Egypt, respectively. The war and occupation had revealed troubling things about Israel. It was not just a vulnerable little nation of socialist pioneers surrounded by enemies. It was powerful and flawed. In 1977, the left's stranglehold on Israeli politics was broken when the right-wing parties, led by Menachem Begin, won power. Begin was a right-wing Zionist, a follower of Ze'ev Jabotinsky, whom many left-wing Zionists considered a fascist. Jabotinsky had been a writer and political activist in Poland in the early part of the twentieth century who advocated for a Jewish state that would stretch from the Mediterranean Sea in the west to the Jordan River in the east. In the 1920s and 1930s, before the rise of Nazism, he warned that the Jews of Europe were doomed. His ideological heirs in Palestine formed the Irgun, the right-wing paramilitary organisation opposed to the Labour-created Haganah that became the Israel Defense Forces after independence.

Begin, too, believed in a Greater Israel that would incorporate the whole of the West Bank. He was not clear about what he believed should happen to the Palestinians in this Greater Israel—just as the ultra-right in Israel today is unclear about what they propose should happen to the Palestinians in the occupied West Bank, and even the Palestinian citizens of Israel. But Begin always made it clear that the Palestinian Israelis were fully citizens of Israel with the same rights as Jewish Israelis—even if the reality was that they suffered from discrimination in housing, in health care, in education.

But the dream of an eternal socialist Israel with the kibbutz movement at its centre was punctured by reality. And a bit like the ex-communists who lived with the psychological and political consequences of their abandoning so much of what had made their lives meaningful, some of the disillusioned leftists, in time, became Zionism's most virulent opponents.

Perhaps the election of Begin was the beginning of the end of the Zionism of those young left-wing Jews I had known and argued with about Zionism and Jewish nationalism and the causes of anti-Semitism. Many have now renounced their Zionism. Such renunciations have become a condition of entry into progressive circles for Jews on the left. But are they now anti-Zionists, these old childhood acquaintances—some of them friends—of mine?

Some are, although few have spelt out just what their anti-Zionism means. It does not mean the sort of anti-Zionism that I once subscribed to, which had nothing to do with racism or colonialism or Israeli fascism. Mine was the anti-Zionism of pre-war Eastern European Bundism, before Israel was established, when there was an ideological battle in the Jewish communities of Eastern Europe over the best way to liberate the Jewish people after two millennia of often murderous persecution — a battle that continued within the Jewish left even for two decades after Israel was established.

Most Zionists believed that Jewish helplessness and the persecution of the Jews could only be dealt with by the establishment of a Jewish nation-state, although there was always a small minority of Zionists, including Martin Buber and Albert Einstein, who believed in a Jewish homeland in Palestine, but not a Jewish state. The alternative was the Bundist ideology that only through the socialist struggle for the brotherhood of man, the creation of a world of unchained workers, freed of class divisions and class-based racism, could Jews be liberated.

What does left-wing — or progressive — anti-Zionism consist of now? It must be the belief that Zionism always was a racist, colonialist — and nowadays white-supremacist — ideology that has forced a racist, colonialist state onto indigenous Palestinian people with the support of the racist and colonialist United States. This is in line with the left orthodoxy whose origins lie in the anti-colonialist and anti-imperialist New Left of the 1960s.

What are the goals, what is the ideology, of anti-Zionism? It seeks to dismantle the state of Israel and replace it with a unitary Palestinian state. There can be no two states on stolen Palestinian land. A Zionist state cannot be abided. For much of the anti-Zionist left, this Palestinian state would be secular and democratic. For the leaders of Hamas, this Palestinian state would be an Islamic republic. Whether the Jews of Israel would be allowed to live in that Palestinian state is a question about which Jewish anti-Zionists, as far as I can tell, have nothing much to offer, except for platitudes about peaceful coexistence.

Non-Jewish anti-Zionists are divided about the fate of the Jews of Israel in the Palestinian state that would replace Israel. The more radical believe all the Jews would have to be expelled and sent back to where they came from—including, I presume, almost half the Jews of Israel who came from North African states such as Morocco, Tunisia, and Egypt, as well as from Middle Eastern countries such as Yemen, Syria, Libya, and Iraq, and also Iran, from which hundreds of thousands of Jews left, many under duress, after Israel was established.

More moderate anti-Zionists believe that only the Ashkenazi Jews—European Jews and their descendants—and especially more recently arrived American Jews—should be expelled. These anti-Zionists feel, frankly, that the proposition that these Jews have a millennia-long attachment to the Holy Land is just colonialist nonsense. Fake history.

The international Boycott, Divestment and Sanctions (BDS) movement has become the centrepiece of anti-Zionism. Its genesis was the NGO Forum at the 2001 UN-sponsored World Conference Against Racism held in Durban, which ostensibly was designed to develop strategies to combat racism and discrimination. Instead, the conference provided a platform for open anti-Semitism and hatred of Israel. The forum formally adopted a Declaration and Programme of Action that called on 'the international community to impose a policy of complete and total isolation of Israel as an apartheid state ... which means the imposition of mandatory and comprehensive sanctions and embargoes, the full cessation of all links (diplomatic, economic, social, aid, military co-operation and training) between all states and Israel'. Australia, the US, and most of the EU refused to attend the fourth UN anti-racism conference in 2021, held in New York, in protest at the open anti-Semitism of the previous three conferences.

From its founding, the stated goal of the BDS movement, as set out by its co-founder, Omar Barghouti, has been to de-legitimise Israel, through sanctions and boycotts, and to replace it with a 'secular, democratic state of Palestine'. To that end, the BDS movement demands that governments, universities, writers, musicians, artists, and businesses boycott — and sanction — Israel, Israelis, and any Israel-related organisations. While this is not always spelt out, the BDS movement, by demanding the 'return' to Israel of an estimated 4 million Palestinians, is in fact demanding Israel's replacement with a Palestinian state 'from the river to the sea' — a slogan chanted at BDS protests.

The BDS movement, so far, has failed to get the support of any government in Europe, the US, Australia, or Canada, and until June 2023, no political party in Australia had formally supported the movement. In a major policy statement, the Greens declared the party's support for BDS, and declared Israel an apartheid state. This was a major change from the 2010 Greens' position on Israel and the Palestinians, which supported a two-state solution and acknowledged Israel's right to exist. There was no longer any mention of Israel's right to exist in the 2023 policy, which the Greens' leadership declared had been developed with the active involvement of the so-called J-Greens — the Jewish Greens, a recognised faction of the party.

In universities, in particular, and in the arts and in publishing, the BDS movement is increasingly powerful and influential. BDS activists have organised protests — sometimes violent protests — against visiting Israeli academics and speakers they consider to be supporters of Zionism. They have managed to convince bands and solo artists to cancel tours of Israel. In 2022, they organised a partial boycott of the Sydney Festival because an internationally renowned Israeli contemporary dance troupe had received some funding from the Israeli embassy—funding requested by the festival organisers.

Whether they are moderate or militant, all these anti-Zionists support Israel's disappearance as a Jewish state. They want to see it dismantled: peacefully, if possible, by Israelis choosing to leave without a struggle, because they believe that their country's disappearance is morally right, or because the international pressure has become too great; or by force if necessary, which can only mean by Israel's military defeat and surrender.

Is this position anti-Semitic? I think this question leads only to dead ends. It is a form of deflection—both by those who make the charge of anti-Semitism and by those who vigorously deny that there is even a scintilla of anti-Semitism among most anti-Zionists. It is tiresome and frustrating and dispiriting and frightening, this constant argument back and forth about whether anti-Zionism can be a form of anti-Semitism. It is also astonishing that, with anti-Semitism on the rise, with things being said about Jews that once would have been unacceptable, with Jews wearing yarmulkes that identify them as Jews feeling less safe, we Jews, and of course non-Jews as well, cannot even agree about what anti-Semitism is.

To be clear, I am not saying that Jews in Australia are confronted with the sort of anti-Semitism that the Jews of France are living with and dying from. But the virus of anti-Semitism is loose in the world, and Australia is not immune. The trouble is that we have no agreement about just what the virus is—indeed, no agreement about whether it even exists.

In a way, the wearisome, unenlightening, obfuscating debate about whether anti-Zionism is a form of anti-Semitism does not matter. It is a way of avoiding what for me is a terrible truth. What matters to me is that Jews sat in silence while Louise served us lunch and someone said rather casually, as if it were a self-evident truth, that Zionism was evil. Jews of the left, former Zionists, and some who were never Zionists have come to believe that Israel is so compromised, so racist, so colonialist and expansionist, so much the creation of an evil ideology, that, one way or another, it must be dismantled.

It is a shocking thing. In the eyes of many leftists, these are the good Jews. I, on the other hand, have, I fear, joined the ranks of the believers in evil. I have journeyed to the dark side, and I am not the only Jew who has done so.

# CHAPTER FIVE

# The Jewish writers' revolt

The disillusioned Jewish anti-Zionists are more influential in the anti-Zionism movement than their numbers would indicate, because they were once believers. And because they are Jews. Peter Beinart, an American academic and journalist, is not anti-Zionist, but rather what some of his supporters label him, a Radical Zionist. Beinart, who was once a liberal foreign-policy hawk, a Zionist, and a supporter of the war in Iraq, is now an influential advocate in progressive circles for the dismantling of Israel and its replacement by a unitary, secular Palestinian state. Beinart is an Orthodox Jew who, he has written more than once, has reserved seats for his family in the New York synagogue where he worships. He is, in other words, a 'substantial' Jew—unlike, perhaps, the anti-Zionist Jews who have only marginal connections to and affections for the Jewish people. Beinart has become a sort of icon, a Jewish icon, for the anti-Zionist left.

I thought about Beinart when student representatives at the University of Melbourne, the University of Sydney, and the Australian National University—Australia's top three universities—passed similar resolutions in 2022 in support of the Palestinians. The Sydney motion, passed on 1 June, labelled Israel an apartheid state, and condemned what it called major institutions in Australia for 'remaining complicit in the Israeli occupation of Palestinian land'. Supporting the cause of Palestine, it stated, 'is a basic anti-imperialist and anti-racist act'.

The motion called on Sydney University to 'divest from Israeli institutions' and to 'uphold the academic boycott of Israeli universities'. This is the BDS action plan. It is now central to every student representative motion at universities on Israel and the Palestinians. It includes a boycott of all Israeli academics, including those who believe that Israel, in the occupied territories, practises a form of apartheid.

And then there is this: the resolution rejected 'the idea that opposition to Israel is anti-Semitic', because 'not all Jewish people support Israeli apartheid'. That's when I thought of Beinart.

I wondered whether, Beinart, who is building bridges between Palestinians, American Jews, and Israelis through dialogue to foster support for a unitary state, supports resolutions, such as these at universities in Australia, the United States, Canada, and Britain, which urge the boycott of Israeli academics, writers, artists, and scientists as a means of getting Israelis to surrender their state. For these are troubling resolutions.

Perhaps most troubling about them was the attempt by these student bodies to remove from Jews the right to define themselves, to decide for themselves what it means to be a Jew. The original University of Melbourne Student Union resolution — which was passed in April 2022 and later rescinded — defined Jews as people who subscribe to the 'Jewish faith'. This was an attempt to de-Jewify all those multitudes of dead and living secular Jews who have defined themselves as Jews and as part of the Jewish people. It would have rendered non-Jewish the multitude of Jews who were secular, assimilated, and who rejected the 'Jewish faith' but were murdered by the Nazis anyway because they were Jews. After criticism from some Jewish groups that essentially supported the motion, the resolution was amended to remove the 'Jewish faith' reference and was passed in August 2022. It condemned anti-Semitism, but, in my view, this was a meaningless condemnation because it did not in any way try to examine what anti-Semitism is and how it may or may not be relevant to the Israel–Palestinian conflict.

Even with the most egregious clause removed in the amended resolution, it remained concerned essentially with defining Jews, separating them into 'good Jews' and 'bad Jews'. Good Jews are anti-Zionists; bad Jews are Zionists, supporters of Israel. This is the way that Jew-hatred is made to disappear, and the way it becomes impossible to explore the possibility that some forms of anti-Zionism are hostile to Jews.

As a result, the Jewish students at these universities can be excluded and vilified, not because they are Jews—heaven forbid—but because they support an evil ideology and are therefore personally responsible for the suffering of the Palestinians. Many Jewish students will feel—many already feel—unsafe. Resolutions such as these have been passed in universities in America, and in Britain, Canada, and Australia. These are resolutions of exclusion: only Jews who support the resolutions are kosher.

I do not mean to suggest that a university such as Melbourne University is an anti-Semitic institution. It is not. Any such suggestion would be an absurd over-reaction to the resolutions passed by the student union. In February 2023, it became the first university in Australia to formally adopt the International Holocaust Remembrance Alliance (IHRA) definition of anti-

Semitism, including the resolution's explanatory clauses, which define some expressions of anti-Zionism—the comparison of Israel with Nazi Germany, for instance—as anti-Semitic in effect, if not intent. While the IHRA definition has been widely adopted by governments and institutions in Europe and America—and by the Albanese government—significant sections of the left, including the Greens, have rejected the definition because they say it is designed to shut down criticism of Israel and Zionism. In this environment, it was a big statement for Melbourne University to formally adopt the IHRA definition.

Even so, I cannot imagine what it is like to be a Jewish student today at Melbourne University—where, not so long ago, I was the inaugural director of the Centre for Advancing Journalism. I am sure it is a darker place for Jewish students who do not renounce Zionism or agree that Israel is an apartheid state than it was even a decade ago. My children were at university a long time ago, but if they were students now, would I lie awake at night worrying about their safety? Would they be confident enough in their Jewishness, knowledgeable enough about the Jews and Israel, to reject such calumnies?

This brings me to the English writer Howard Jacobson. I have loved some of his novels—*Coming from Behind* is a hilarious early novel, but I particularly liked *The Finkler Question*, which won the Booker Prize, and his later novels, including *J*, which is about memory and forgetting, and *Shylock is My Name*, Jacobson's reimagining, in twenty-first-century England, of *The Merchant of Venice*. I also greatly admired the columns he wrote over two decades or more for the now-defunct *Independent* and, later, for *The Observer*. Even more than in the novels, it was in these columns — funny, biting, satirical, and so very English — that Jacobson charted his journey towards his embrace of his Jewishness.

In 2021, Jacobson wrote an essay for the *SAPIR* journal, which is funded by the Maimonides Foundation and is edited by Bret Stephens, the *New York Times* columnist. The essay is in the form of a commencement speech, 'Advice to a Jewish Freshman', to Jewish students at the beginning of their time at university. Jacobson does not specify any university, or even country, for that matter, because this speech could be given to Jewish students at any American or British or Australian university.

Jacobson begins his address like this:

> It's customary to begin an Induction Address by congratulating you on the hard work that has got you here and expressing the hope that the next however many years will exceed your expectations. I would like to add the wish that you not be distracted from your studies or made to feel unwelcome or uneasy in this place of disinterested learning by depictions of Jewishness, which you, as a Jew, will find hard to recognize, let alone share.

He goes on to describe the various strategies the students could employ to mitigate the pain of being confronted by the anti-Jewish — if not anti-Semitic — behaviour of students and faculty. This is Jacobson writing about what anti-Zionism has meant for Jewish university students in Britain, in the United States, and in Australia who would not declare themselves anti-Zionist. It is not the first time that Jacobson has written about anti-Zionism, but the power of the piece, the heartbreak of it, is that he is addressing young people who have been told they are supporters of evil. It is particularly hard for Jews like Jacobson and me because we never had to live with this sort of hatred — not at Monash University in the 1960s when I was a student, and not at Sydney University, where Jacobson taught in the same decade.

No summary of what Jacobson has to say can capture the power of the writing, its richness and charm, its savage, wounded humour. At its heart, he is urging these students to be courageous and to commit themselves to the pursuit of knowledge, to arm themselves with an awareness of history, so that, at the very least, they will know that what they are being accused of being is all lies. In a sense, this is Jacobson fully accepting his fate as a writer and as a human being — that, for him, being a Jew, connected to the Jewish people, was not a choice but a birthright.

Shortly after the publication of this essay, Jacobson's memoir, *Mother's Boy: a writer's beginnings*, was published. I think most literary editors who work for newspapers of the left, the moderate left — and most of those employed by papers on the moderate right, for that matter — have their go-to Jewish reviewers of books written by Jews about Jews. Louise Adler is one of the designated reviewers in Australia of Jewish-themed books, which is not surprising, given that she was a leading Australian publisher and is now the director of a major Australian literary festival. While I once did not much care that these reviewers were all on the left and clearly not Zionists, I am no longer sanguine about it. I wonder whether a known Zionist-identifying Jew would ever be asked to review a book like Jacobson's. This is a rhetorical question. Only Jews like the Jewish writers who sat around that lunch table at Louise's place are asked to review books like *Mother's Boy*. And I am sorry to be so blunt, but only Jews like Louise, who sign letters like the one she signed—letters that want to silence the purveyors of 'tired narratives' about Israel and the Palestinians—could be appointed as director of Adelaide Writers' Week.

A search for reviews of Jacobson's book is revealing. The Jewish reviewers are overwhelmingly progressive, and secular, and they exhibit a sort of Jewish cultural nostalgia—for Yiddish literature, for instance, and for a Jewish culture that includes Jewish religious rituals such as the Passover Seder and strips them of any Jewish religious or spiritual dimension, so that they become mainly about food and whatever they can extract that fits their progressive, secular, universalist values.

One review of *Mother's Boy* encapsulates why only progressive, secular reviewers are chosen to review books about Jews. And let me describe the almost hilarious—although also disheartening, upsetting, and infuriating—consequences.

I do not intend to review *Mother's Boy* here, but suffice it to say that it is the story of the author's journey to becoming a writer, a particular kind of writer—a Jewish writer. Jacobson writes about how his childhood in Manchester with his immediate family and his aunts and uncles, the influence of his teachers and his time at Cambridge, his girlfriends, his marriages, and his divorces all led, eventually, when he was almost forty years old, to his writing and publishing his first novel. The thing is, it was not just a first novel, but, in Jacobson's own words, it was a Jewish novel.

*Mother's Boy* is a memoir about how Jacobson became a Jewish writer, and about all that this has meant for him. I know of no other writers in English—not Saul Bellow, not Philip Roth, not Norman Mailer, and certainly no English writer—who has described himself or herself as a Jewish writer. They were all writers who happened to be Jewish. Indeed, all of them rejected the 'Jewish writer' label.

In *The Guardian* on 27 February 2022, under the headline 'Mother's Boy: a literary titan ill at ease in the world', Joe Moshenska begins his review of the book with a memory of his grandmother, who reminds him, he writes, of Jacobson's mother:

> I thought often of her and her life as I read *Mother's Boy* and its insights into the frustrations, possibilities and intensities of human lives and of the lives of British Jews in particular.

The 'possibilities and intensities of human lives ... of British Jews'. What could that possibly mean? Moshenska is a professor of literature at Oxford.

Moshenska then writes of Jacobson's tortured and anxiety-filled journey to becoming a writer. While this part of the review is not too bad — not great, mind you, but not too bad — it hints at what is to come. Moshenska writes that a 'sense of a necessarily ill fit with his environment is what, for Jacobson, makes being a British Jewish writer the most naturally unnatural thing to be'. Again, I literally have no idea what 'naturally unnatural' can possibly mean. Except it must be something not too good — who wants to be naturally unnatural?

Jacobson's memoir ends at the point when he finally manages to write a novel, after years of dreaming of writing one, pretending to write one, not writing one, and despairing that he never will write one. And how does he finally manage it? When he realises that if he is to be a novelist, he will be a Jewish novelist, and that the main character in his first novel and in most of his subsequent novels will be Jewish. He goes on to write about what it has meant for him to come to this realisation.

It doesn't quite end there. Jacobson writes in the final

chapter that after decades of being immersed in the great works of English literature, he is reading Gershom Scholem, and Maimonides, and the Talmud. He writes about how, after two marriages to non-Jewish women, in 2005 he married the documentary producer Jenny de Jong, in a religious ceremony conducted by Britain's chief rabbi, Jonathan Sacks.

These are interesting revelations from one of Britain's most renowned contemporary writers, no? It certainly put in context for me that piece he wrote for *SAPIR*, addressed to Jewish university students, in which he so powerfully identifies with and proclaims his membership of the Jewish people.

How does Moshenska deal with this?

The ending of Jacobson's book is underwhelming, as the nomadic and contorted lost soul, unable comfortably to write or to be, makes way for the celebrated novelist. The belated success of his first novel makes it easier for Jacobson to be a writer but also easier for him 'to enjoy some of the more humdrum pleasures of unquestioning tribalism'.

'Unquestioning tribalism'. What a strange and demeaning term that is. Moshenska is made uncomfortable because he does not consider himself a 'tribal' Jew. He misunderstands—because he must—what Jacobson means when he writes of how finally accepting that he is a Jewish writer made it easy for him to accept the trivial and not-so-trivial features of being a Jew who feels a deep connection to the Jewish people.

In the final paragraph of the review, Moshenska writes of his real problem with Jacobson. Here we get to understand again why only Jews like Moshenska get to review books like Jacobson's in the left-leaning media:

It's been a funny old time to be Jewish in the UK in the past five years (by which I mean a deeply unfunny time) … Jacobson's book makes clear that he is more concerned than I am about the spectre of left-wing anti-Semitism, which, while it certainly exists, troubles me less than … the unedifying spectacle last year of minor celebrities and Twitter personalities grinningly accepting the gift of a tree planted in Israel 'on behalf of "the Jewish community of the UK", without questioning whether there is such a single entity or who has a right to speak on its behalf.

Here's what Moshenska meant when he wrote that being Jewish in the UK in the past five years had been 'deeply unfunny'. It was not deeply unfunny because the British Labour Party led by Jeremy Corbyn — who, at the very least, did not like Jews very much — had a serious anti-Semitism problem that led many Labour-supporting Jews and several Jewish Labour MPs to quit the party. It was not deeply unfunny because an independent inquiry later concluded that British Labour had a serious anti-Semitism problem and, as a consequence, anti-Semites were (finally) expelled from the party.

None of this was what Moshenska found hard to take. To him, left-wing anti-Semitism was a minor problem. No, what concerned him instead was the 'unedifying spectacle of minor celebrities and Twitter personalities' accepting the gift of a tree to be planted in Israel. Not just that, but these lumpen, brainless personalities accepted the gift 'on behalf of the Jewish community in the UK'. They'd been fooled by the Jews because, Moshenska writes, there is no such thing as a Jewish community, a 'single entity', and therefore those who claim to speak on its behalf are speaking on behalf of no one but themselves.

All this, over the gift of a tree that would be planted in Israel! What is Moshenska doing here, what is he thinking and feeling and wanting to make clear? I think he is signalling that he is a good Jew, an anti-Zionist, unlike those bad Zionist Jews who fooled those brainless celebrities into planting a tree in Israel. And he is saying that good Jews do not accept that they are part of a 'single entity', the Jewish community, for such a thing as the Jewish community or Jewish peoplehood does not exist.

There is more to Moshenska's dismissal of left-wing anti-Semitism as a minor issue than his implied defence of Corbyn and Corbyn's followers in the Labour Party. The Labour Club at Oxford University, where Moshenska is a professor of English, was the subject in 2016 of accusations that it had been infected with institutional anti-Semitism, leading to an inquiry that confirmed many of the allegations. A co-chair of the club resigned because, he said, many members of the club and the Oxford student left generally had a problem with Jews. He said Jewish club members were regularly called Zios, which the inquiry found was an unequivocally anti-Semitic term. Moshenska has nothing to say about any of this in his review of Jacobson's book. I assume that the last thing he wants is to be seen criticising anti-Zionists.

Implicit in this, I believe, is an acceptance by Moshenska of the widespread left position that Zionists or Jews who charge that some forms of left-wing anti-Zionism might be anti-Semitic do so in order to silence criticism of Israel. No inquiry and certainly no claim by students about anti-Semitism in the Oxford University Labour Club could change that position: Jews who complain about anti-Semitism do so for nefarious reasons. In this way, left-wing anti-Semitism is reduced to a minor issue, if it is an issue at all.

Like Moshenska, David Mamet, the renowned American playwright, is a dissident Jew, but a dissident whom Moshenska would despise. Unlike Jacobson, Mamet is not a 'Jewish' writer. His thirty-six plays and twenty-nine screenplays are not about Jews. Perhaps his most lauded play, the Pulitzer Prize-winning *Glengarry Glen Ross*, is set in a Chicago real estate office where four unethical and morally broken real estate agents play out their disappointments and failures. Mamet, an eclectic and wide-ranging playwright and screenwriter, whose film credits include the political satire *Wag the Dog, The Untouchables*, and *Phil Spector,* was for most of his writing life a self-identified American liberal, although one not entirely on board with every element of the liberal playbook.

But late in life — he is in his seventies — Mamet has become a Jewish writer. Not of plays or screenplays, but of polemical essays and columns, often brilliantly written; satirical, vicious pieces of writing mostly published by the conservative magazine *The National Weekly.* A collection of the columns was published in book form early in 2022. *Recessional: the death of free speech and the cost of a free lunch* is essentially an excoriation of contemporary liberalism, of identity politics, of the social justice movement, of the ideology of anti-racism, and, yes, of anti-Zionism and anti-Semitism.

Mamet has travelled a long way down the road from a sort of inherited liberalism — his Jewish parents were first-generation Americans from Poland and Lithuania, and were, according to Mamet, communists — to the populist right-wing radicalism of Donald Trump. He is for Donald Trump. Apart from receiving notes of dismissal, faux sadness, and disappointment in the few brief reviews of his book in American mainstream newspapers and magazines, Mamet's stance has disqualified him — perhaps America's greatest playwright of the last half-century — from any serious consideration of his views and analysis of American culture.

A decade or more before this book was published, before Mamet had arrived at his Trump epiphany, but when he was already well down that road, Howard Jacobson wrote a column in *The Observer* about appearing with Mamet at a literary event organised by a Jewish communal organisation in London. The organisers, for obvious reasons, had wanted Jacobson and Mamet to talk about being Jewish writers. Mamet refused. Jacobson was left alone to talk about his journey back into that place where he felt connected to and part of the Jewish people.

In the column, Jacobson considers Mamet's conversion to a Trump-supporting populist unimportant, arguing that Mamet is a writer and that he should be judged on his literary work. He says that great writers do not necessarily have political views that mean very much at all. Jacobson does not share Mamet's journey to the populist right; nevertheless, there is part of the journey they do share: their journey into what it means to be a Jew. For both, it involves their immersion into Judaism and its holy texts. Their rejection of anti-Zionism and what they both insist is a form of anti-Semitism — Jacobson despises Jeremy Corbyn and his acolytes — is both a product of this immersion and, at the same time, pre-existed it, and had been a trigger for their journeys into Judaism and Jewish peoplehood.

In the spring 2022 edition of *SAPIR*, Mamet published a biting, savage, lacerating essay entitled 'Zionism and the Necessity of Choice'. Its targets are the Jews — American Jews, in particular — whose Jewishness involves reducing Judaism to 'good works', the way that many left-wing secular Jews and Reform Jews, especially in America, regard Judaism as an exhortation for Jews to perform and embrace *tikkun olam* (repairing the world):

> To reduce Judaism to 'good works' (the current *reductio ad nihilo* of Reform) is to denature it not only to an identity with Christianity; but, beyond, into po-faced agnosticism …

Here is Mamet on Jewish fate and the impossibility of assimilation through reducing Judaism to good works:

> The trouble, for the Jews, is the necessity of choice: In or out. Are you, that is, siding with your people, or betting that, uniquely in human history, the host culture in which you live will not, eventually, revert to destroying you, should you attract its notice, awakening envy by your success and savagery by your differences? How do the frightened propitiate their opponents? What could be a greater proof of sincerity than indictment of one's kind?
>
> One might stand with his people from a sense of joy, or responsibility, or gratitude, or even obligation. Or one might do so from the most practical consideration: Who is likely to defend me when the general population loses its mind?

Reading this, I thought of the Jews of France—the largest Jewish community in Europe—who are emigrating in increasing numbers to Israel and to the United States because they feel increasingly unsafe. The numbers are not large, not yet, but amount to hundreds a month, and they are increasing. The killing of Jews—in schools and supermarkets, in their apartments, and on the streets of their cities—has become somehow normalised. The fact that Jews cannot walk down the streets wearing signifiers of their Jewishness has been normalised. Perhaps the most widely reported attack was on 9 January 2015, two days after the *Charlie Hebdo* shootings, when a gunman entered a kosher supermarket in Paris. He held the staff and patrons hostage, and demanded that the suspects for the *Charlie Hebdo* murders, who were at the time surrounded by police, not be harmed. He shot and killed four of the Jews in the supermarket before police stormed the supermarket and killed him.

And in this environment, where Jews were being murdered with a sort of morally deadening regularity, several leading French philosophers and public intellectuals — including André Glucksmann, Alain Finkielkraut, Pascal Bruckner, and Bernard-Henri Lévy — came out as supporters of Israel and as trenchant critics of the part of the left that was, at best, silent about the attacks on Jews by radical Islamists and who, in the main, excused the attackers on the basis that they were the victims of racism and colonialism. These philosophers — most but not all of whom are Jews — were part of a group of former Marxist intellectuals that in 1976 Lévy labelled the New Philosophers.

The New Philosophers were originally disillusioned Marxists — their eyes opened to Marxism and communism by Aleksandr Solzhenitsyn's *The Gulag Archipelago*, by the revelations of Mao's crimes against the Chinese people, and by the murderous brutality of the Khmer Rouge in Cambodia. They were apostates — despised, as is inevitably the case on the left, by their former comrades. They still are despised; as are, even more so, the Jews among them who support Israel's right to exist.

Lévy is perhaps the most despised by his former comrades. In many ways, his has been a French version of Mamet's journey away from the left, although Mamet was never a Marxist, and Lévy remains, in his view, a person of the left, though not of the mainstream left in France. Their journeys are different because Mamet is American, and Lévy is French, and their experience of anti-Semitism and anti-Zionism on the left is different. In the main, there is no significant Islamist population in America like there is in France.

The French right has a long—and dishonourable—history of anti-Semitism, manifested perhaps most vividly in the false accusation that French army officer Alfred Dreyfus, a Jew, had spied for the Germans against his nation. It was the conviction of Dreyfus, in 1894, on concocted evidence, and his imprisonment on Devil's Island, that convinced the Austrian Jewish journalist Theodor Herzl, the founding father of political Zionism, that Jews needed to be 'normalised', to live in their own state and to be actors in their own destiny, rather than helpless victims.

Right-wing French anti-Semitism did not die with the Holocaust. Jean-Marie Le Pen, the founder, in 1972, of the National Front, remains a Holocaust denier, or at the very least a minimiser, who has dismissed the Holocaust as an irrelevant detail in French history. The front was later renamed National Rally, and is now led by his daughter, Marine Le Pen. She received over 40 per cent of the vote in the run-off for the presidency against Emmanuel Macron in 2022.

But what troubles these former New Philosophers most are French radical Islamists, who are responsible for most of the anti-Semitic murders of Jews in France over the past decade or longer, and their supporters on the left. In an interview with the German magazine *Der Spiegel* on 4 December 2019, Alain Finkielkraut, one of the most influential of the New Philosophers, had this to say about Islamism, anti-Semitism, and the French left:

> In France, [anti-Semitism] is part of the extreme left and a growing part of the population with a migration background. It is particularly worrying that the extreme left defends radical

anti-Semitic Islam for two reasons: ideologically because, for them, the Muslims are the new Jews, the disenfranchised; but also, for tactical reasons, because today there are many more Muslims than Jews in France …

Because of the existence of Israel, the Jews are now considered racists. 'Filthy Jews'—that was a morally disgraceful term. 'Dirty racists'—that is highly moral today. Memory [of Nazi and fascist anti-Semitism] blinds us to the reality of the present … we do not recognise the new forms of anti-Semitism and when we do recognise them, we underestimate them.

In September 2022, the Jewish People Policy Institute, a non-profit Jerusalem-based NGO, released the results of a survey of Jewish communities in Europe and the US. It confirmed Finkielkraut's characterisation of French anti-Semitism: coming from 'the extreme left fringe', this anti-Semitism 'often conceals itself behind the mask of human rights and egalitarianism':

The Jewish State is frequently described by activists in these movements as the last bastion of colonialism, an evil entity that should be dismantled. This is often accompanied by age-old anti-Semitic tropes, creating a hostile environment for Jews.

According to the report, 20 per cent of French Jews have been physically assaulted; 37 per cent feel insecure often or from time to time; and 45 per cent of Jewish parents 'ask their children not to disclose their religion'. The report does not identify the perpetrators of the assaults and threats, but it implies that the rhetoric of anti-Zionist left-wing extremists creates an environment in which some Islamists feel encouraged to go out and attack Jews—even to kill Jews.

Finkielkraut is not afraid to talk about Islamist attacks on Jews. For his trouble, he has been subjected to hate campaigns on Twitter. During a yellow vest protest on 16 February 2019, Finkielkraut, a sixty-nine-year-old man, was surrounded by a gang of protesters who shouted anti-Semitic abuse at him. He had to be rescued by the police. He is fearless, and so is Bernard-Henri Lévy.

At an event to publicise his book *The Genius of Judaism*, held at the 92nd Street Y in Manhattan in January 2017, Lévy stated his unequivocal support for Israel, and labelled anti-Zionism 'the new dressing for the old passion of anti-Semitism'. He is the most forthright supporter of Israel among these former New Philosophers, and the most forthright in labelling anti-Zionism as a form of anti-Semitism:

> If you are anti-Zionist, that means you wish for a huge disaster for the Jewish people ... I am unconditionally partisan to Israel. Israel's story is one of the greatest human and political adventures of modern times.

Lévy has maintained that position through two wars in Gaza and through a time of growing pessimism about the possibility of a two-state solution to the conflict between Israel and the Palestinians being achieved. In his unswerving support of Israel, in his view that Israel's existence is essential for Jewish continuity, his Jewish journey is not that different from Mamet's. Like Mamet—and like Howard Jacobson, for that matter—Lévy is convinced that the Jews are in greater danger, subjected to more hatred, disguised as anti-Zionism, than they have been since the Holocaust.

In the *SAPIR* piece, Mamet writes that Zionism is:

... the defended assertion that a people has the right to live in peace in its own home — a right endorsed by the UN and all human-rights councils; their endorsement withheld from but one group. We know from the Torah that Hashem says of Israel, *Those who bless you will be blessed, and those who curse you will be cursed.* Normalizing the indictment of Israel is anti-Semitism. Historically, it is an entry-level step to chaos.

While I believe there is no evidence in Jewish history to suggest that HaShem, or God, curses those who curse the Jews, something in me reacts viscerally to the power, the bluntness, the un-equivocation of Mamet's words, his lack of concern for what the *goyim* may think of him and the Judaism that separates him from them.

I am not traveling down Mamet's road towards Trumpism. It is a mystery to me that a writer of Mamet's stature could be a Trump supporter. Neither are Finkielkraut, or Lévy, or Jacobson travelling down Mamet's road. They may have been cast out of the left, but they have not flown into the arms of the populist right. I remain — and believe I will remain — a Jew of the left, even if, in some parts of the left, my membership might be, at best, suspended. In the end, I don't understand how a Jew like Mamet can support Trump, given what he must surely know of Trump's racism, misogyny, authoritarianism, and brutality, and his dislike of the Jews.

But Mamet's view of the progressive Jews, the non-Zionist and anti-Zionist Jews who have reduced Judaism to a social justice movement — universalised it — resonates with me. For a long time, I have struggled with this Jewish universalism. I grew up with it. We universalised everything that we felt made

us Jews—our Yiddish culture, our commitment to the socialist
creed of the brotherhood of man, our love and support for the
powerless of the world, the Stranger, the victims of racism and
capitalism.

Many years ago, I wrote a script with an old friend of mine
for a musical show that told the history of the Jews through
Yiddish music and song. We had grown up together in Skif.
I wrote a draft that he didn't like very much. He sent it back
to me with his corrections and changes. What he had mostly
done was eliminate all references to Jews. The script became a
history of people who wrote and sang in Yiddish, and who were
often oppressed and who suffered discrimination and racism,
like many other people in the world. He transformed Yiddish
into a universal, de-Jewified language, and Yiddish song into
the songs of oppressed people everywhere. Yet the music and
songs were full of Jewish particulars. How could it be otherwise,
given that these songs and this music came from the shtetls of
Eastern Europe, where the Jews were mostly pious, and where
Yiddish songs, the greatest of them, were about these pious
Jews?

One of the greatest of these songs was 'Oyfn Pripetshik—In
the Fireplace'—in which a group of small children sit in
a classroom by the open fire and their teacher, their *rebbe*, is
talking to them, teaching them the Hebrew alphabet, the
Hebrew of their prayer books. Two verses go like this:

Remember, dear children
What you are learning here.
Repeat it again and again,
*Komets-alef* [a letter in the Hebrew alphabet] is pronounced
'o'! …

When you are older, children,
You will understand
How many tears and laments
These letters contain.

How, then, was it possible for my old friend, a writer widely admired and loved, especially by those on the left, to de-particularise, to almost entirely delete, the word 'Jew' from our script, which was a history of Eastern European Jews — most of whom were not universalists — told through song and music? Until the Nazis murdered most of them, Eastern Europe hsd been the centre of Jewish life, and the home of the greatest thinkers and rabbis of Judaism.

It was possible because we grew up as universalist, secular, and left-wing Jews, and Yiddish was our secular, left-wing language. We spoke and were taught a Yiddish that contained less of the *loshn-koydesh* (Hebrew and Aramaic) component than the written or formal language. This meant we had difficulty understanding a lot of the vocabulary deriving from religious teachings, debates, or texts that Yiddish-speaking male Jews with a traditional, pious upbringing had no trouble with.

The Yiddish of the great foundational Yiddish writers is full of words and phrases deriving from the Hebrew and Aramaic of the Torah, Talmud, and other holy books of Judaism, and without exposure to these holy books, this style of Yiddish is hard to follow. That was not our Yiddish. Ours was the language of Jewish universalism, and we were taught that the Zionists were determined to destroy Yiddish. So our attachment to Yiddish was an ideological as well as a cultural stance.

The Bolsheviks and the Soviet Union did a more drastic job of making Yiddish a secular, revolutionary language than the Bundists did. Once Stalin came to power, the Soviet Yiddish poets, novelists, and playwrights were forced to write in the approved socialist-realist style, with all references to Judaism removed except negative ones, such as the corruption of the rabbinical tyrants. Many of these writers were later murdered on Stalin's orders. In the end, try as they might, they could not escape their Jewish fate. Their corruption of Yiddish, because that was what was demanded of them, did not save them.

Of course, I am not saying that my mentors from the Bund were Stalinists. Quite the opposite—most dedicated their lives to the anti-communist cause. And if I am at all educated, it is because they inspired me to read and study and think—and not necessarily at school. Nevertheless, their movement produced few great works of literature or great music. There are songs about workers and their struggles that I still love when I hear them. But most are not great songs, because, as with all ideological art, the language is sort of dead.

Among some anti-Zionists and Jewish social-justice activists, anti-racists, and trans activists, there is a movement to resurrect Yiddish as their language—the language of Jewish secular progressivism. Hebrew, on the other hand, is the language of abhorrent Jewish nationalism. Yiddish is 'good' because it is not a national language or the language of the powerful, and it is a language that Zionists always associated with the diaspora and Jewish helplessness.

It is true that, from its birth in the late-nineteenth century, political Zionism, despite the fact that the Zionists overwhelmingly were Eastern European, Yiddish-speaking Jews, rejected the idea that Yiddish could be the language of the Jewish state. Instead, Hebrew—which was the language of prayer and of the holy books—was to be resurrected as the national language of the Jews in the state of Israel.

And it was a singular achievement, this resurrection of

Hebrew as a secular language. Hebrew is the language of Israel and of Israelis. Its writers write in Hebrew; modern Hebrew literature is astoundingly rich. Israel's songwriters write in Hebrew. Its great universities are Hebrew universities. But there was a price paid for this, and that price was paid in part by those hundreds of thousands of Holocaust survivors who were Eastern European Jews whose first language was Yiddish, and who managed to get to Palestine and later Israel in the late 1940s and early 1950s.

From the start, they were discouraged from speaking Yiddish. Yiddish was not taught at any schools or universities, not then and not for decades afterwards. The political class — most of which was Yiddish-speaking — was determined to force the Yiddish-speaking Holocaust survivors to live in Hebrew. There was an unofficial ban on Yiddish theatre and most Yiddish-based cultural organisations. As a result, Yiddish, which had been mortally wounded by the Holocaust, died in Israel, and was regarded by most Israelis — certainly young Israelis — as a dead language of the pre-state Jewish diaspora.

But none of this makes Yiddish a progressive language. In a sense, it is a Jewish pre-Enlightenment language. Most Yiddish speakers always were — and still are — Haredim, the ultra-Orthodox Jews you see in some southern suburbs of Melbourne, or on the streets of Jerusalem, or Antwerp, or New York City.

I think what is happening with Yiddish, in its adoption by leftist Jews — some even talk about resurrecting the Bund — is part of that universalising of the Jews, their language, their culture, and, in particular, their history. It's what Mamet was talking about when he said that progressive Jews are reducing Judaism to 'good works'. As a result, Judaism is being stripped of any particularity.

# CHAPTER SIX

# Good Jews

*People love dead Jews. Live ones, not so much.* I like these two sentences. They are perfect, in the sense that they are direct statements and at the same time allusive, hard to pin down in their meaning, knowing and funny. I first heard these sentences uttered in a podcast interview with the writer Dara Horn. She said she had been unsure about the title of her new book of essays, *People Love Dead Jews,* but that her publisher had loved it and had insisted on using it. It became what *The Washington Post* called 'a contender for the most arresting title of the year'. But for me, her second sentence was the more arresting. Horn said it while laughing, I think, in what I took to be a broad Brooklyn Jewish accent—'Live ones, not so much.'

Dara Horn is a scholar of Yiddish and Hebrew literature. She knows a lot about dead Jews. Yiddish literature is a half-dead language, the characters who people it long dead. Yet Yiddish is there in her English, in the rhythms of her sentences, and in her sharp, quietly lacerating humour. She nails something about Yiddish literature that would be uncomfortable for Americans and American Jews who read only English: there are few, if any, happy endings in Yiddish literature, most certainly not in the Yiddish literature of the Holocaust. There are no lessons, no moral fables, no fantasies of hope out of the darkness. In what is now a voluminous Yiddish Holocaust literature—which comprises mostly memoirs and biographies, with some fictional accounts—there are only dead Jews murdered because they were Jews, and survivors who are angry, vengeful, guilt-ridden, and inconsolable.

In one essay in her book, Horn describes how the Nobel Peace Prize winner Elie Wiesel removed most of the anger and despair from his Yiddish memoir, originally titled *And the World Was Silent*, for the French edition. This version became the basis of subsequent editions, notably *Night* in English. For Wiesel, it seems, it was okay to be angry in Yiddish, but for non-Jewish readers who liked hope at the end of depictions of terrible experiences, too much anger would be off-putting.

*People Love Dead Jews* was published in the middle of 2021, when the Covid pandemic ruled our lives. We were in the dangerous age range, my wife and I. We were anxiously waiting for vaccines. And I was devasted that I could not see my four-year-old grandson, who had lived with us for the first year of his life, along with his mother and father. I had written a couple of short essays about being old in the time of this plague. I wrote of how old people in old people's homes were dying alone, abandoned, because of the virus, but also because many families in my generation had opted to put their ageing parents in homes. My one surviving sister was ninety-one, and in a home. Every day I prayed that at the time of her dying, I would be allowed to be there with her. When I visited her, she sang Yiddish songs with me, remembering every line of every song. She had once sung beautifully. Now she sang from somewhere unknowable, but her raspy voice held the tune, and the Yiddish words were beautiful.

It was in this world that I read Horn's book. I would wake in the middle of the night with something from the book—a sentence, an image, a question—in my head.

Horn has written five novels. Each examines a period of Jewish history. A number of her characters are historical Jewish figures, some renowned and some more obscure. *People Love Dead Jews*, her first book of non-fiction, consists of twelve essays, some having appeared in a range of publications over the previous decade or so. They all feature dead Jews in a variety of historical settings. There are the Jews killed in the Holocaust who have been rendered 'non-Jews' in Holocaust museums and movies and novels—the talismanic Holocaust victim, her Jewishness erased in her memorialisation, being Anne Frank. There are the Soviet Jewish writers killed in Stalin's purges—Jews who had given up their Jewishness but were murdered because they were Jews. There are the Jewish intellectuals, artists, and writers who were rescued from the Nazis by a heroic but complicated American called Varian Fry. For reasons that are unclear, but that suggest they did not want to acknowledge they had suffered persecution and threats to their lives because they were Jews, they later refused to publicly acknowledge their rescue.

Three essays examine the murder of Jews in recent years in France and the United States, and the great reluctance in France and America, including in progressive media such as *The New York Times*, to acknowledge that these Jews were the victims of anti-Semitism. At the centre of these essays, their unifying theme, is the erasure of the Jewishness of millions of Jews who were murdered because they were Jews. They are turned into universal victims: a Nazi-like genocide could have happened to anyone, and it was random bad luck that it happened to Jews. On the left, that erasure of Jewishness in contemporary America and in Europe takes the form of the widespread minimising and sometimes denial of anti-Semitism as a motive for violence against Jews — violence by supporters of anti-Zionism and the 'Palestinian cause'.

The erasure of Jewish particularity is most stark and powerful in the chapter 'Everyone's (Second) Favorite Dead Jew', about Anne Frank and the Anne Frank House in Amsterdam. Horn cites the most-often-quoted line in Anne Frank's diary: 'I still believe, in spite of everything, that people are truly good at heart.' These words, Horn writes, flatter us:

> They make us feel forgiven for those lapses of our civilization that allow for piles of murdered girls ... It is far more gratifying to believe that an innocent dead girl has offered us grace than to recognize the obvious: Frank wrote about people being 'truly good at heart' before meeting people who weren't.

What happened next — the betrayal of her family in hiding, their transport to concentration camps, Anne's death, the survival of her father, Otto — is mostly quickly passed over. Why they were in hiding and why they ended up dead — because they were Jews — is hardly ever discussed. Instead, Anne Frank has become a redeemer of humanity. Almost Christlike. Certainly not Jewish, except for the fact that, like Jesus, she happened to be a Jew.

Profoundly sad and yet full of hope: that's now the Anne Frank story. But what is truly shocking in Horn's Anne Frank chapter is not how Anne Frank has been erased as a young Jewish girl, but how the museum established in her name, which is visited by more than a million people a year, has come to regard the Jews. In 2017, a young Orthodox Jewish man started a job there. He wore a yarmulke, as you would expect and as his faith dictates. He was not a Haredi Jew, dressed in black with a black hat and with *tzitzit*—fringes—from his prayer shawl hanging down his trouser legs. Apart from his yarmulke, he looked like any resident of Amsterdam. Nevertheless, he was asked by the museum management to remove his yarmulke and replace it with a museum baseball cap. He was unhappy with having to do this, and asked his managers to reverse the decision. They considered this request at several meetings over several months. Reluctantly, they finally rescinded their ruling. In the museum that honours the life of a hidden Jew, a young Jewish man had been asked to hide his Jewishness. This is the most damning illustration of the way that the millions killed in the Holocaust have been de-Jewified. Dead Jews are good Jews, and live Jews, like the young man in the yarmulke, not much good at all.

Why did the museum do this? I think the most likely explanation is that it was worried that visitors would be offended by the young man, this religious Jew. Not that they had anything against him, but they may have worried that an identifiable Jew working in the museum might lead to protests and arguments and even violence by people who harbour, for various 'reasons', an animus against Jews. It was better to erase him. This is happening not just in the Anne Frank House. Across European cities, Jews are being advised—and, for a time in France, ordered—to shed all evidence that they are Jews when they are among non-Jews on the streets, on public transport, and at work. It is now too dangerous for European Jews—in Europe, after the Holocaust and the murder of millions of them—to be Jews in their own cities.

What remains largely unspoken and unexamined is that the threats to Jews in Europe—from France to Sweden—come largely from radical Islamists: young men, the children of immigrants and refugees. The Jews who have been murdered in France over the past two decades in terrorist attacks were killed by young men born in France. They were French citizens.

In Sweden, the dwindling Jewish community of around 20,000 is confronting anti-Semitic threats from Islamist radicals among the 800,000 mostly immigrant Swedish Muslim community. In Malmö, where there has been an organised Jewish community since 1871, violence against and intimidation of the Jews — now down to around 500 people, in a city where there are 45,000 Muslims, 12 per cent of the population — is commonplace. In September 2022, Sweden held a general election, as a result of which a right-wing coalition supported by a populist anti-immigrant party won government. The previous centre-left social-democratic government had decried the attacks on Jews, but had never been able to bring itself to call out where those attacks were coming from.

Australia is not France or Sweden, but there are armed guards at Jewish institutions and synagogues and schools. And some Jews are removing their Jewish-identifying clothing and symbols. They are erasing themselves publicly as Jews because they feel unsafe. But why they feel unsafe — in Europe, America, and increasingly in Australia — and where the threats to them come from is not open for discussion. It comes from neo-Nazis and the far right, that is true, but that is far from the whole story. Some anti-Semitic threats cannot be called out, because that would be labelled Islamophobia, and because the left cannot bring itself to call out the anti-Semitism of people and groups they consider powerless and victims of oppression.

All of this is implied in Horn's chapter on Anne Frank and, in particular, in her anecdote about the young Jewish worker at the Anne Frank House who was asked to remove any evidence that suggested he was a Jew.

Horn manages to give shape to the powerful but vague discomforts, doubts, and even anger I had felt over the years about what has happened to dead Jews. I felt it when I visited Holocaust museums. I felt it when I read about how Anne Frank's diary, which was perhaps the first Holocaust book I came across, had been edited and stripped of direct references to Jewish practice before it was published, probably as part of the effort to turn her into a symbol of hope in the midst of darkness.

I felt anger — or was it despair? — when I read recent Holocaust fiction, much of it concentration-camp porn, and when I watched Holocaust fairy-tale fantasies such as *Life is Beautiful*, the Italian film that won an Oscar, and Steven Spielberg's Hollywood 'masterpiece' *Schindler's List*, which ends with a procession of Holocaust survivors laying flowers on the grave of Oskar Schindler, their rescuer. In the darkness, there was humanity. There were good Germans. And after the darkness lifted, there was hope. There is nothing like this in Yiddish Holocaust literature, because it is pure Hollywood bullshit.

Before I read Horn's book, I understood that I was on a journey, along with other former universalist Jews, to find my Jewishness. What sort of Jew was I? How should I regard the Jew I was as a young man, when I felt little connection with anything Jewish, beyond an affection for Yiddish and its music and song? How should I regard the Jew that my mother and father and my Bundist mentors crafted me to become? I think that Dara Horn is on this journey with me, along with Howard Jacobson and Bernard-Henri Lévy, in his exploration of his Jewishness in his book *The Genius of Judaism*. In *People Love Dead Jews*, Horn points to where my journey might lead me. She is comfortable with and immersed intellectually and emotionally in the Jew she has become. She understands and celebrates her Jewish particularity.

There is much in Horn's book that is confronting, especially for universalist Jews of the left. The easy part of what Horn has to say is that the Holocaust has been transformed into a universal metaphor for the capacity of human beings to do terrible things to other human beings. It has been robbed of any Jewish particularity; it could have happened to Americans, French, English, any people. Much of contemporary Holocaust fiction in English consists of stories of love and hope in concentration camps—romance in Auschwitz! Apart from the fact that writing 'true romances' set in death camps is problematic, to say the least, it too is part of the process of minimising the Jewishness of the Holocaust. The millions of people who were murdered by the Nazis were just people like you and me, children like your children. Maybe they were murdered because they were Jews, but there is nothing Jewish in the way they are rendered or thought of. Reviewers of Horn's book in the centre-left newspapers in the US, most of them Jewish, understand all this. They praise Horn's bravery in calling out US Holocaust museums for their love of dead people who just happen to be Jews. I think they get it because some of them seem to believe that Jewish history began with the Holocaust. De-Jewifying the Holocaust doesn't feel right, even for universalist Jews.

But what they can't bring themselves to wrestle with is Horn's assertion that, more and more, anti-Semitism is being so narrowly defined by progressives that only neo-Nazis can be deemed anti-Semites. Attacks on Jews by Blacks are hardly ever called out as anti-Semitism. Attacks on Jews by pro-Palestinian gangs can't be acts of anti-Semitism. That's the hard part of Horn's book that progressive reviewers in the main ignore.

But even the easy part is not very easy. Should universalist Jews on the left reclaim the central role of the Jewish people in the Holocaust? Expose once again that what motivated the

Nazis was the genocide of these particular Jews? What would be the purpose, and how would it be achieved? And before I or others go about resurrecting and particularising the murdered Jews, don't we need to explore just what Jewish particularity means? What made their fate unique? Was it just the numbers of Jews murdered—was that it?

What made their fate unique is now no longer much discussed. The largely successful genocide of European Jews was carried out by a modern, Western, post-Enlightenment state, renowned for its cultural and scientific achievements, for its philosophers, novelists, poets, and composers. The killers and the victims lived together. It was a genocide of Jews of all types—Haredi, conservative, secular, socialist, Zionist, Jews who didn't consider themselves to be Jews in any meaningful way, and Jews who didn't even know they were Jews. It was carried out on the basis of an irrational, ridiculous, insane conspiracy theory. Each group of exterminated Jews was Jewish in a particular way. What united them was that their murderers defined them as Jews.

When Jews are accused of exploiting the Holocaust for nefarious political and economic reasons, what does this mean? It is true, for instance, that Jews are still claiming property and artworks that their murdered family members owned before the war in countries such as Poland. Is this an example of Jews exploiting the Holocaust for economic reasons? Perhaps it is, but only in part, as their cause is just. What the accusers also mean is that American cultural entrepreneurs—in Hollywood, for instance—have commercialised the Holocaust—in books and films and television series. What else can the exploitation of the Holocaust mean? When Jews say the Holocaust is a uniquely Jewish horror, why do they say such things, and for what purpose? To what end?

The end, according to many anti-Zionists, is to hide, deny, and deflect from the reality of the oppression of the Palestinians, the racism of Zionism, and Zionism's foundational role in the establishment of apartheid Israel. That's what the constant harping about the Holocaust and the constant refrain that the Jews and only the Jews were its victims is all about—about justifying the occupation and the powerlessness of the Palestinians by claiming the title for the Jews as the greatest victims in human history. Jews, Jews, Jews, Holocaust, Holocaust, Holocaust. Enough already. Anti-Zionists are sick of hearing about Jewish suffering, murder, dispossession. As if they, the anti-Zionists, are somehow responsible for what happened long ago. As if this gives Jews the right to ethnically cleanse Palestine of Palestinians. Aren't there more recent, even current, genocides and racist horrors to worry about? And, anyway, the Jews do not own the Holocaust. It belongs to all of humanity.

Perhaps the weirdest chapter in *People Love Dead Jews* is about Harbin, where the provincial government spent $30 million on restoring buildings and sites with a connection to the former Jewish community, including a hotel that was once owned by a prominent Jewish family.

Harbin was built by Jews at the turn of the twentieth century. These Jews had been brought to Harbin, which, back then, was a collection of small villages, by the Russian company that had been contracted by the Chinese authorities to build part of the Trans-Siberian Railroad through Manchuria. Thousands of Russian Jews signed up to build Harbin, which would be a hub for the railroad project. Most did so to get away from the pogroms and the vicious and discriminatory anti-Semitism of tsarist Russia.

The story of Harbin's Jews, what they built and how they

eventually vanished, is beautifully told by Horn. The way the Chinese have rebuilt the Jewish presence in Harbin—now a city of over a million people—with only one Jew living there, often reads like a short story by Kafka. The Chinese, without apology, have said that they have rebuilt Jewish Harbin to attract wealthy Jewish tourists and investors. People not only love dead Jews, but they build heritage sites to them, not to honour them but to profit from them. How the Jews disappeared—in fact, the Japanese occupiers persecuted them throughout the Sino-Japanese war from 1931 to 1945, the Soviets who replaced the Japanese in 1945 sent the surviving Jewish community leaders to gulags, and the Chinese communists who finally took over in 1949 confiscated the property and finances of the remaining Jews in a successful effort to force them to leave—is not told. The Jews just vanished.

The Harbin chapter made me think of how Poland, a country that was once home to almost three-and-a-half million Jews, most of them murdered by the Nazis, has become a place of pilgrimage for Jews like me. My parents and ancestors were Polish Jews. My parents are dead, but had they been alive when I went to Poland—twice—they would have been horrified. When, from time to time, I asked my father whether he would ever go back to see the place where he grew up, he would answer that Poland was just a Jewish cemetery, nothing more. A country of dead Jews. Why go back there? To visit the land where millions of the Jews of Poland were murdered? He never called them Polish Jews.

The first time I went to Poland, in 1985, I was with a group of travel writers on what we journalists call a junket. We visited Russia, East Germany, and Poland, all at the time either part of the Soviet Union or, like Poland, a Soviet-controlled country. I met no Jews. There were no Jewish communal centres. As far as

I could tell, there were no organised tours for Jewish tourists of Jewish landmarks.

I visited Poland again in 2013, in a trip organised by a Polish organisation dedicated to resurrecting, marking, and honouring the history of the Jews in Poland and the role that the Jews had played in Polish life and history. More than that, the organisation had a program for Polish high schools, in which the students researched the history of the Jewish communities where they were based. The students were formed into work groups that worked to repair the old and neglected Jewish cemeteries of their area. Sometimes, they were even put to work helping to renovate old buildings, including libraries that the pre-war Jews of their city or town had built. But there were no books in these libraries, and no Jews to read them.

I was taken to Jewish communal organisations, newly formed after the fall of communism. I met young and not-so-young Jews who, after the end of communism, had gone in search of their roots and discovered that they had Jewish parents or grandparents and ancestors. The Jewish population of Poland has grown from several thousand to somewhere between 10,000 and 20,000. I was taken to the old Jewish part of Krakow, where several historic synagogues have been magnificently restored. In the main square, I saw Jewish organised tours, their participants mostly American Jews waiting to catch the tour bus for Auschwitz, which was a bit over an hour away. Poland, like Harbin, in a way, is full of Jewish heritage sites. Most of them are cemeteries.

I do not mean to criticise or belittle the work of the Poles who want to reconnect those high-school kids to the vanished Jews of their towns and villages. I was moved by their work, I admired what they were doing, and I was moved, in some cases to tears, when speaking to those kids about their holy projects.

One day, at a school in a town in central Poland, not far from the town where my father was born, I spoke with a group of students who were repairing and cleaning the graves in a small nearby Jewish cemetery. We were sitting at a café opposite the cemetery. One of them asked me where my parents had come from. I said they came from a town not too far away and that their families, their ancestors, had lived in Poland for maybe a thousand years.

'So you are Polish, yes?' she asked. 'Like your parents?'

I answered, 'Yes, I suppose so.' What else could I say to this girl who so eagerly wanted to take me into the Polish family—unlike thousands of her ancestors, who had been, to put it mildly, less than eager to accept my ancestors? People love dead Jews. The resurrection of Polish Jewish history, of the Jewish presence in Polish history, in which these children and their instructors play an honourable role, is based on avoiding the central truth of the Holocaust: the Jews of Poland, of its towns and cities and villages and countryside, three million of them, did not just vanish, somehow just cease to exist. They were murdered by the Nazis. But sometimes they were murdered by their Polish neighbours.

The children are told that Poles and Jews were murdered by the Nazis. They are not told that the Jews were gassed in death camps. The Holocaust history of their towns—of how the Jewish community in their town was annihilated, of how many were murdered and why there might have been non-Jewish Poles who killed Jews—this is not taught. Fixing those tombstones in that little cemetery, no one translated the Hebrew or Yiddish lettering on the stones to name the dead and make it possible to redeem them, to discover who they were, and to know how they lived and how they died. They were just this thing called Jews; I felt that the word had no deep meaning to them, except that these Jews were dead.

Live Jews — especially historians who are researching the killing of Jews by Poles, not only during but after the war, when the few Polish Jews who had survived returned to search for family — are despised and are threatened with legal action and jail. This applies even to Polish scholars such as Barbara Engelking and Jan Grabowski.

The current right-wing populist Polish government is determined to control the Holocaust narrative when it comes to Poland. What is the point of their narrative? It is to erase the exceptionalism of the Jewish experience and to deny that non-Jewish Poles played any part in the Jewish genocide. To suggest that non-Jewish Poles were complicit in the killing of Jews is a slander, because the Germans were responsible for all the killing and suffering in Poland, including the deaths of three million non-Jewish Poles. But research by Polish historians makes it clear that Poles were complicit in the murder of thousands of Jews, both during the Holocaust and in the post-war years. It is this research that the Polish government has wanted to outlaw.

The erasure of Jewish particularity — and, as a result, the minimising almost out of existence of anti-Semitism — is not confined to the work of right-wing populist governments or movements. In three chapters of *People Love Dead Jews,* Horn writes about the aftermath of attacks on Jews and Jewish communities in the United States.

These attacks, all violent and some deadly, elicited different, sometimes profoundly different, responses from American progressives, including in newspapers such as *The New York Times.* The newspaper described it as a horrifying race crime when a neo-Nazi white man gunned down eleven, mostly elderly, worshippers in a synagogue in Pittsburgh.

There was no need for 'context' for the crime. Easy. That's

what anti-Semitism is, a hate crime of the racist right. Anti-Semitism ends up being about neo-Nazis and Proud Boys, or some other white-supremacist groups.

After attacks such as this one, Horn was approached to write op-eds about the murdered Jews: 'a job that I did not apply for, but one that I accepted out of fear of what someone less aware of history might write instead'. But then came a violent attack on Hasidic Jews in Jersey City, in a predominantly Black neighbourhood. The attackers were Black. It is a neighbourhood with a small, but growing, Hasidic community.

The two attackers had killed a man with a Jewish-sounding name—he was not Jewish, as it turned out—who had been sitting in a parked car. They then shot and killed a police officer who was examining their stolen van, before going to a kosher grocery store, where they killed the store owner, a customer, and a store worker. The two gunmen were subsequently shot dead by police in a gunfight.

In media coverage of the attacks, the reports provided a supposed context for them—there was tension between Blacks and the Hasidic Jews who had moved into this predominantly Black neighbourhood. The Associated Press report about the murders, which was picked up by many news outlets, including NBC, said: 'The slayings happened in a neighborhood where Hasidic families had recently been relocating, amid pushback from some local officials who complained about representatives of the community going door to door, offering to buy homes at Brooklyn prices.' The Newark *Star-Ledger* reported that the attacks 'highlighted racial tensions that had been simmering ever since Ultra-Orthodox Jews began moving to a lower-income community'. *The Washington Post* said at the beginning of its coverage that Jersey City 'is grappling with whether the attack reflects underlying ethnic tensions'.

But the rest of the *Washington Post* report found little evidence of such tension between the Hasidic Jews and the Black community. Indeed, it found that, in the main, the two communities lived in relative harmony. And the killers did not come from Jersey City. They were virulent, murderous anti-Semites; there was no 'context' for their crimes. But it seems that Black people can't be racist, that the murders might have happened because Haredi Jews offered to buy the houses of Black residents in a Black neighbourhood. Black people are the victims of racism. And Jews? Well, Jews are white, and white people always cling to their white privilege. How can they be victims of racism? *The New York Times* did not ask Horn to write a piece about this attack.

In May 2021, a ten-day battle broke out between Hamas and the Israel Defense Forces, which involved thousands of rockets fired into Israel and Israeli airstrikes that killed more than 200 Palestinians. During that conflict, Jews in Los Angeles and New York were attacked in restaurants and on the street by gangs of men who were ostensibly motivated by their outrage at what Israel was inflicting on the people of Gaza. These attacks were either not reported or, if they were, they were reported in the context of the Gaza conflict, and that context was partly the terrible things Israel was doing. The view of many on the left was that these might have been anti-Semitic attacks, but the anti-Semitism, at least in part, was Israel's responsibility. Israel was partly to blame for these bicoastal attacks on Jews.

Where does this narrowing of what can be called anti-Semitism lead? If you erase the Jewish particularity of the millions of Jews murdered in the Holocaust, and transform the Holocaust into a lesson about how monstrous human beings can be, and how anyone, every group of people and nationality, could be victims of such monstrosity, why not take the lesson to mean that Israelis are behaving monstrously, just as the Nazis had behaved monstrously? Okay, not quite as bad, but on the road towards that dreadful place?

What then follows is that it is not anti-Semitic to compare Israelis to Nazis, to describe Zionism as evil and racist at its core, to deny the fears of Jews who feel that anti-Zionists and Palestinian supporters who equate Jews to Nazis are at least on the road to being anti-Semitic. It also follows that Jews who accuse progressives of using anti-Semitic language and tropes are Jews exploiting the Holocaust in order to silence criticism of Israel. By restoring Jewish particularity to the Holocaust, putting Jews and anti-Semitism at the centre of it, these Jews are cynically and dishonestly using the Holocaust and the whole history of Jew-hatred to silence all those anti-Zionists, anti-racists, Black Lives Matter activists, and social-justice warriors who want to legitimately criticise Israel. This exploration of the narrowing—the rewriting—of the concept of anti-Semitism is central to Horn's book.

The only anti-Semitism that is recognised or criticised is the anti-Semitism of white supremacists and neo-Nazis. There is no other kosher anti-Semitism. Not among Islamists, for instance, in the Muslim communities of France, where Jews have been killed by Islamists shouting *'Allahu Akbar'*. Not in Black communities in America. Not in the British Labour Party during Jeremy Corbyn's leadership. Instead, these are all treated as examples of Zionists weaponising the Holocaust and using accusations of anti-Semitism to silence critics of Israel.

People love dead Jews, but live ones—Zionists, funny-looking religious ones, rich ones, rude ones, greedy ones, even loud ones—not so much.

After more attacks on Jews by neo-Nazis, Horn decided she would write no more pieces for *The New York Times* and other papers of the soft left. There was no point. If she was to write, she would have to call out the way these papers had covered other attacks, the way they had avoided raising the possibility that these were anti-Semitic attacks. It was too late, she felt, to particularise the attacked Jews and their attackers. Who would listen?

Several weeks after the Jersey City attack, the Jewish community organised a 'No Fear, No Hate' march in New York City. Some 25,000 people turned up, although almost none were from the Hasidic community that had been attacked by the gunmen who had killed two of their members. There was condemnation of anti-Semitism in general terms — but no reference specifically to the increasing number of violent anti-Semitic attacks against Haredi Jews, and there was a motherhood rejection of hate in all its forms.

Horn did not go to the rally. 'And while I knew the march was intended as an act of pride and defiance and that those who attended found it empowering and inspiring,' she wrote, 'its mere existence felt profoundly depressing to me, almost like an admission of defeat.'

Instead, Horn turned to find comfort — and particularity — in reading the Talmud, celebrating Judaism with a community of readers, a decision sparked by a massive Jewish gathering at a stadium near where she lived in New Jersey. It was attended by people like those who had been attacked at the kosher grocery store and in other places in New York City and Brooklyn. This gathering dwarfed the 'No Fear, No Hate' protest. Ninety thousand Jews, nearly all Hasidim, came to the stadium, not to protest anti-Semitic attacks on their communities, but for a ceremony, repeated at gatherings around the world, to celebrate the completion of a communal reading of the Talmud 'a page at a time'. The reading takes seven-and-a-half years, and on completion, the readings, a page at a time, start again.

'I suddenly knew what I wanted to do,' she wrote. 'Along with hundreds of thousands of people around the world, I opened to the very first page [of the Talmud] and began.'

She still follows what she calls 'the old old news' about the Jews in the liberal media, but she is no longer the go-to Jew for *The New York Times* or any other media when there is an attack on Jews. She is glad of this, because she has nothing to say that can be said in 800 or 1,000 words.

Horn is reaffirming her own Jewish particularity in the face of its erasure — in live Jews, in Holocaust victims, and in those Hasidim shot dead in Jersey City — mainly by progressives if this particularity has anything to do with Zionism or Israel. I think I am following in her footsteps, as are Jacobson and Leevy, and others, too.

As I write, a memory comes to me of the late Amos Oz at a writers' festival event at a packed Melbourne Town Hall a decade or more ago. His fellow Israeli writer A.B. Yehoshua, who died in June 2022, often infuriated American Jews when he told them that diaspora Jews were only partly Jewish. He said they wore their Jewishness like a coat they could take off at any time, when being Jewish might be inconvenient. But if they made aliyah and migrated to Israel, their Jewish coats would become their Jewish skin.

Amos Oz was not quite as blunt. What he said at the Melbourne Town Hall was that only in Israel could Jews lead a fully Jewish life. In a way, I am writing something approaching a rebuttal to Yehoshua and Oz. Writing it involves not worrying what non-Jewish people will think, whether I will feed the fantasies of people who don't much like Jews, who think they are some sort of secret society more concerned about themselves and their interests than the interests of the wider community.

And what will they think when I write that I love the Jewish people? Will they understand what I mean? Can I explain what I mean? This question of *Ahavat Israel*—the Hebrew phrase meaning 'love of the Jewish people'—has occupied me ever since I read an exchange of letters between two of the great German Jewish intellectuals of the twentieth century. The two had been friends for decades before their friendship ended suddenly. One was considered perhaps the greatest scholar of Jewish mysticism—of the Kabbalah and its influence in Judaism—and the other was a renowned philosopher and writer whose work on totalitarianism remains foundational in the study of the twentieth century's wars, genocides, and bitter ideological disputes.

The two letters that ended their friendship were about this question that I am wrestling with, about their sense of themselves as Jews. At the centre of the letters written by these two German Jews, both in different ways exiled and rejected by the country and culture they had loved, are the questions of whether they loved the Jewish people, what such a love meant, and whether or not loving a people—as opposed to individuals—is meaningful, or even possible.

# CHAPTER SEVEN

# Hannah Arendt, and loving the Jews. Or not.

Gershom Scholem and Hannah Arendt had a friendship in letters. For twenty-five years, they wrote to each other, in German, these two formidable intellectuals. Scholem, a decade older than Arendt, had been immersed from an early age in a lifelong study of Judaism, Jewish mysticism, and Jewish history. Arendt was a philosopher trained in German universities.

Scholem left Germany for Palestine in 1923, never to return. Arendt fled Germany in 1933, the year Hitler became chancellor. She settled in Paris, but after the Nazis invaded France, she was briefly interred by the Vichy regime before she, along with other Jewish intellectuals, writers, and artists, was rescued in Marseille by Varian Fry and taken to the United States, where she lived until her death in 1975. Her great work included two seminal studies of totalitarianism. She wrote several challenging studies of anti-Semitism and Zionism, and of course the book that made her both famous and notorious, *Eichmann in Jerusalem: a report on the banality of evil*. All of this was written and published in New York, where she was a celebrated public intellectual.

Scholem and Arendt met several times over the decades

of their correspondence, but these meetings were fleeting and frustrating for both—they were, they often said, too busy to spend a great deal of time with each other and, anyway, they were hardly ever in the same country. But like many intellectuals and writers, their relationship in their letters was long and substantial. They lived in different worlds, in a sense, but their letters were about what they shared, about their Jewishness, and about their increasingly bitter disputes. It is clear from their letters, certainly from the 1940s onwards, that they differed profoundly about what it meant to be a Jew, and over the promise and fulfilment of Zionism, and of Israel, its progeny.

Two letters, one from Scholem and a reply from Arendt, written after *Eichmann in Jerusalem* was published in 1963, ended their friendship. It was Arendt who ended it. Perhaps the most poignant part of this ending is that Scholem wrote to Arendt months after this bitter exchange to tell her he was coming to New York to give a series of lectures and that he would love to see her. Arendt did not reply to Scholem's letter. They did not write to or see each other again.

In the letters between Scholem and Arendt about *Eichmann in Jerusalem*, in an admittedly oblique but nevertheless powerful way, they wrote about what it meant to each of them to be Jewish, and about whether the notion of Jewish peoplehood had any meaning. By the time the letters were written, less than two decades after the end of the war, Scholem had lived in Palestine and then Israel for forty years. He was an Israeli. Arendt had become an American citizen.

The letters need a context. *Eichmann in Jerusalem* was to become for many people a seminal text for their understanding of the Holocaust—what motivated the Nazis to try to exterminate the Jews, the Jewish complicity in the Nazi project, and the nature of the evil that so gripped so many Germans that they could actively participate in and organise a genocide.

I first read *Eichmann in Jerusalem* in the early 1970s, when I was starting out in journalism and when *The New Yorker* was my journalism bible. I loved the long, sometimes edition-length, articles of more than 10,000 words. They were deeply reported and written in that *New Yorker* style, in clear and elegant and dispassionate prose, the pieces narrative-driven, with commentary and analysis buried in the story. This was the sort of journalism I wanted to do.

Over the forty years I spent writing for newspapers and magazines, I did occasionally manage to wangle the time and space from my editors to research and write long pieces like the ones I loved in *The New Yorker* when I was first starting out. I was not given quite as much time, nor was I ever allowed 10,000 words, but, in Australian terms, I was blessed. However, the blessings of editors were still years off when I bought a copy of *Eichmann in Jerusalem,* mostly because it had been published first in *The New Yorker.* Given that it is now fifty or more years since I bought and read the book, there are certain things about it that I cannot recall, and these are all about what I believed back then about Jews and Zionism and Israel.

What I knew about the Holocaust had come in the main from eyewitnesses—my father, and my older sisters, who had escaped Poland and had spent the war in Siberia—and from the survivors who spoke at the annual Holocaust remembrance evenings of the Bund held on 19 April—the anniversary of the Warsaw Ghetto uprising on 19 April 1943. My closest Bundist mentor was a Holocaust survivor. I had not read any Holocaust histories: not, for instance, *The Destruction of the European Jews,* written by Raul Hilberg, the first and one of the greatest Holocaust historians; nor Primo Levi's *If This Is a Man*; nor André Schwarz-Bart's *The Last of the Just*, published in French in 1959, which I believe is one of the greatest Holocaust novels. I had read some Yiddish Holocaust poetry with my father—he had insisted that I do so—but I do not recall it making any deep impression on me.

I read *Eichmann in Jerusalem* not knowing that many New York Jewish intellectuals, who in the 1960s were perhaps the leading public intellectuals in America—among them, Norman Podhoretz and Irving Kristol—had written scathing reviews of the book. And not just American Jewish intellectuals. The renowned British political philosopher Isaiah Berlin, a Russian-born Jew, told the critic Edmund Wilson that Arendt's book had too many faults for him to enumerate, but that, in essence, it was a 'bad book'. Reading some of the criticisms, it is not hard to understand why Arendt felt targeted and despised—betrayed, even cast out—by her fellow Jewish intellectuals. Did she consider Gershom Scholem, an old friend, to be among them?

Ignorant as I mostly was about the Holocaust and about Hannah Arendt; ignorant about, and not that interested in, Israel and Israelis; and ignorant as I was about the fierce controversy swirling around *Eichmann in Jerusalem*, I nevertheless read the book in a few nights. I read it after I finished my police-reporting shifts, which started in the early afternoon and ended before midnight. I read it as a piece of journalism. Perhaps I was expecting a piece of New Journalism, which was all the rage back then, maybe something like Norman Mailer's work, say *Miami and the Siege of Chicago*, about the US presidential conventions in 1968.

I read it when I was an ambitious reporter, a young man who had found his calling after trying teaching and a public service job as an economist, who had dreams of writing stories like those in *The New Yorker*, who hoped one day to be another Norman Mailer, but who, meanwhile, was ready and eager to write short, formulaic pieces, day in, day out, about a traffic accident or a fire, or, even, if I was lucky, a murder.

I can't remember in detail my response to the book, but I think I did not find it thrilling. It was not what I expected from a piece of writing that had taken up two whole issues of my favourite magazine. Sent to cover the trial of one of the main implementors of the Holocaust, Arendt didn't report the trial, but instead wrote what we called back then a very long 'think piece' about Eichmann, the Holocaust, and even Israel.

When I read the book again, a decade later, it puzzled and disturbed me. I thought it was an important and challenging book. It was dense, although there was nothing academic about the writing. I found the central idea — that Eichmann, far from being the personification of some inexplicable evil, was a mediocre and banal bureaucrat who did not believe in anything much except self-advancement — troubling. I was also troubled by Arendt's accusation, offered in passing, that the leaders of the Jews in Nazi-occupied Europe had co-operated in, and to a certain extent facilitated, the rounding-up and murder of millions of fellow Jews.

But this was not journalism. It lacked a narrative. Arendt did not create a story from the progression of the trial, the unfolding of the evidence against Eichmann, the voices of witnesses, Eichmann's own testimony, the way the defence and prosecution put their cases and examined witnesses, or the atmosphere in a courtroom full of survivors — many in audible pain in the middle of wakeful nightmares. There was no sense of Arendt sitting in the courtroom witnessing the trial, listening to the testimony from survivors, retelling almost indescribable horrors.

Instead, the tone seemed both detached and invested in a theoretical, philosophical belief about what was taking place in the courtroom. There was too much commentary, too much analysis, too many judgements—many of them scathing and vicious—of the participants in the trial. Arendt was especially vicious about the chief prosecutor, Gideon Hausner, and Israel's first prime minister, David Ben-Gurion.

And there was her wholesale dismissal of the survivors who had come to bear witness as irrelevant to the proceedings. Their testimony, in her view, transformed the Eichmann trial into a show trial, serving the political interests of Ben-Gurion to showcase Israel's legitimacy by suggesting that the old, helpless, and powerless diaspora Jews had been superseded by the powerful new Jews of Israel, with Hausner as Ben-Gurion's willing political enabler.

And Adolf Eichmann, there in that Israeli courtroom, being judged for his role in the Nazi annihilation of six million Jews, became a pathetic, insignificant figure. He became, above all—and this is always the greatest journalistic sin—uninteresting to Arendt. Even in my almost total ignorance of the Holocaust, I knew this trial was a momentous event, and that Arendt had not captured it.

I read the book again a few years ago. By then, I had spent years—sometimes months at a time—reading nothing but histories of the Holocaust, Holocaust memoirs, survivor testimonies, writers like Primo Levi and Elie Wiesel, and the brilliant journalist Gitta Sereny. I read Yehuda Bauer's study of the *Judenräte,* the Nazi-appointed Jewish councils that ran the day-to-day life of the ghettos and concentration camps—not the death camps—of Nazi-occupied Europe.

In this most recent reading of *Eichmann in Jerusalem,* what most troubled me was not so much the book itself, but the way it had become the defining book about the Holocaust for many people, including Jews—particularly Jews of the left.

The Arendt view of Eichmann, her indictment of the Jewish leaders in Nazi-occupied Europe, and, critically, the absence of any sense that anti-Semitism had played a part in what Eichmann did—or even of the ideology that motivated the Nazis—has had a big influence on the way the Holocaust has been de-Jewified over the past half-century. It has become a crime against humanity, not against the Jews. The Jews do not 'own' it. As if the Holocaust could not be both a crime against the Jews specifically—for that is what it was—and a crime against humanity.

But it was a book by Holocaust historian Deborah Lipstadt, *The Eichmann Trial*, published in 2011, that crystallised for me what I felt was profoundly wrong with Arendt's portrayal of Eichmann. Lipstadt had been sued by the Holocaust denier David Irving, and had won the case, in a famous victory against Holocaust denialism. *Denial*, a 2016 film based on the case, with Rachel Weisz in the role of Lipstadt, was a critical and commercial success.

*The Eichmann Trial* is not a direct attack on Arendt's reporting of the Eichmann trial and her portrayal of Eichmann as a mediocre, low-level bureaucrat who couldn't think and who, as he claimed in his evidence, just did what was asked of him. It is, nevertheless, a devastating rebuttal of Arendt's central thesis in *Eichmann in Jerusalem*.

Lipstadt rejects Arendt's view, so strongly put in her book, that David Ben-Gurion and Gideon Hausner had turned the proceedings into a show trial. Instead, she argues, the trial gave survivors a voice for the first time, a voice in the country of the Jews. The victims sat in judgement of the perpetrators. Jews had agency. And, for the first time, the unimaginable horror and extent of the Holocaust started to emerge.

At the centre of this horror, Lipstadt makes clear, was

eliminationist anti-Semitism, without which there would not
have been the thousands and thousands of Germans and others
who were prepared—often eager—to dirty their hands in this
attempted genocide of the Jews.

Lipstadt establishes that Eichmann was not just a minor
cog in the Nazi killing machine—a self-description that
Arendt accepted—but one of its principal organisers. And
she establishes beyond doubt that Eichmann was a committed
and ferocious anti-Semite, although a cunning one, who in his
trial brilliantly played the part of a minor bureaucrat who had
nothing against the Jews.

By the time I read Arendt's book a third time, researchers
had discovered recordings of conversations between Eichmann
and a Dutch Nazi journalist, Willem Sassen, that were made
at Sassen's house in Argentina, where Eichmann and other
escaped Nazis regularly met to talk nostalgically about their
past. The district was home to a number of Nazi officials who
had managed, like Eichmann, to escape to South America.

These audio recordings, released by the German archival
authorities in 2021, reveal just how completely Arendt had
misunderstood and been fooled by Eichmann. The recordings,
which an Israeli producer and director made into a three-part
television documentary series, *The Devil's Confession: the lost
Eichmann tapes*, demolish Arendt's view of Eichmann, on which
she based her central concept of the banality of evil.

Eichmann emerges from these recordings as a dedicated and
ferocious anti-Semite, committed to Nazi ideology and to the
Nazi plan for the 'Final Solution' of the Jewish question, and
unapologetic about his major role in the murders of millions
of Jews. He is articulate and passionate, his German close to
perfect, and he talks endlessly, as if he is talking for posterity.
As if this is his testament to what he had achieved and what, in

the end, he had been unable to achieve—the total genocide of the Jews:

> In conclusion, I must say to you ... I regret nothing. I have no desire to say that we did something wrong. If we had killed 10.3 million Jews, I would say with satisfaction, 'Good, we destroyed an enemy.' Then we would have fulfilled our mission. And thus, to my regret, it was not to be.

Similarly, Eichmann's letters to fellow Nazis when he was in hiding in Argentina, and the testimony of people who knew him there, show that, far from being inarticulate, Eichmann was clear and dramatic in his language, committed without apology to anti-Semitism and the Nazi plan to rid the world of the Jews. He expressed no regret, and no pity. There was no drawing back from the Nazi view of the Jew as the mortal enemy of Germany and of mankind. This was an Eichmann very different from the man of Arendt's imagining, the mediocre if ambitious bureaucrat with no ideology or worldview, let alone a murderously anti-Semitic one. He was very different from the man summoned up by the phrase that forms the subtitle of her book, *a report on the banality of evil*—a phrase that has become a cliché of genocide studies, used to describe every sort of mass murderer, authoritarian, and dictator.

Another thing struck me as strangely simplistic for an intellectual of Arendt's standing. The Nazis appointed Jewish leaders to 'run' the ghettos into which they herded the Jews in the European countries they conquered. In time, when the Nazis embarked on the Final Solution, these Jewish leaders were given the task of choosing the Jews who would be sent to be murdered in the death camps. In Arendt's view, these Jewish leaders should have refused to co-operate with the Nazis from the start, even if it meant their certain death and the death of all their families.

But, of course, it was not that simple. There were cases of great moral failure, by leaders who did everything they could to save their own lives and the lives of their families. There were leaders who behaved like petty tyrants. There were leaders who, confronted with the terrible choices offered them by the Nazis, committed suicide. And then there's this: what was happening to the Jews was literally unimaginable, even when stories of what was happening leaked out of the death camps. How could an intellectual giant like Arendt not instinctively know all this?

There is a connection in her book between Eichmann and his role in organising the slaughter of the Jews, and the Jewish leaders who organised the orderly round-up of Jews destined for the death camps. The provision of trains and their often-complex scheduling was the responsibility of Eichmann and the Nazi units he ran. To do his work efficiently required him to travel from one country to another to make sure the trains were running on time, and to schedule the round-up of Jews in time for the train arrivals. In his capacity as chief organiser of the gathering and despatching of the Jews to their deaths, there were times when Eichmann had to deal with Jewish leaders. Eichmann and the Jewish leaders: complicity everywhere.

The consequences, according to Arendt, were beyond appalling. She maintained that, had these Jewish leaders refused to take on the leadership of the Jewish communities in occupied Europe, they most likely would have been sent to a death camp—most ended up there anyway—but the Jews of the ghettos and the cities and in the countryside could not have been delivered so efficiently and with such little resistance to the Nazis. Millions of Jews would still have been murdered, according to Arendt, for the Nazis were zealously committed to annihilating as many Jews as they could—diverting soldiers and equipment and trains that were needed to take food and guns and clothing to the front. Nevertheless, she claimed, had the Jewish leaders refused to do the Nazis' dirty work, perhaps half of the murdered six million Jews would have survived—millions of men, women, and children.

It was this thesis of Arendt's, that the Jewish leaders were responsible for millions of dead Jews, that elicited Gershon Scholem's most passionate and scathing criticism of *Eichmann in Jerusalem.*

In the letter to Arendt that ended their friendship, Scholem wrote, 'It is the heartless, frequently almost sneering, and malicious tone with which these matters, touching the very quick of our life are treated, to which I take exception.'

I shall come back to the letters, but I think Scholem is right about Arendt's heartlessness. More than that, her brief and shallow consideration of the fate of these often-tragic figures, who were designated by the Nazis to lead their shattered and dying communities, is pitilessly devoid of any hint of empathy.

But the central failure of Arendt's book is her portrait of Eichmann. It was always superficial and unconvincing, but Lipstadt's book about the trial, and the transcripts of the interviews conducted by Willem Sassen, show that it was also fundamentally flawed. And that failure was due in part to Arendt's reporting.

Arendt may have been a great academic, but she was a poor observer. Her description of the first time she saw Adolf Eichmann, when he was led into the courtroom, is instructive. She describes him as a small man, suffering from a cold. He did not look like a mass murderer of unimaginable, unprecedented proportions. She had to stifle an urge to laugh at this little bloke who sweated a lot and looked bewildered, sitting there in his glass booth.

Arendt attended the trial for a month at the start, then left for a five-week holiday in Switzerland, came back for a time, and left again. During the periods she was absent, she missed a lot of witness testimony and, crucially, some of Eichmann's testimony and his cross-examination.

Every reporter who has covered criminal trials knows that a violent man who has done terrible things to other human beings can be made to look like you and me, and like the police who interrogated him. In my years spent witnessing trials and reading records of police interrogations, this mystery would confound and obsess me — how an ordinary-looking man, quietly spoken, often tongue-tied, tidily dressed, even polite, could have committed acts of terrifying violence, often in a terrible rage, although sometimes with a calm, conscience-less determination.

Did Arendt not know that there are no horns or demon's eyes to find, no physical embodiment to discover, in a mass murderer? Did she not know what I knew, even as a cub reporter, that many men who have a capacity for massive, often heartless, and uncontrollable violence are great actors, method actors, able to convince themselves of the roles they are playing, and able, during police interrogations and courtroom trials, to talk and walk and look like the opposite of what their crimes reveal them to be?

On what did Arendt base her conclusion about Eichmann's thoughtlessness, mediocrity, and lack of intelligence (the evidence for which, according to her, was his inability to express himself in good German)? It was based on transcripts of the Israeli police interrogations, on his listless demeanour in court, and on his evidence and his responses during cross-examination, which she described in general terms but drew no examples from — she cited no exchanges between Eichmann and his defence attorney, or between him and the prosecutor. Had she ever seen and reported a trial?

When I read the book recently, I wondered how this brilliant woman, there to cover the trial of one of the architects of the attempted genocide of the Jews, hardly covered the unbearable testimony of Holocaust survivors, which often provoked cries of pain and anguish from the scores of other survivors who were seated in the gallery. She hardly covered any of this, but instead raised the question of the Jews' complicity in the attempted genocide of their own people.

Writing this now, I wonder how Janet Malcolm or Helen Garner would have covered the Eichmann trial. It would not have been the way Arendt covered it, I'm sure. They would have had a determination to overcome their biases and prejudices, to see something for the first time, which is the way that all good non-fiction writing is created—with an open mind.

Instead, Arendt came to the trial with the baggage of an intellectual who had written a seminal book on totalitarianism (*The Origins of Totalitarianism*), and challenging papers and articles about anti-Semitism and Zionism. And as a German Jewish refugee from the Nazis who had once been a Zionist but had become disillusioned with the Zionist project. She came to Israel eager to validate that disillusionment. She came with the question of what makes a person capable of being instrumental in an attempted genocide already answered. Had she known what Eichmann had said before he was captured, how he revealed himself to be a pitiless anti-Semite determined to kill as many Jews as he could, would she have changed her mind? I don't think so. She came to Jerusalem in thrall to a philosophical notion.

In the time since I first read *Eichmann in Jerusalem*, as I grew older and then old, I became less ignorant about the Holocaust.

I read some of Arendt's books and some of her writings on anti-Semitism. And I read about her relationship with Martin Heidegger.

Heidegger, whom many consider to be the greatest philosopher of the twentieth century, mentored Arendt, and they were lovers for four years. Heidegger joined the Nazi Party in 1933, ten days after being appointed as rector — vice-chancellor — of Freiburg University. He supported the Nazis and their ideology. When he joined the party, he said that 'the Fuhrer alone personifies German reality and German laws, now and in the future'. As rector, he oversaw the expulsion of all Jewish faculty members, a process that had begun before his appointment.

Luckily for her, Arendt was still in her twenties and not on the Freiburg faculty. Would Heidegger have expelled her if she had been? Heidegger never apologised for his expulsions of Jews from Freiburg University, and never repudiated his support for Nazism. I don't pretend to understand this. Perhaps you need to be a renowned intellectual to get it. I do not understand how Arendt, given Heidegger's lack of contrition, could have worked to get his philosophical work published in America. How she could accept his lack of contrition.

Nor do I understand why Arendt never acknowledged her rescue, or that of her husband, mother, or thousands of other European Jewish intellectuals, from Nazi-occupied France by the young American Varian Fry, in the face of opposition from the US State department. As previously mentioned, many of the others rescued by Fry and his committee — gifted people who went on to transform American literature, art, and philosophy — similarly never acknowledged his role in their salvation.

Arendt could, in the main, forgive Heidegger his Nazism,

but she could not acknowledge that she, a precocious and intellectually gifted German Jewish refugee, in love with German culture, its music, its writers, and its philosophers, had needed to have her life saved from her murderous German persecutors, among whom Heidegger was, at best, a fellow traveller.

Still, this is not what struck me most as I read more of Arendt's writing and the work of her many admirers and, yes, of some of her detractors. What struck me most was that Arendt had come to the trial with her mind made up—not just about Eichmann, but about the complicity of the Jewish leaders in the Nazi annihilation of millions of Jews. She had come as an admiring student of Heidegger, whose concept of thoughtlessness was central to his philosophy.

I am not going to pretend to have a deep understanding of this concept, but if thoughtfulness is the opposite of thoughtlessness—and we must assume it is—how could Heidegger join the Nazi Party and proceed to expel Jewish academics, some of whom had been his students? How could he stay in the Nazi Party during the implementation of the Final Solution? He did not suffer from thoughtlessness. He was not rendered mediocre by it, like Eichmann supposedly was. His German was perfect. He was one of the world's great thinkers. And he became a Nazi.

I was in part prompted to re-read *Eichmann in Jerusalem* by the 2012 film *Hannah Arendt*—a dramatisation by German director Margarethe von Trotta of responses to Arendt's book from her critics and supporters, although I must say that the film is unkind to the critics and too soft on her supporters. What struck me was that *Hannah Arendt* was a piece of hagiography. It revealed, though, how little research the real-life Arendt had done in preparation for her reporting of the

Eichmann trial. She had read Raul Hilberg's *The Destruction of the European Jews,* which was published in 1961 and was the first major history of the Holocaust.

At that time, there was no way Hilberg could be anywhere near definitive or comprehensive, given the vastness of the Holocaust, its reach across so many European countries, the virulent, eliminationist anti-Semitism at its centre, the machinery of killing of the German industrial state, and the role of mainly Eastern European collaborators in the attempted genocide. Most of Hilberg's study is based on Nazi documents. He had no survivor testimony, and none of the diaries and journals that Jewish groups wrote and collected in the ghettos and even in the concentration camps. He did not have access to the Soviet archives.

When those archives were made available to historians after the fall of the Soviet Union, they shed great light on the 'shooting' Holocaust in Ukraine, Russia, and Belarus, where Nazi death squads and their Eastern European helpers shot more than a million-and-a-half Jews after 1941, when the Wehrmacht invaded the Soviet Union.

Nor did Hilberg have much more than a limited number of Nazi documents available to him when he wrote about the Jewish councils and their leaders. There had been a handful of books by survivors that described the work of the councils, but no real analysis of the way they were appointed and how they operated. Since then, there have been many studies of them, and novels published about them by writers who lived in the ghettos and who were ruled by these councils and these elders. There have been documentaries about them—I am thinking particularly of *The Last of the Unjust*, a documentary about Benjamin Murmelstein, a Viennese rabbi who became the leader of the Jewish Council in the Theresienstadt concentration camp in 1944 after the two previous leaders had been killed. The film was made by Claude Lanzmann, and was based on six hours of interviews by Lanzmann with Murmelstein in Rome, where the former rabbi had settled after the war. The film was an offcut of Lanzmann's nine-and-a-half-hour-long *Shoah*, which is widely regarded as a work of surpassing power.

When I read *Eichmann in Jerusalem* for the third time, I did wonder whether Arendt would have changed her mind—or at least acknowledged the moral complexity of the victims' collaboration with their oppressors—had she read or seen any of this voluminous work on the councils and their leaders. Again, I doubt it. When I read some of her writing on anti-Semitism, and read some of the critics of her work, I realised that Arendt believed that the way diaspora Jewish community leaders had operated for centuries—doing deals with and offering special expertise to the kings, princes, and authoritarian rulers of the countries in which they lived—was a fundamental cause of the anti-Semitism from which the helpless and hapless Jews these leaders were meant to serve suffered so grievously.

It was this thesis, that the Jewish leaders of diaspora communities, far from combating anti-Semitism, were in part to blame for it, that Arendt brought to the Eichmann trial. Those earlier Jewish leaders had their equivalents in the leaders of the Jews in the ghettos of Nazi-occupied Europe.

Why is this important now, more than sixty years after Eichmann was hanged on specially constructed gallows—the only person to have been executed in Israel, since its justice system does not impose capital punishment for any crime? There are many reasons.

The trial, the first since the end of the war to expose the extent and unique evil of the Nazis' attempted genocide of the Jews, was big news. That it was held in Jerusalem confirmed, for many Jews, the miracle of Israel. For the first time in millennia, the Jews were delivering justice to their murderers and persecutors—in this case, to a man who had helped to organise the attempted genocide of their people.

Survivors told their stories. They bore witness. The prosecution laid out in graphic detail what the Nazis had done, and how that evil empire worked.

Hannah Arendt did not acknowledge any of this. She came to Israel with settled views about the country—a Jew who was once a Zionist but had become a trenchant critic of Zionism and of Israel's political class and system, and, above all, of Israeli nationalism. She quickly came to intensely dislike Israelis. She wrote to the philosopher Karl Jaspers of her disdain for the 'Oriental mob' outside the courthouse, who were behaving as if they were in Turkey or some other 'half-Asiatic country'. These 'Orientals' were Mizrachi Jews who, after Israel was established in 1948, had fled from the Arab countries where they had lived for centuries.

She excoriated Gideon Hausner, the chief prosecutor, for what she regarded as wildly overstating Eichmann's seniority in the Nazi hierarchy, and for calling Holocaust survivors to give evidence of the horrors they had suffered, when, in her view, this testimony had no direct connection to Eichmann and the charges against him. Hausner, she wrote to Jaspers, was doing Ben-Gurion's bidding. Even if this were true, she also despised Hausner personally for reasons that were not clear until much later, with the publication of her letters to Jaspers, in which she described Hausner, who was born in Lviv, in Ukraine, as a 'typical Galician Jew, very unsympathetic, boring, constantly making mistakes. Probably one of those people who don't know any language.'

There is a lot like this in Arendt's letters to Jaspers, and to other friends and colleagues she wrote to during the trial. She felt contempt for virtually every Israeli involved in the trial whose origins were in Eastern Europe. The only court officials she praised were the three judges, who, like Arendt, were all German Jews. The only Israelis she could abide were the *Yekkes,* German and Austrian Jews, some of whom, like the three judges, 'represented the best of German Jewry'.

This class and ethnic snobbery, this disparagement of Jews from Eastern Europe, where the Holocaust was centrally located and where Jews had been murdered in the greatest numbers, is disturbing. Arendt was a German Jewish snob.

What this illustrates for me is that even great thinkers like Arendt, after what had just happened to the Jews, after what she herself had been through, could blithely express not just an elitist sort of prejudice grounded in her 'Germanness', but a blunt racial prejudice towards the 'Oriental mob'.

I am not comparing Eichmann to Arendt in any way, of course. What I want to explore further is not Eichmann, but Arendt's fantasy of him. Arendt claimed that Eichmann's thoughtlessness and, consequently, mediocrity and banality explain what he was able to do. But I think Arendt, a renowned intellectual, and a proud product and lover of German culture — especially its language — was guilty of thoughtlessness herself in those prejudices and in the racism she so unapologetically expressed.

CHAPTER EIGHT

# Universalist Jews

'In the Jewish tradition, there is a concept, hard to define
and yet concrete enough, which we know as Ahavath Israel:
"Love of the Jewish people."'

— Gershom Scholem in a letter to Hannah Arendt,
23 June 1963

'I have never in my life "loved" any people or collective —
neither the German people, nor the French nor the American
... I indeed love "only" my friends and the only kind of love
I know of and believe in is the love of persons.'

— Hannah Arendt in a letter to Gershom Scholem,
20 July 1963

Hannah Arendt was what David Mamet called an anxious Jew.
I think he meant by this a Jew who is uncomfortable with any
Jewishness that in any way sets the Jews apart from other people.
Anxious Jews reject anything but the most superficial sort of
Jewish particularity. They are ashamed and angered — as Arendt
was during the Eichmann trial — not just by the Oriental mob,
but by the black-hatted Haredi Jews, with their long sidelocks

and black coats, and their babbling away in guttural Yiddish. This perceived flaunting of Jewish difference angers anxious Jews.

Universalist Jews are anxious Jews. And *Eichmann in Jerusalem* is the work of an anxious and universalist Jew. It is there in the tone of Arendt's writing, in her sarcasm, in her detachment, and in what the historian Walter Laqueur called her imperiousness and flippancy. It is there in her conclusions about what motivated Eichmann—his thoughtlessness, which has nothing to do with hatred of Jews. The only Jewish particularity she recognises is the complicity of those Jewish leaders in the Nazis' Final Solution. She removes anti-Semitism from the attempted—and almost successful—genocide of Europe's Jews. Nearly sixty years later, the actress Whoopi Goldberg—who I imagine has never read Arendt—could say that racism had nothing to do with the Holocaust, that it was not about anti-Semitism at all. It was just white guys being violent and murderous to other white guys.

And the anti-Semitism in sections of the British Labour Party under Jeremy Corbyn was often manifested through the suggestion—famously made by the former lord mayor of London, Ken Livingstone—that the Zionists in Germany had co-operated with the Nazis in the early 1930s in their goal to deport the Jews of Germany to Palestine. Arendt suggested as much in *Eichmann in Jerusalem*. When taken together with her charge that the Jewish elders had co-operated with the Nazis in the murder of millions of Jews, it is fairly clear why *Eichmann in Jerusalem* remains the seminal and foundational text of the Holocaust universalists, in which Zionism is somewhere adjacent to Nazism, and both Jewish particularity and anti-Semitism are made to vanish.

The two letters between Gershom Scholem and Hannah

Arendt that ended their friendship are really an argument about what it means to be a universalist Jew. Does it have to mean that they do not think of themselves as part of the Jewish people, if they would be expected to feel a greater love and concern for Jews than for the goyim, among whom Jews live in nations where the goyim are the vast majority?

Scholem was not an anxious Jew. He chose to live in a place—it was not yet a nation when he moved there in 1923—where the idea of the anxious Jew is meaningless. Jews in Israel might be anxious, but they are not anxious about being Jewish. This is what Amos Oz meant when he said that only in Israel could a Jew be fully a Jew.

Scholem writes to Arendt from Jerusalem, several weeks after the publication of *Eichmann in Jerusalem*. Arendt by then is back in New York, and Scholem apologises for not having written earlier. He writes that he will not deal with the factual errors or distortions in Arendt's book—others will no doubt do that work, he says—although he rejects Arendt's view of Eichmann, dismissing 'the banality of evil' as a meaningless cliché. But what he really wants to address, he writes, is the pitilessness of the terrible accusations against the Jewish leaders during the Holocaust, some of whom, he writes, acted honourably and others less so.

He writes that the question the Israeli youth was asking—why did the Jews allow themselves to be slaughtered?—is a fair and important one:

I see no readily formulated answer to it. At each decisive juncture, however, your book speaks only of the weakness of the Jewish stance in the world. I am ready to admit that weakness, but you put such emphasis upon it that, in my view, your account ceases to be objective and acquires overtones of bitterness and malice. The problem I have admitted is real enough. Why then should your book leave one with so strong a sensation of bitterness and shame—not for the compilation but for the compiler? Insofar as I have an answer … it is an answer that goes to the root of our disagreement. It is that heartless, frequently almost sneering, and malicious tone with which these matters, touching the very quick of our life, are treated in your book to which I take exception.

In the Jewish tradition, there is a concept, hard to define and yet concrete enough, which we know as Ahavath Israel: 'Love of the Jewish people'. In you, dear Hannah, as in so many intellectuals who came from the German left, I find little trace of this. A discussion such as is attempted in your book would seem to me to require—you will forgive my mode of expression—the most old-fashioned, the most circumspect, the most exacting treatment possible—precisely because of the feelings aroused by this matter, this matter of the destruction of one-third of our people—*and I regard you wholly as a child of our people and in no other way.* (Emphasis added.)

The rest of the letter is harsh. There is no 'I write more in sorrow than in anger' tone, which you might expect from someone writing to an old friend. Scholem, in essence, accuses Arendt of distorting the role played by the so-called Jewish elders in the ghettos and even in the concentration camps into which the Jews were herded by the Nazis. He argues that what she does is blur the line between tormentors and victims: 'What perversity! We are asked, it appears, to confess that the Jews, too, had their 'share' in these acts of genocide.'

And what makes this 'perversity' so unforgivable, so painful, is that Arendt is a 'child of the Jewish people'. For Scholem, the book is a betrayal of Arendt's people. This was a terrible charge to make when the black cloud of the Holocaust still hovered over Jews in Israel, America, Europe, everywhere. Scholem is saying that after the deaths of millions because they were Jews—some defined as such even when they had only a distant Jewish relative, and in many cases had converted to Christianity—how could Arendt write, in such a heartless, flippant way, that Jews had been complicit in their own destruction? Do you have no love, he cries, for the Jews, even though you are a child of our people?

Arendt responded eight days after she received Scholem's letter. She begins her letter with 'Dear Gerhard', using his German name, rather than Gershom, the name he took for himself when he went to live in Palestine in 1923, and the name he signed in the letter to her. After rejecting one of his accusations—that she came from the German left—as factually wrong, Arendt states:

> I found it puzzling that you should write 'I regard you wholly as a child of our people, and in no other way.' The truth is I have never pretended to be anything else or in any way to be other than I am ... It would have been like saying I am a man and not a woman—that is to say, kind of insane ... This attitude makes certain types of behaviours impossible—indeed precisely those which you chose to read into my considerations ...
>
> To come to the point: Let me begin, going on from what I have just stated, with what you call 'love of the Jewish people' or Ahavath Israel. (Incidentally, I would be very grateful if you could tell me since when this concept has played a role in Judaism, when it was first used in Hebrew language and literature etc.) You are quite right—I am not moved by any 'love' of this sort and for two reasons: I have never in my life

'loved' any people or collective—neither the German people,
nor the French nor the American ... I indeed love 'only' my
friends and the only kind of love I know of and believe in
is the love of persons. Secondly, the 'love of the Jews' would
appear to me, since I am myself Jewish, something rather
suspect. I cannot love myself or anything that is part and
parcel of my own person ... I do not love the Jews, nor do I
believe in them. I merely belong to them as a matter of course,
beyond dispute or argument.

Does it mean anything at all, anything consequential, her
acceptance of the fact that she is, in Scholem's words, a child of
the Jewish people? Later in the letter, she writes this: 'But I can
admit to you that the wrong done by my own people naturally
grieves me more than the wrong done by other peoples.'

Nowhere does Arendt say anything about how she
feels—whether it 'naturally' aggrieves her more—when it is
the Jews to whom serious wrong has been done. How are we to
understand what she is saying? That she feels a special grief when
Jews do wrong, but feels no special grief when Jews are wronged?
As I write, more than sixty years later, I think that this exchange
on the matter of what it means to be Jewish, on the question of
attachment to the Jewish people—on whether there is even such
a thing as Jewish peoplehood—is more compelling and relevant
than it ever was.

On the one hand, there is the Jew writing from Jerusalem
who has dedicated his life to the study of Jewish history and
aspects of Judaism, who unequivocally loves the Jewish people
and feels no need to examine how and why he is connected to
them, because they are his family. He is a Jew in full, as Amos
Oz might describe him.

On the other hand, there is the Jew writing from New York,

who rejects the notion of love, or any special feeling, for the Jewish people, but who somehow feels extra grief when Jews do bad things. She is an anxious universalist Jew who does not deny her Jewishness, but who sees it as no more than an accident of birth. Yes, her fate, I suppose.

Is that fate anything more than the fact that she was born Jewish, along with the universal values she and leftist secular Jews like me ascribe to Judaism and Jewishness — justice, equality, anti-racism, love of the stranger. What else is there that makes her Jewishness meaningful, if there is no love or deep connection with the Jewish people?

I was once a universalist Jew. Thirty years ago, I would have read these letters differently from the way I read them now. I do not know exactly how differently, but I know that the road I am on must not take me to the dead end of the word 'Jew' defining all that I am. How, then, to embrace Jewish particularity in a meaningful way while remaining true to the values and principles of social democracy that I grew up with and still hold dear? What does Jewish particularity mean for someone like me, who has been a leftist secular Jew for most of his life?

I know, I know, the conflict between Judaism's particularity and its universalism has been wrestled with and argued over by greater minds than mine, although not so much by secular leftist Jews. I do not want to be defined by my Jewishness, but nor do I want to be an anxious Jew, constantly aware that many Jews out there are giving Jews a bad name, causing them to be disliked, even hated, and that they must do everything they can to deny any association with these Jews. I do not want to go where many leftist Jews have gone, to become the sort of Jew that the German Jewish communist Rosa Luxemburg was when she was murdered by German fascists in 1919. This is what she wrote to a friend two years before her death:

What do you want with this theme of the 'special suffering of the Jews'? I am just as much concerned with the poor victims on the rubber plantations of Putumayo, the Blacks in Africa ... They resound within me so strongly that I have no special place in my heart for the ghetto. I feel at home in the entire world ...

I go back to Scholem's question to Arendt: has she no love for the Jewish people? Her answer was: I do not love a people, but only individuals. This was disingenuous. Scholem was not talking about the sort of love you have for individuals. Arendt's response, 'I indeed love "only" my friends and the only kind of love I know of and believe in is the love of persons', is really a deflection from the hard question, which is this: since you are a child of the Jewish people, do you have no special feeling for them? Being a child is being a member of a family, isn't it? I think that's what Scholem meant by love, a sort of love of fellow Jews that is familial, that you are born into.

There is no love of her fellow Jews in *Eichmann in Jerusalem*. The 'banality of evil' has become a piece of conventional wisdom for those the left, including some left-wing Jews. Eichmann's evil—Nazi evil, by implication—had nothing to do with any adherence to anti-Semitism, but was about mediocrity, an inability to think, combined with a singular ambition to get ahead. Arendt did not raise Eichmann's anti-Semitism, because to her it was not relevant to understanding his motivations, and, by implication, it was not relevant to understanding why the Nazis attempted the genocide of the Jews. I think Arendt was one of the first major thinkers—certainly one of the most consequential—to de-Jewify the Holocaust, to dismiss its particular uniqueness, its Jewish particularity, and to transform it into a crime against humanity—which it was, of course—in which the Jews, as Jews, are absent.

That's what Dara Horn was on about. People love dead Jews because they are not particularly Jews at all. They are like all of us, people who were unlucky enough to be singled out by the Nazis—but, really, it could have been any people. And any people could have been mass murderers, prepared to murder millions on an industrial scale, given the right circumstances.

And both anti-Zionists and anti-Semites have used Arendt's condemnation of the Jewish leaders in Nazi-occupied Europe to suggest that the Jews colluded in their own genocide. The Russian foreign minister, Sergey Lavrov, said as much in 2022 when someone pointed out that the president of Ukraine, Volodymyr Zelenskyy, was Jewish. Lavrov replied that he was only arguing that Jews helped the Nazis, and that not only was Hitler partly Jewish, but that some anti-Semites are Jews. Lavrov went further, and suggested that Hitler may have been a Jew, a suggestion that even his boss, Vladimir Putin, apparently said was not quite right.


Hannah Arendt had heirs, Jewish heirs, including people like Noam Chomsky—once voted the world's greatest public intellectual—who, like Arendt, had been a Zionist when he was young, but became deeply disillusioned by the 'reality' of Zionism and the state that it created. He became—and remains—an inspirational figure for anti-Zionists. The influence of these disillusioned Jews is much greater than their numbers, because their anti-Zionism, regardless of its exact nature, is exploited by pro-Palestinians and the BDS movement, and is used to dismiss accusations of anti-Semitism.

Some of my old friends from Skif, the Bundist youth group, seem to have remained anti-Zionist, even when the meaning of the term today is so different from when we were *Skifistn*. They have come to despise Zionists and Israel, not because of what Zionism once was or what Israel has become, but because of what they now believe Zionism and Israel always were—racist, colonialist, even evil. Not all my fellow *Skifistn* have taken that road, but some have become fellow travellers with Chomsky and other disillusioned former Zionists.

A few days after the University of Melbourne's Student Union passed the motion, part of which was subsequently rescinded, that branded Israel a colonial apartheid state and narrowed the definition of Jewishness to those who practise the 'Jewish faith', an old friend of mine, a former fellow *Skifist*, responded to criticism of the resolution, which had come mostly from Jews, by registering her strong support on Facebook for the resolution. Perhaps my friend did not absorb the students' definition of who is a Jew. Had she done so, she could not have prefaced her support for the student union resolution with the words 'I am a proud Jew'. She went on to write that she fully supported the resolution's description of Israel as a colonialist, apartheid state, and of Zionism as an essentially colonial and racist ideology. She embraced the resolution's support for the BDS movement, which essentially seeks to dismantle Israel as a Jewish state and replace it with a new state, Palestine—the character of which is never spelt out, although, whatever it might be, the Jews would be a minority in it.

Had we still been in touch, I would have asked her what she meant exactly when she said she was a proud Jew. Proud of what? Surely not her attachment to Judaism, for my old friend is a committed secularist who, I would guess, grew up knowing nothing or next to nothing about Judaism. She clearly is no Zionist and has no pride in—or even connection with—Jews who are Zionists, or even Jews like me who have a soft place in their hearts for Israel. It may even be that she despises these

Jews who make life hard for her, these Jews who support an evil ideology. What, then, is she proud of? It's a meaningless word in this context, isn't it? Whether consciously or not, it's a rhetorical trick designed to make it impossible to argue that she is supporting a resolution that in places is close to being anti-Semitic. How could it be anti-Semitic when Jews like my old friend support it?

While my old Skif friend was declaring her support for the resolution, over 170 academics and students from universities across Australia signed an open letter headed 'MSU stands with Palestine: an academic solidarity statement'. The statement offers support for the student union resolution and its characterisations of Israel. I would question how academics who teach in this area could publicly support such a resolution, knowing, for instance, that some of the students they teach are Jewish, and that these students, at the very least, would be concerned about how they might be treated by these solidarity-statement signers. They would find it difficult to believe that they would be treated fairly by these academics — unless, of course, these Jewish students were anti-Zionists, and basically supported the views of their academic mentors.

But what is truly astounding about the academic solidarity statement is the accusation it contains that student union members who passed the resolution are being subjected to 'bullying, harassment, and intimidation privately and publicly by Zionist groups inside and outside the University'. The statement goes on to say that Palestinian and pro-Palestinian students 'are subject to repression, fearmongering, surveillance, silencing and censorship on university campuses'. These academics then go on to demand action by university authorities to 'ensure the safety of students who take a stance against apartheid and settler colonialism'.

This is Orwellian. The only evidence the open letter provides for the very serious charge that there is a campaign by Zionists in and outside the university of harassment and intimidation—not to mention repression, fearmongering, and surveillance—is that, at the student union meeting held to vote on the resolution, students—mostly Jewish students—who opposed the resolution subjected the students involved in drafting and passing the motion to 'bullying and harassment'. What form this took is not explained. How such harassment and intimidation was possible when a large majority of the students were supporters of the resolution—which was passed comfortably—is not explained.

There is not a single piece of evidence provided for the open letter's claim that pro-Palestinian students require protection because of the activities of Zionists, and no evidence has been furnished subsequently. These are accusations untethered from facts or evidence. To the complaints from Jewish students—backed up by evidence of both the intimidation of individual students and protests aimed at silencing so-called Zionist students, the open letter, far from considering these complaints, deflects them by declaring, without any evidence, that the reverse is true, that Jewish, Zionist students and their backers outside the university—the Israel Lobby?—are making universities unsafe for the brave opponents of racism and colonialism.

One of the organisers of the petition, Jordana Silverstein, is a senior research fellow in the law school at Melbourne University. She is a cultural historian of migration and aspects of the Holocaust. The fact that she is Jewish means for some that the statement could not possibly be hostile to Jews.

This solidarity statement received very little coverage in the media. Why not? The accusations were grave. Students requiring protection is a serious problem. Bullying is a serious problem.

The idea that people outside the university were bullying and intimidating students was a very serious matter. It might even have been criminal. What was the university doing about this? What steps were being taken to make these students feel safe again?

It was a good and important story, so why the lack of interest from journalists, many of whom would have had sympathy for the pro-Palestinian students? I can only guess that it was because the accusations were literally unbelievable, so the whole thing was ignored. In any case, it was too messy, too likely to upset the people on the right side of the conflict between the Palestinians and the Zionists.

It is a sign of how much has changed in little more than a decade or so that when I was editor of *The Age*, I hardly thought about—or felt the need to debate—what was a good or bad definition of anti-Semitism, whether anti-Zionism was or was not anti-Semitism, whether a Jew like me could ever fairly run a paper's coverage of the conflict between Israel and the Palestinians, or even whether I should oversee the coverage of business, especially business where Jews were heavily involved.

I thought all these questions were settled, that the answers were self-evident. I thought those things even when the fact of my Jewishness became an issue, first for the journalists on the paper, whose career progress to some extent depended on me, and then for journalism in general, and for the wider Australian community and for the Jews.

## CHAPTER NINE

# Bad Jews

In June 1981, I arrived back in Australia after three years in London, where I had been a correspondent for The Herald and Weekly Times newspaper group. A few weeks later, I was asked to come to what I was told would be a panel discussion about the way the media covered the conflict between Israel and the Palestinians. I assumed I had been invited because of the articles I had written a few months earlier, during my first visit to Israel, which had caused something of a stir in the Melbourne Jewish community.

By the time I arrived back in Australia, I had forgotten the articles, and was surprised by the invitation. I did not know the people who issued it, and I somewhat reluctantly agreed to be on the panel. I thought the other panellists would be journalists.

The event was held in a suburban community hall on a Sunday afternoon. On stage, at the front of the hall, were six or seven chairs, with another chair set a small distance away. When I arrived, I was told I should sit on that chair. About 200 people trooped into the hall, most of whom I did not know. In the row of chairs sat not journalists, but a group of youngish men. Each of them had copies of the articles I had written. For the next hour and a half, these articles were analysed, criticised, dissected, destroyed. I was on trial!

When it came to my turn to defend myself for what I had written about Israel, I don't think I did a magnificent job. I felt I had been misled about the composition of the panel. Still, I could not help but see that these Jews were forensic, knowledgeable, articulate. They knew much more than I knew. This taking on and re-educating me, a Jewish journalist, was a mission for them. Back then, there were few Jews in journalism. It was a trade, and a poorly paid one. Few Jewish mothers would have encouraged their children — their sons, in particular — to become reporters.

I had moved on from those articles. Journalists are always moving on to the next story. But we forget that while we move on, for the people we write about, and for people like the Jews in that hall interrogating me, there is no moving on, because the stories are central to their lives and their life's work.

Like all foreign correspondents returning home, I felt unsettled, unclear about what the paper I was returning to had in store for me. I had loved the freedom of the correspondent's life. London in the late 1970s and early 1980s was the capital city of a country in decline. The empire was gone. Northern Ireland was racked by the violence of what was essentially a civil war. Racism against Blacks and South Asians was widespread. British industry was in decline; its industrial centres — Manchester and Liverpool, and other northern cities — were becoming industrial wastelands, where the future looked bleak. This was about the time, in 1979, when Margaret Thatcher came to power. Before her election, she was known as 'Thatcher the milk snatcher' because, as education minister in the Heath government during the early 1970s, she had removed free milk from Britain's schools.

We had lived in the south of London. We did not have close Jewish friends, and we were not involved in Jewish communal life. We had acquaintances who were Jewish, people my wife had known when she lived in London in the early 1970s, who we would visit from time to time. But there was a distance between us and them that we never overcame. The ancestors of these Jews had come from Eastern Europe a century before and had settled in the East End or in Manchester, but their roots were now in the middle-class suburbs of north London. They were determined not to make a fuss of their Jewishness. They were so damn English.

More than forty years later, I wonder about the English Jews we knew back then, what happened to them after Jeremy Corbyn became leader of the Labour Party. Were they still the quiet, polite, anxious, hoping-to-be-invisible Jews that we had known? They were so different from the Jews in that community hall in Melbourne who were interrogating me, those unapologetic Jews who were unashamedly defenders of Israel.

This was my first encounter with some of the Jews who would eventually become part of what came to be regarded by many on the left as the Israel Lobby, a powerful, international, secret, almost demonic group of Jews who the former premier of New South Wales and former foreign minister Bob Carr, once a passionate supporter of Israel, has described as 'the most powerful foreign influence operation in our country'—a terrible accusation that borders on a warrant for treason.

It is particularly troubling for Jews, because it carries echoes of classical Jewish conspiracy theories about Jews both being extraordinarily powerful and holding dual loyalties—that Jews are, above all, loyal to their fellow Jews.

Half a century ago, on that stage in suburban Melbourne, before they had become part of the Israel Lobby, they were a bunch of young and early-middle-aged men, none of whom I knew, but all of them punchy, smart, deeply knowledgeable about Israeli politics in a way I was not—not even close. And they were relentless. I had no great affection for them that day. Later, when I had more contact with them, and especially when I was editing *The Age,* I would often think that if their goal was to educate journalists, editors, and politicians about the conflict between Israel and the Palestinians, they were not very good at it, this so-called Israel Lobby—which is a misnomer, for it suggests they represent a foreign government, which is not true.

These young men were too ready to accuse journalists of sloppy work, too quick to see bias when, even if there happened to be bias in an article, it was not all that important. This tendency to accuse too quickly, to elevate every biased bit of reporting into something fundamentally significant, persisted even when these young men became professional lobbyists in support of Israel. I often thought that accusations of bias were not the way to influence journalists and editors. I often wondered whether other journalists disliked them more than I did. The answer to that question, I was to discover, was that there were journalists who despised the Israel Lobby and who despised its leaders. These journalists felt threatened and bullied. They believed that these lobbyists threatened to harm their careers, that they had influential friends and contacts they would lobby to try to get them sacked. They felt bullied, because these people were relentless with their complaints, constantly challenging their reporting, constantly demanding meetings with editors.

Was any of this true? Were media executives—even board members of media companies—contacted and urged to 'do something' about a particular journalist or editor? I am pretty sure it did happen. But was a journalist or editor ever moved or sacked as a result? I think not. During my seven years as editor of *The Age*, there were many instances when a politician, or a business leader, or another public figure contacted me to complain about the work of a particular journalist. Peter Costello, when he was treasurer, would call to complain about the work of Tim Colebatch, *The Age*'s veteran economics editor. Frankly, he wanted Colebatch sacked. Did he complain to the CEO or the board about this? I do not know. But I do know that, often, when they were not satisfied with my response, politicians and others went to the CEO or to members of the Fairfax board. Occasionally, the CEO or a board member would call to tell me about a complaint they had received. I would listen, but that was all. I do not remember any calls from senior Fairfax executives or board members complaining about the paper's reporting of Israel and the Palestinians.

Towards the end of my time as editor, when the prominent businessman Ron Walker was chairman of the board, Walker called me two or three times a week to suggest how I might improve the paper, and every now and then he gave me the benefit of his opinion about a particular journalist. He complained about the way the paper was 'covering Melbourne'. What he meant was that we were not enthusiastic enough about the Grand Prix or the great benefit of the Casino to Melbourne's cultural life. None of this ever went anywhere.

I thought that editors should listen to what the CEO or a board member had to say, and then ignore it. I also thought that editors — and journalists — needed to listen to complaints about the paper's journalism. Editors had power over what was published. The people who complained didn't.

I thought — and still think — that it was ridiculous for editors to whinge too much about people, such as members of the Israel Lobby, who were regular complainers. There is nothing worse than editors whingeing about what they have to put up with; thin-skinned (senior) journalists are not much better. Yes, as I've said, sometimes these complainers went above the head of the editor and complained to the CEO or a board member. That's their right. The editor has the power to decide what appears in the paper, and how it's treated. Part of the job is to listen to complaints and to meet from time to time with people — even people you don't like very much — who have problems with the paper.

In 1981, when I was on trial in that small community hall for my articles about Israel, I was found guilty of having raised unwarranted questions about Israel's survival, although no formal verdict was pronounced. There were Jews, most of them volunteers, who did *hasbara* — there is no English equivalent for the word, but it means taking on the role of explaining — for Israel. They were my interrogators at my trial.

These hasbara volunteers were keen and smart and knowledgeable, but their relentlessness, their criticism of even minor factual errors, for instance, was often counter-productive. The creation of a team of professional hasbara lobbyists was born later out of a growing dissatisfaction among Jewish community leaders with the work of the unpaid, untrained hasbara volunteers. In the 1970s and 1980s, the Israel Lobby, with its supposed power and influence, and its supposedly malign effect on Australian foreign policy, lavishly funded by wealthy Jews, did not yet exist.

There were Jewish organisations — the Zionist Federation, the Executive Council of Australian Jewry — that advocated for a close relationship between Australia and Israel. Sometimes, these organisations sent delegations to Canberra to meet with foreign ministers, even prime ministers, to discuss Australia's position on Israel and the Palestinians. But they were not considered to be a dark and nefarious and secretive cabal of

Jews doing the bidding of Israel, acting in Israel's national interests rather than Australia's. What they were doing was straightforward: they wanted to convince Australian politicians and journalists and the Australian people of the need to be 'friendly' to Israel—they called it being 'fair'. These organisations and the small group of volunteers doing hasbara wanted to put the case that friendship with and support for Israel was in Australia's national interest.

I don't think the idea that Zionism was racist and evil was widely held on either side of Australian politics, nor within Australian journalism. This was the case even though the UN General Assembly had passed a resolution in 1975 stating that Zionism was racist. That resolution had come at the height of the Cold War, and had been pushed by the Soviet Union as part of its attempt to strengthen its influence in the Arab world. The New Left, which in the aftermath of the Six-Day War in June 1967 regarded Israel as a neo-colonial state, supported the resolution, and some in the Socialist Left of the Victorian Labor Party supported it, but mainstream Labor did not. That held even after the 1982 invasion of Lebanon by the Israeli army and the massacre of Palestinians by Christian Phalange forces—Israel's allies—in two Palestinian refugee camps.

The UN resolution was rescinded in 1991. Earlier, in 1986, the Australian parliament had passed a resolution calling on the UN General Assembly to reverse its 1975 vote. Bill Hayden, the foreign minister at the time, spent a year preparing for the motion and ensuring Labor Party support for it. Australia was the first country to pass such a resolution; the US Congress followed its example, as did Britain and France. It would be an exaggeration to say that Australia played the lead role in rescinding the Zionism-is-racism resolution, but its role was significant. Hayden at the time was a leading federal member of the Centre Left faction, and yet he took on this campaign to reverse the UN resolution. While there was some disquiet on the left in the Labor Party, there was no significant pushback to Hayden's campaign.

In retrospect, this was a sort of high point — a low point for much of today's left — in the relationship between the Jewish community and the Labor Party. It is inconceivable that a Labor government today — the Albanese government, for instance — would allow a foreign minister to do what Bill Hayden did: help lead the charge to overturn a UN resolution on Israel. It would not happen, even with a Labor government that is, on any reasonable reckoning, pro-Israel.

What else has changed? The small group of Jews doing hasbara back when I first met some of them grew into a professional operation funded by donations from the Jewish community. The Australia/Israel & Jewish Affairs Council, formed in 1997 with the merger of Australia-Israel Publications and the Australian Institute of Jewish Affairs, is independent, and not answerable to the peak Jewish community organisations. But, increasingly, because it is well funded and staffed by professionals, it has come to be regarded by the political class and by journalists as the voice of the Jewish community on everything to do with Israel and Palestine. Some former senior Labor politicians who were once enthusiastic supporters of Israel believe that this well-funded and professional group of Jews has seized extraordinary powers for itself. For many on the left, this group of Jews has been able to dictate Australia's foreign policy, especially policies on the conflict between Israel and the Palestinians, to the detriment of Australia's national interest.

To me, this is both laughable and shocking. Shocking,

because I grew up a Jew a heartbeat after the Holocaust, in the shadow of Jewish powerlessness and its terrible consequences. Laughable, because, like most conspiracy theories, it is bullshit, but powerful bullshit because it is rooted in ancient prejudice.

# CHAPTER TEN
# Powerful Jews

The former New South Wales premier and foreign minister Bob Carr's journey has taken him from being a supporter of Israel to becoming a bitter enemy of the Jews who lobby for Israel. He has been on this journey since 1986, when he supported Hayden's campaign against the UN's Zionism-is-racism resolution. In 1977, he co-founded the Labor Friends of Israel group with Bob Hawke. Both Hawke and Carr had extensive contacts with the Israeli Labour Party and trade union movement. Some forty-five years later, Carr is perhaps the most prominent, relentless, even obsessive critic—hater, I'd say—of those Jews and their Jewish supporters who run the Australia/Israel & Jewish Affairs Council (AIJAC). Carr calls them variously the 'Zionist Lobby', the 'Jewish Lobby', and, ever more frequently, the 'Israeli Lobby' to signal that these Jews are corrupters of Australian foreign policy.

I am prepared to do a little psychoanalysis on Carr. Writers of long-form journalism do this all the time without declaring it. You don't need training to do a little psychoanalysis. Anyone can have a go, and many writers do, although too often they try to hide it. In fact, I have been the subject of psychoanalysis by journalists and cartoonists and media commentators over decisions I made when I was the editor of *The Age*. I always thought that was their right, even when I thought they were bad psychoanalysts. So here is my psychoanalysis of Carr.

The tone and language of Carr's distaste for the Israeli Lobby is much like the tone and language of the many critics of Israel, and particularly of the lobby in Australia and elsewhere. The dislike—hatred—is personal, as if these critics have been personally wounded by Israelis and by the powerful Jews who support them.

Carr is very angry and nasty when he writes about Israel, and particularly about the Israeli Lobby. He has been disrespected, made to feel bad by people for whom he has done so much. The Israeli Lobby is made up of ungrateful Jews. And Carr has turned these Jews into virtual Israelis. They are not even Australians, because they act in the interests of a foreign power.

When I was doing research for *The Powerbroker,* my biography of the Jewish Zionist leader Mark Leibler, published in 2020, I interviewed Carr about his relationship with Leibler when Carr was foreign minister in the Gillard government. It took some time to get Carr to agree to the interview. I had already interviewed Julia Gillard. She and Leibler were friends. She was reluctant to say too much about her relationship with Carr, a relationship that had been fractious, to say the least, basically because Carr thought Gillard was a captive of the Israeli Lobby. Gillard made it clear to me that she found this insulting, if not sexist.

When I finally spoke to Carr, his booming, theatrical voice down the phone line made it hard to get a word in edgewise. He was determined to have his say and not to be interrupted. And what he wanted to say was that he, Bob Carr, had defeated the Israeli Lobby and had broken its hold on the Labor Party; he, Bob Carr had won his long and bitter battle against these powerful Jews—though that's not what he called them, not then anyway—and he was now done with them.

What had happened? Well, Carr had initiated and promoted resolutions, first at the New South Wales Labor Party conference and later at a national conference, that called for the recognition of the state of Palestine. The resolutions were passed at both conferences with little opposition, and although they would not be binding on any future Labor government, they represented significant changes in Labor's position on the conflict between Israel and the Palestinians.

But just how this represented an ultimate victory for Carr against the forces of darkness represented by the Israeli Lobby is hard to fathom, except in the context of his personal bitterness about the way members of the lobby, Leibler among them, had treated him. After all he had done for Israel and for the Jews.

In his memoir, *Run for Your Life*, Carr writes about how these ungrateful Jews first revealed themselves when, in 2003, the lobby organised a campaign to force him, as New South Wales premier, to withdraw from the ceremony where he was to present the Sydney Peace Prize to the Palestinian activist Hanan Ashrawi. It is true that AIJAC lobbied Carr and others to withdraw from the prize-giving ceremony on the basis that Ashwari was not a peace activist. And it is true that the lobbying was a bad mistake—a mistake that Mark Leibler conceded when I spoke to him about it during my research for *The Powerbroker*. The attacks on Ashwari were extreme and mostly unjustified. This, to me, was an example of the way the so-called Israel Lobby can damage its cause by over-reaction. Nevertheless, it did not call for Ashwari to be 'banned' from entering Australia, nor did it try to silence her. The lobbying was all about getting Carr to disinvite himself from the prize-giving ceremony—a hopeless and counter-productive campaign. His reaction, though, was over the top and revealing:

The storm of criticism that then occurred was a shock ...
Soon after my participation was announced, Jewish leaders
launched an 'international petition' to force me to withdraw
from the award ... There were threats of funding being
withdrawn from the Sydney University. Letters of protest
were dispatched about the awards going to a Palestinian,
switchboards were set aflame with indignation.

Switchboards aflame. Letters dispatched. International forces
gathered to mount their attack. Threats made to withdraw their
(Jewish) money from the university if Carr was not brought
into line, although just how Sydney University was meant to
get Carr to cave and refuse to hand the prize to Ashrawi is
unclear. Of course, no such threat — if it was even made, and
there is no evidence that it was — resulted in Jewish money
being withdrawn from the university. I could find no evidence
of any sort of 'international petition' against Carr. There were,
no doubt, phone calls and letters, and no doubt some of these
were organised, but this lobby — these bullies who ran the
international campaign against him, who could set switchboards
aflame — how did it come to be so powerful?
    Carr never answers this question, because it is unanswerable
except in terms that I believe Carr would disavow. Ever since
the Ashrawi affair, Carr has regularly returned to his obsession,
one of the enduring goals of his public life: the exposure of the
nefarious nature of what he has recently come to refer to as the
Israeli Lobby. He calls it 'Israeli' in order to emphasise that it
acts on behalf of a foreign power, which, if not challenged, will
continue to distort Australia's foreign policy position — against
Australia's interests — on the Middle East, and particularly
on Israel and the Palestinians. And far from being 'done' with
the lobby, far from having achieved a total victory over it, as

he claimed to me in 2021, the lobby had to be exposed and defeated again and again. This was very personal.

So it was that after the 2022 election and the Labor Party's victory, Carr wrote a piece for the website *Pearls and Irritations* in which he celebrated, again, the thwarting of the Israeli Lobby's plans—this time, to re-elect the pro-Israel Morrison government. It is a strange piece, to say the least. It argues that the Israeli Lobby—and by now, Carr means every Jewish organisation, no matter how big or small, whether mainstream or extreme—had organised a (failed) campaign to make sure that Australian Jews voted for the Coalition, especially in the handful of seats in Melbourne and Sydney with sizeable Jewish populations. (There were nowhere near Jewish majorities in any of these electorates.)

Virtually every Jewish organisation, according to Carr, urged Jews to vote for the Coalition, as if the future of Israel depended on it. He even criticised the *Australian Jewish News* for interviewing *The Australian*'s star investigative reporter Sharri Markson, as if interviewing a journalist were a sinister thing for a newspaper to do. This is where a belief in a conspiracy theory often leads—to bullshit. It is true that Markson is a fiercely pro-Israel journalist. There are things about her work that make me uneasy. Her articles in *The Australian* during the election campaign about Albanese's long-ago political past, when he was a committed left-winger, were not examples of outstanding journalism, but it is simply ridiculous to suggest that the fact that the *Jewish News* interviewed Markson was sinister enough to condemn the paper as a member of the dreaded lobby.

To confirm its role in the Israeli Lobby's campaign, Carr wrote that the *Jewish News* had published an editorial urging a vote for the Coalition. *The Australian* newspaper had also been captured by the lobby, according to Carr. What was the evidence for this startling claim? In its final editorial before the election, the paper had argued that Albanese's views on Israel disqualified him from becoming prime minister. Amazing, the power of the lobby!

What was Carr on about? Two things: first, he wanted to show Albanese and his foreign minister, Penny Wong, that when it came to Israel, they did not need to appease the Jews, to be trapped by them or to give in to their pressure, because 'no matter what concessions Labor gives to the Lobby it will always in the end support the Coalition'. And why? Because the lobby, according to Carr, was moving to the hard right, and no Labor government could ever win its support:

> The lobby is accommodating new right-wing voices, specifically the Australian Jewish Association, which stakes out conservative positions on social issues as well as the hardest of hard lines in support of ultra-nationalism in Israeli politics.

But the second point Carr wanted to make was that the lobby's campaign had failed. Dismally. This was cause for celebration, and Carr was celebrating.

As I write, I wonder whether Carr is worth all this attention. After all, he was an insignificant foreign minister, an appointment by Julia Gillard that she no doubt came to regret. Carr is a more significant and consequential activist in Australia's relationship with China, a much more critical issue for Australia than Israel or the Palestinians. And on China, Carr, who ran the Australia-China Relations Institute at the University of Technology Sydney from 2014 to 2019, with funding from a wealthy China-based businessman, has hardly been trenchant in his criticism of China's human rights record, including the attempted genocide of the Uyghurs.

But I think he is worth the attention because his obsession with the Israel Lobby is not singular. It is common, not just among anti-Zionists — and Carr is not an anti-Zionist, at least not yet — but among large sections of the left, including the Jewish left, in Australia, the United States, and Canada.

The obsession leads to startling distortions and so-called facts that are fictions. Convinced of the power and influence of the Israel Lobby, everything that happens and that is said must be made to fit into this conspiracy theory about Jews and Jewish power.

This is what actually happened in the 2022 Australian federal election. It is simply not true that any of the major Jewish organisations that presumably constitute the Israel Lobby — the Executive Council of Australian Jewry, the Zionist Federation of Australia, and AIJAC, which is openly a pro-Israel lobbying outfit — came out in support of the Coalition or urged a vote against Labor. As for the Australian Jewish Association, cited by Carr above, it may have advocated a vote for the Coalition, but I don't know if it did and, frankly, why would anyone care? Except for Bob Carr?

The AJA — a laughable and grandiose title if ever there was one, is a fringe group of mainly elderly Jews — some of whom drove me crazy when I was editor of *The Age*. It might have 100 members, but this is unknowable, as they do not reveal their membership. Every major Jewish organisation has repudiated the AJA and has emphasised that its politics are not shared by their organisation or by the vast majority of Australian Jews.

Why, then, would Carr elevate this fringe group into a powerhouse of Jewish influence that has pushed the Israel Lobby to the right and somehow forced it to organise the campaign against Labor in the 2022 election? I think the answer is obvious: this is where conspiracy theories end up, in a fantasy world of shadowy and malevolent groups out to rule the world.

Nor is it true that *The Australian Jewish News*, in its election editorial, urged a vote for the Coalition. It did not. The major Jewish organisations did what they do at every election: they asked the major parties to answer questions about a whole range of issues, ranging from Jewish welfare concerns, their support for Jewish education, their attitudes to and funding of Jewish security challenges, and their position on the conflict between Israel and the Palestinians. The answers were then published on the websites of the organisations and, in abbreviated form, in the *Jewish News*. Not one of these organisations urged a Jewish vote against Labor.

And what about *The Australian*, which, according to Carr, stated in its election editorial that Albanese's views on Israel meant he should not be prime minister? This is what the editorial says:

> Mr Albanese is a formidable politician. A man of great depth, if little non-political experience, thoughtful, considerate: an authentic man who over many years has shown himself to be a collegiate and capable figure of substance in the labour movement who seems to have transformed himself from the loony university left of Labor to a centrist.

The editorial then suggests — disgracefully, in my view — that Albanese's old left-wing views cannot be ignored:

> ... he has failed to explain how and why he has changed his mind on so many substantial obsessions of the hard left, including their attitude to Israel.

This is nonsense, but the paper is not saying that the old

hard left's attitudes to and positions on Israel, which Albanese may or may not have shared, but certainly does not now support, means that Albanese should never be prime minister. This is just a Carr distortion, because he is fixated on the power of the Israeli Lobby. Look, those Jews can even get a newspaper—okay, only *The Australian*, but still—to rule out Albanese as a prime minister because he was once a member of the Labor Party 'hard left' that was hostile to Israel!

A fixation on the Israel Lobby is commonplace among the left, and particularly among the anti-Zionist left. Like any conspiracy theory, it is impervious to questioning or criticism. If you suggest, for instance, that some anti-Zionism verges on anti-Semitism because it uses classic anti-Semitic tropes—such as the spectre of rich, secretive, and super-powerful Jews running the media—this is taken as proof that you are either part of the lobby or have been captured by it. If you say that the so-called Israel Lobby cannot be behind every pro-Israel decision and position taken by every government, politician, and journalist, you will be invariably called out as part of the Israel Lobby trying to silence the critics of Israel.

Here is an example of this sort of tactic. After *Pearls and Irritations* published Carr's post-election piece, Michael Easson, a former vice-president of the Australian Council of Trade Unions, a long-time senior official in the New South Wales branch of the Labor Party, wrote a response pointing out some of the errors in the piece. Easson's article was conciliatory. He and Carr had known each other for decades, and had both been members of Labor Friends of Israel. Easson has remained in the group, whereas Carr long ago went in a different direction. In response to the Easson piece, Carr wrote what any reasonable person would describe as a personal and at times vicious attack. Easson asked for a right of reply. He submitted a short and again conciliatory piece suggesting that he and Carr could try to sort out their differences.

This was the response from John Menadue, the editor and publisher of *Pearls and Irritations*, a former diplomat and senior public servant who, many years before, had gone on to become a senior executive in the Murdoch empire: 'I will not be posting [your piece]. You have had a good run. I think your views are indefensible and offensive towards others.'

That was it. Nothing more. No details were needed about what was indefensible or offensive to others in Easson's piece. It was understood. It was the pro-Israel and pro-Zionist Easson, the person, who was offensive and indefensible — not anything in particular that he wrote.

When and where did this start, this obsession on the left with the power of the Zionists? The Zionists, who cowed prime ministers and presidents into supporting Israel, no matter what Israel did to the Palestinians, and no matter that this support was against the national interests of America, Canada, or Australia?

I was living in Washington, DC, in 2006 when, on 23 March, the political scientists John Mearsheimer and Stephen Walt, both eminent academics at major American universities, published a long piece in the *London Review of Books*. The essay bluntly stated, without qualifications or leaving any room for debate, that something they called 'the Israel Lobby' had distorted American foreign policy to such an extent that, for decades, presidents and Congress had acted in Israel's rather than America's national interest.

The piece became a sensation — a rare thing in journalism, especially in a small and elite publication such as the *London Review of Books*. It was widely quoted and debated. Mearsheimer and Walt became regulars on cable TV and on the major free-to-air television networks. It felt like a shift had taken place in the debate about US foreign policy on the Middle East, on Israel in particular.

What was most startling for me about this piece was the authors' use of the term 'the Israel Lobby'. Mearsheimer and Walt never said exactly who it comprised — they called it 'a loose coalition of individuals and organisations without a central headquarters'—but, reading the piece, it becomes clear that, for them, every Jewish institution and organisation in America is part of the lobby. Perhaps all Jews, no matter whether they are progressive Zionists, or supporters of Likud, or supporters of the Religious Zionist extremists who want to expel the Arabs from Israel and from the West Bank, are part of this powerful lobby? So successful had these Jews been that they had dragged America into a foreign policy that resulted in the attacks of September 11 and the wars in Afghanistan and Iraq. The Jews were ubiquitous, in the universities, in congressional offices, in the national security organisation, in the administration, everywhere, and their power was unmatched:

> Other special-interest groups have managed to skew foreign policy, but no lobby has managed to divert it as far from what the national interest would suggest, while simultaneously convincing Americans that US interests and those of the other country — in this case, Israel — are essentially identical.

To some, it seemed that Mearsheimer and Walt had shone a light on malevolent Jewish influence in — but not only in — the George W. Bush administration. It was also there in publishing, in American universities, and in the American media — nearly everywhere in American life. Then Mearsheimer and Walt turned their article into a bestselling book: *The Israel Lobby and US Foreign Policy*.

In journalism and in academic life, timing is everything. In 2006, the invasion and subsequent occupation of Iraq was a failed enterprise at best. The occupation was a shambles, and the raison d'être for the invasion—that Saddam Hussein had weapons of mass destruction—had been shown to be a fiction, a huge intelligence failure by US intelligence agencies. How had America got into this mess? Who was responsible for this catastrophe? George Bush, after all, was widely regarded as a know-nothing idiot—I remember the contempt with which my American friends spoke of him—which meant that some person or group was pulling the strings, the shadowy puppet masters of an illiterate president. These puppet masters—all neo-conservatives, many with close links to the Israel Lobby, according to these two scholars—had manipulated Bush and other senior people in his administration into invading Iraq, because that was what Israel wanted.

Mearsheimer and Walt maintained that Israel shared much of the responsibility for both 9/11 and the subsequent war in Iraq, because it had warped US foreign policy. It was America's siding with Israel against the Arab countries and the Palestinians—against America's national interest—that had been a major contributor to the terrorism that had delivered the 9/11 attacks on America.

Who were these people in the Bush administration who worked secretly and zealously to advance the interests of Israel? Well, according to Mearsheimer and Walt, they were a small number of staffers concentrated in the offices of the vice-president, Dick Cheney, and the defense secretary, Donald Rumsfeld, many of whom were Jews. They were also neo-conservatives, supporters of a foreign policy position developed by, among others, Jewish intellectuals such as Irving Kristol and Norman Podhoretz. Podhoretz ran *Commentary* magazine, for decades the favoured journal of neo-conservatives, run and financed by Jews and Jewish organisations.

Neo-conservatives believed in the use of American military power to spread democracy in the Middle East. They argued that, after the collapse of the Soviet Union, the US military should be used to change the regimes in those countries in the Middle East and South Asia that supported and gave succour to the terrorists responsible for the 9/11 attacks. The neo-conservatives were for an interventionist foreign policy backed by US military power. But Mearsheimer and Walt implicitly suggested that their patriotism was feigned and that their stated position on American foreign policy just a ruse. They were, in fact, agents of influence for Israel buried in the heart of the Bush administration.

It is true that most neo-conservatives were supporters of Israel, and it is true that most of them were Jews. I met some of these people in Washington. Paul Wolfowitz, who was a deputy secretary of defense working for Donald Rumsfeld, was a polite and quietly spoken man, self-deprecating about his 'power', and bemused, at least publicly, by allegations of dual loyalties—a charge that anti-Semites had used for centuries to smear the Jews and justify their persecution.

When I read Mearsheimer and Walt's article, and later their book, I looked for evidence for their charge that Wolfowitz's neo-conservative colleagues were largely responsible for the Iraq War, that they had advocated and planned for it in a way that served the interests of Israel. What magical power did they possess, these Jews who worked in the Bush administration, in cahoots with the leaders of American Jewish organisations? How could they manipulate their superiors, Bush and Cheney and Rumsfeld and Condoleezza Rice—in the cases of Cheney and Rumsfeld, politicians of long experience, and in the case of

Rice, a person with significant foreign policy expertise — into acting against US interests?

Where was the proof that Osama bin Laden, as Walt and Mearsheimer argued, had been motivated to organise the 9/11 attacks because of the US's support for Israel? Where was the real proof that Israel was desperate for the US to take on Saddam Hussein, or that the US had invaded Iraq at Israel's behest? There was none. There was nothing to show that support for Israel was Bin Laden's motive for attacking the US — the Great Satan — and there was no proof that the US had invaded Iraq at Israel's behest. The evidence they provided was scanty, and all of it was contestable.

In the end, I believe this is a proposition for which there is no hard evidence. Iraq was no threat to Israel. Surely it would have all come out, one way or another, if Israel had advocated for a war in Iraq, insisted on it, and organised support in Congress for it? But, as far as I can tell, nothing came out — certainly, Mearsheimer and Walt produced no real proof of Israel's advocacy for the war in Iraq.

The neo-conservatives had their moment of glory during the Bush years, but it did not last. The Iraq fiasco was the beginning and the end of their influence. They had no place in the Obama administration because, by then, the idea of an interventionist foreign policy was anathema among both Democrats and Republicans in Washington. Both Obama and, later, Trump were determined to get America out of its foreign entanglements, wars, and security commitments, to get out of Iraq, Afghanistan, and Syria, and, in Trump's case, to even get out of NATO.

The neo-conservatives were dead as a force in US foreign policy, but Mearsheimer and Walt's Israel Lobby did not die with the neo-conservatives, according to much of the left of the

Democratic Party. Instead, it became even more powerful and sinister as it continued working to distort US foreign policy in the interests of Zionists and Israel. Born in the US, the Israel Lobby now lives, thrives, and grows in power in the minds of many in Australia, Canada, and Britain as an international force that is responsible for much of what is wrong with the world.

I am exaggerating, but not by much. Haven't some people always believed that Jews control everything? *The Protocols of the Elders of Zion* was long ago shown to be a forgery written and published in Russia on the orders of the tsar, but it lives on as an 'authentic' document in much of the Muslim world, and in countries such as Japan where there are no Jews. While I do not think that those who have invested the Israel Lobby with magical powers believe that *The Protocols of the Elders of Zion* is anything but an anti-Semitic forgery, there is some echo, isn't there, of it in their loathing—and fear, in my view—of this cabal of Jews?

One consequence is that for much of the left, no government, prime minister, or president, indeed no politician on the left, can express pro-Israel views, even of the most moderate kind, and be taken at their word—that they believe what they are saying, and have come to such views after careful consideration.

According to Israel Lobby obsessives, these politicians have simply surrendered to the lobby. Every politician and journalist who has not denounced Zionism and has refused to see the conflict between Israel and the Palestinians in black-and-white terms is part of the Israel Lobby, or has been captured by it.

In terms of winning elections, Tony Blair was the most successful prime minister in the history of British Labour. His government had a substantial record of what I would call social-democratic achievements, including strengthening the social welfare safety net and significantly increasing funding for the National Health Service. But, in the end, Blair became a figure of hate for many in the Labour Party, and that hatred has grown ever fiercer. The hatred is ostensibly about Blair's support for the war in Iraq, but it is about more than that. What really made him such a hated figure was that he openly praised and supported the idiot George Bush, and therefore American imperialism. According to many of his colleagues, he was a supporter of Zionism and Israel, and, in their eyes, a captive of the Israel Lobby.

Julia Gillard, Australia's first female prime minister, appointed two foreign ministers — first Kevin Rudd and then Bob Carr — who both came to believe that Gillard had been rendered a captive of the Israel Lobby. Even before she deposed him as prime minister, Rudd had concluded, as he writes in the second volume of his memoir, *The PM Years*, that Gillard had become a 'subsidiary' of the lobby, of Mark Leibler in particular. Leibler had cultivated her, and she had allowed herself to be cultivated. Leibler had transformed her views on Israel and the Palestinians. When I asked Carr whether Gillard had been captured by the Israel Lobby, he answered that because he had defeated the lobby, had destroyed its influence in the Labor Party, there was no longer any point in talking about what had happened to Gillard.

Would this not have been a fabulous story for a political journalist to have followed up? How two senior Labor politicians, one a former prime minister, both having served in the cabinet of Australia's first female prime minister, came to regard her as a captive of the Israel Lobby? It was not simply that she had views about Israel and Palestine — and the power of the lobby — that they did not share. No, at least as far as Rudd was concerned, Leibler had been party to the plot to replace him as PM with Gillard. Perhaps this was just too far-fetched for the federal press gallery journalists to follow up. Perhaps it was too hard, because Gillard was not prepared to comment on any of it—not directly anyway. Apparently, it was not a worthwhile story, for none was ever written or broadcast about Carr's and Rudd's allegations.

In Britain, the hatred of Blair by much of the Labour Party led, in part, to the eventual elevation to the party leadership of Jeremy Corbyn, for long an obscure backbencher and a left-wing ideologue who was everything that Blair was not. Apart from anything else—and there were lots of anything elses—Corbyn and his supporters were fiercely anti-Zionist, fiercely critical of Israel and its racist, colonialist nature, and fierce believers in the Israel Lobby conspiracy theory.

What did this mean? It meant that even when independent investigations concluded that the Labour Party under Corbyn had a significant anti-Semitism problem, Corbyn and his supporters insisted—and continue to insist—that anti-Semitism in the Labour Party was an oxymoron, since Labour was the party of anti-racism. Moreover, the suggestion that Labour might have an anti-Semitism problem was the work of the Israel Lobby, and was designed to silence criticism of Israel and support for the Palestinians living under a brutal apartheid regime.

Every Jewish Labour MP who said they had been subjected to anti-Semitic attacks was dismissed as a Corbyn opponent doing the work of the lobby. All Jewish groups—from the British Board of Deputies to representatives of local synagogue communities who complained about anti-Semitism in the Labour Party, expressing what they felt, viscerally, in the way that people subjected to racism always feel these things—were dismissed as anti-Corbyn right-wingers and as shills for Zionism and Israel.

This has become the standard response to any claim that anti-Zionism and opposition to Israel's existence as a Jewish state can sometimes use anti-Semitic tropes. For part of the left, anti-Semitism on the left does not exist. Rather, it is a weapon used by powerful Jews to silence the truth-tellers, including those righteous Jews who are brave enough to call out the evils of Zionism and apartheid Israel.

In his 2017 book, *Contemporary Left Antisemitism*, David Hirsh, a British secular leftist Jew and former Marxist, argues that some expressions of anti-Zionism are anti-Semitic. I think the case he makes is compelling. Hirsh is an academic sociologist, but while his book is in part based on the methodologies of sociology, it is not an academic book. It is permeated by fear, full of foreboding about anti-Semitism in the British left, of which he is a long-time member — fearful that its growth is unstoppable, particularly in British universities, where being a Jewish academic or student who does not condemn Zionism is to be cast out of university communities, including the academic trade unions. Hirsh, who once saw himself as not a particularly Jewish Jew, now finds that, for his critics, everything he writes, every example he gives of left-wing anti-Semitism, is dismissed as an example of propaganda from a Zionist, which is to be a particularly dishonourable sort of Jew.

Even people who are not Jews can be made Jewish under these new definitions. In his book, Hirsh refers to a column by the English journalist Nick Cohen that was published in *The Observer* in March 2016, a year after Jeremy Corbyn was elected Labour leader.

At this point, it is important to say that Cohen resigned from *The Observer* in January 2023 and moved his column to Substack. In an article published in *The New York Times* on

1 May, he was accused of sexual harassment at *The Observer*, where he had been a columnist for 20 years. The article reported that seven women had made allegations against Cohen of harassment and, in some cases, of groping. In the article, Cohen is quoted as saying that until 2016 he was an alcoholic and is ashamed of how he behaved before he 'got clean'. The accusations are entirely credible. The question is, does that disqualify him from having a voice on any issue? He is ashamed, he has left mainstream journalism, and he deserves the public shaming. But I do not believe he should be totally cancelled, vanished for good from public life. He is an award-winning journalist, has been considered a major voice on the British left, and was a brave critic of Jeremy Corbyn. And so I quote him here.

Cohen was 'a red-diaper baby', an American term used to describe people whose parents were communists. Although Cohen is not a communist or Marxist, he remains on the left. Yet he criticises those leftists who he believes support autocracies and radical Muslim fundamentalists because they are anti-American and therefore anti-imperialist. He was a critic of Corbyn's support for Hamas and Hezbollah, which, in Cohen's view, were opposed to everything the left stood for.

Cohen also thought that Corbyn and some of his followers failed to call out anti-Semitism in the Labour Party. Not only that, he argued, but they also employed what Hirsh labelled 'the Livingstone manoeuvre'—after the former mayor of London and Labour veteran Ken Livingstone, who responded to Jews in and outside the party warning that Labour had an anti-Semitism problem not by rebutting their claims, but by labelling them as Zionist stooges who were using the accusation of anti-Semitism to destroy Corbyn as leader of the Labour Party.

This is how Cohen started his column:

It took me 40 years to become a Jew. When I was a child, I wasn't a Jew and not only because I never went to a synagogue. My father's family had abandoned their religion so he wasn't Jewish. More to the point, my mother and my grandmother weren't Jewish either, so according to orthodox Judaism's principles of matrilineal descent, it was impossible for me to be a Jew.

All I had was the 'Cohen' name …

Like his parents, he did not think that being a Cohen would ever be a cause of concern for him. Yes, some people might mistakenly take his name to mean he was Jewish, but so what? Being mistaken for being a Jew is not a great burden in twenty-first-century Britain. Or so he thought.

Cohen's name did become a burden. He became his name. Everything he wrote was considered through the prism of his 'Jewishness'.

When I first responded to the antisemitism that has spread so far from the extreme left into the mainstream that it now threatens to poison the Labour party, I am ashamed to say I considered two disgraceful replies.

I might, I thought, not stop at opposing the Israeli occupation of the West Bank, and pledging support to leftwing Israelis and Palestinians who wanted a just and peaceful settlement for both peoples, but go on to behave like a grotesque from a Howard Jacobson satire. I would reassure fanatics that their 'anti-Zionism' (that is, their call for the total destruction of the world's only Jewish state) was not remotely racist.

Cohen did not do that, but he did say to anyone who asked—and some who did not—that, despite 'appearances to the contrary, I am not Jewish':

> And that was as dishonourable. I sounded like a black man trying to pass as white or a German arguing with the Gestapo that there was a mistake in the paperwork.
>
> I stopped and accepted that racism changes your perception of the world and yourself. You become what your enemies say you are. And unless I wanted to shame myself, I had to become a Jew. A rather odd Jew, no doubt: a militant atheist who had to phone a friend and ask what on earth 'mazel tov' meant. But a Jew nonetheless.
>
> As one of the finest liberal ambitions is to find the sympathy to imagine the lives of others, you should become a Jew too. Declare that you have converted to Judaism or rediscovered your Jewish 'heritage' and see the reaction. It's not just that, if you are middle class and fortunate, you might experience racism for the first time, which in itself would be a 'learning experience' worth having. You might also learn the essential lesson that antisemitism is not about Jews. Like rape, it is about power.

I have no idea what sort of response there was to this astounding column, but I imagine that it was essentially ignored, especially by the Corbyn-supporting left. By this time, it had so thoroughly demonised Zionism and Zionists that Cohen's column would have been seen as yet another example of Zionist perfidy. But what it illustrates, I believe, is that 'Zionist' and 'Jew' have become interchangeable, and that calling someone a Jew is no different from calling them a Zionist. Both are insults.

And it is Jews who have long been warriors of the left who are most often targeted by anti-Zionists. In a paper published in *Fathom* magazine in 2021, the Australian academic Philip Mendes quotes the British radical-left activist Steve Cohen parodying the way he has been targeted by anti-Zionists:

> Every Jew on the left will know that terrible syndrome whereby, whatever the context and wherever one is, we will be tested by being given the question; what is your position on Zionism? Wanna support the miners—what's your position on Zionism? Against the bomb—what's your position on Zionism? And we all know what answer is expected in order to pass the test. It is a very strong form of anti-Semitism based on assumptions of collective responsibility. Denounce Zionism, crawl in the gutter, wear a yellow star and we'll let you in the club.

Under the 'terrible syndrome' that Cohen identifies, Zionists become less people and more a collection of conspiracists with little if any capacity for love and empathy and fear. Nor do Israelis possess any of these human qualities, since they live in the Zionist state. Nothing said or done to such people can be anti-Semitic, since they are oppressors and supporters of oppressors.

The erasure of anti-Semitism has spilt over from anti-Zionist and anti-Israel positions into the social justice and anti-racist movements, where the Jews are defined as possessors of white privilege, at best, and adherents of white supremacy, at worst. To put it another way, since Jews are powerful, they cannot, by definition, be the victims of racism.

Where does this lead? Alice Walker, the celebrated Black American writer, author of *The Color Purple*—a bestseller that

Steven Spielberg made into an award-winning film—was asked by *The New York Times* in 2018, as part of an interview series, to nominate the books she had on her nightstand. The second recommendation on her list was *And the Truth Shall Set You Free*, by the British writer David Icke. By any reckoning, the book is full of anti-Semitism, including its suggestions that a Jewish clique created the Russian Revolution and the two world wars, as well as the Holocaust. The Jews, Icke has written elsewhere, are lizard people, aliens doing evil in the human world.

When Walker was criticised for selecting Icke's work, and the newspaper was criticised for running her selection without comment, she dismissed the charge of anti-Semitism against Icke as an attempt to silence him. But Walker is simply a classic anti-Semite, whose history of Jew-hatred has nothing to do with her professed support for the Palestinian cause. In a poem first published in 2017, 'It Is Our (Frightful) Duty to Study the Talmud', Walker expresses the most paranoid and scurrilous libels against Jews and the Talmud, which she describes as 'poison' and as justifying making goyim slaves of Jews.

While several Jewish writers called out Walker's anti-Semitism, there was little outrage or condemnation of her views from literary critics and commentators. Mostly, there was silence. Several years later, in June 2022, *Gathering Blossoms Under Fire: the journals of Alice Walker* was published to great acclaim. A glowing review from Helen Elliott in *The Age* ends like this:

> In Walker's case, beauty is a bulwark.
>
> So are these journals. She needs a bulwark because, lately, she's been saying some very crazy things. The journals show her at her peak and at her best.

Elliott is one of Australia's best literary critics, which makes it incomprehensible to me that she could write such a paragraph, and that *The Age*'s literary editor could wave it through without asking Elliott what these 'very crazy things' that Walker had been saying lately were. How was a reader meant to know what the hell Elliott was talking about?

It seems to me obvious that Elliott did not want to reveal the fact that this most revered Black female writer was an anti-Semite. She'd said crazy things, that's all. Nothing else to see here. And even then, Elliott got it wrong. Walker had not started to say crazy things lately. She started saying such things more than a decade ago. And not just saying them, but writing them in her poetry and prose.

Why did Elliott find it so hard to call Alice Walker an anti-Semite — or, at the very least, call out what is clearly anti-Semitic in her public pronouncements and in some of her writing? The answer is that the erasure of anti-Semitism is now widespread, especially if it is not clearly and definitively neo-Nazi in character. And it cannot be anti-Semitism if it comes from victims of racism, from Black or Brown people, or from the victims of colonialism. If it comes from a Black woman such as Alice Walker, it cannot really be anti-Semitism. It is just a victim saying 'some very crazy things'.

# CHAPTER ELEVEN

# The Jewish editor

I was appointed editor of *The Age* in September 1997. On the Saturday before my appointment was announced, Princess Diana died in a car accident. I thought I should write something for the paper about this, even though I was not on staff. I was at the football. I left at half-time and ran through the parkland in Princes Hill to *The Age*'s building. I was younger then.

The piece I wrote was terrible. I had been a journalist long enough to know when I had nothing interesting to say. I should not have written it, and it should not have been published. Journalists find it hard to admit that they do not know much about a particular issue. But their editors ought to encourage them to be frank about the limits of their knowledge, and if they then write something, the limits to what they know should be made clear.

In the online world, for journalists to say they do not know something or have nothing new or interesting to offer is close to impossible if they want to keep working. On social media and on that seemingly endless list of news websites, even those of major newspapers, with their minute-by-minute deadlines, there is no time for thought and reflection, and so time — past, present, and future — collapses in their work.

I am not saying these things to offer up some sort of

retrospective from an old man who paints his long-ago journalistic past in golden hues. I say them because these issues about journalism sit here with me ever more acutely as I write. The way things change with time, with looking back and forward, and the way the writer ages and changes — all these things sit with me. The most important questions for a journalist working on a story should be: what is factual, and how much do I know about the subject? This is not a matter of aiming for objectivity or even fairness. It is a requirement for self-interrogation about honesty — about declaring what you know, the limits to what you know, and, often, the seeming endlessness of what you don't know.

I believe that much of the reporting and commentary from the Middle East is full of certainties that are far from certain. The lack of any sense of doubt or of the limitations of what can be known, the lack of nuance, makes me doubt not so much its factual accuracy as its truthfulness and fairness.

In the age of the multitudes of what were once called, rather optimistically, citizen journalists on social media — particularly Twitter — is it asking too much of us journalists to be modest about what we know, and honest about what we don't? I fear the answer might increasingly be that it is asking too much or, more likely, 'This question is so out of date, you old, privileged white man.' Some might even add 'Jewish'.

But I think self-interrogation remains important for journalists, despite the pressures on them to abandon it. I think admitting the limits of what you know, and saying that some things might be unknowable, remains important. I interrogate myself as I write this book, and I ask myself why I have offered no commentary so far on the conflict between Israel and the Palestinians. The answer is not simple.

One reason is that I have done no reporting from Israel,

Jerusalem, Ramallah, or Gaza City for more than a decade. There is much I simply do not know.

In *The Powerbroker*, the biography I wrote in 2019 of Mark Leibler, a prominent and uncompromising Australian Jewish leader and advocate for Israel, I did not offer up my opinion about his views, nor did I suggest what my views about Zionism and Israel might be. I have not written any commentary on the conflict between Israel and the Palestinians for decades. I have been asked to do so, but I have declined. I had nothing original or new to say that has not been said by others, many times over.

But I am now not able to maintain this position, not in a book like this. In the past, some people, including colleagues at *The Age*, no doubt saw my silence as cowardice. They would have concluded that I was silent because I wanted to deny the fact of my being a Jew, because, in their eyes, being a Jew should have disqualified me not just from reporting on the conflict between Israel and the Palestinians, but from running *The Age*'s coverage of the Middle East. In fact, I believed—and still believe—that journalists, reporters, and editors need to avoid, as far as possible, the perception that they are activists for a cause. And, yes, I did not want everything I wrote to be seen through the lens of my Jewishness. But I will now, for whatever it may be worth, enter into that hot and fearful space where reporting and commentary on the conflict between Israel and the Palestinians lives, and where, it seems to me, good intentions and humanity and history are never accepted at face value.

It was not that long ago in years—but pre-digital time feels like centuries ago—when, as editor of *The Age*, a quality daily newspaper, I shaped and oversaw the paper's coverage of Israel and Palestine.

I was a Jewish editor. A decade ago, that had a meaning and consequences vastly different from its contemporary meaning and consequences. In the history of the Jews, being a Jew has hardly ever been a matter of self-definition alone. Jews were also Jews because the non-Jews around them — the communities and nations in which they had lived for generations and were citizens — saw them as Jews first and hardly ever as Poles, Hungarians, or Russians, or even as English, French, or German. They were Jews, and often 'You are a Jew' was an accusation that had dire consequences, for the Jews of Europe in particular.

For a period after the Holocaust, being Jewish became essentially a question of self-definition. The non-Jews had no say in whether I was a Jew. This was so for various reasons, but the main one was that after the Holocaust, the Nazi definition of a Jew, which was wholly related to blood, had been discredited. The Nazis had a formula for deciding who was a Jew: a percentage of Jewish blood in your ancestry decided it. Even Jews who thought of themselves as non-Jews — those who had converted or whose parents had converted to Christianity — were classified as Jews if they had the percentage of Jewish blood required to make them Jewish. And they suffered the consequences.

But those several post-Holocaust decades, during which Jews were allowed to self-define their Jewishness and what it meant to be Jewish, have passed. Increasingly, especially on the left, whether you are a good or bad Jew — and even whether you are a Jew at all, in some cases — are matters to be determined on the basis of whether you are a Zionist or an anti-Zionist. That was what the University of Melbourne student declaration in 2022 sought to determine: not just who is a good Jew and who is a bad Jew, but who is actually a Jew. As we've seen, in their declaration, they defined Jews as those who follow the Jewish religion. That's it. Secular Jews are not Jews. Jews born of Jewish mothers but who are not religious are not Jews. Most of the world's Jews, according to this definition, are not in reality Jews.

I cannot recall ever thinking about any of this sort of madness, not when I was a reporter and not when I was an editor. I hardly thought about or felt the need to debate what was a good or bad definition of anti-Semitism, whether anti-Zionism was or was not anti-Semitism, whether a Jew like me could ever fairly run a major paper's coverage of the conflict between Israel and the Palestinians, or even whether I could oversee the coverage of business, especially businesses in which Jews were heavily involved. The fact that I was a Jew did not disqualify me — nor, I believed, would it disqualify any Jewish journalist in the future — from being appointed the editor of a paper with a storied history like *The Age*. I thought these issues were settled and self-evident, even when the fact of my Jewishness became a problem from time to time.

When did it become clear to me that I was no longer able to define who I was, and what it meant to be a Jew? For some people, including some journalists on *The Age* who worked with and for me, my Jewishness mattered. It certainly mattered from time to time for the online newsletter *Crikey*, which on various matters thought it important to point out the fact that I was a Jew. It mattered, according to *Crikey*, when I wrote a profile of the retail magnate Solly Lew, a profile that had been commissioned by the editor of *The Good Weekend* magazine. It needed to be made clear that I was a Jew when I was considering writing a biography of Jewish businessman Joe Gutnick — a proposal that came from a publisher when I was a freelance writer. It needed to be declared when I was editor of *The Age* and there was big news out of the Middle East.

I was a Jew and … what? I was 'soft' on the Jews, that's what. Many conspiracy theories were published on far-left websites about how I was part of the Israel Lobby, that I was a Zionist, that I was serving Jewish rather than Australian interests.

Mostly, I ignored this stuff. I could do so because Twitter and Facebook were still science fiction. But with the prominence of Twitter and Facebook and Instagram, and whatever else there is for people of bad faith and a conspiracy mindset to deploy, I imagine that no journalist or editor can ignore this way of seeing the world. Our new reality coincides with a time in which people are increasingly defined by their race, ethnicity, gender, and religion. Were I a Jewish editor today, the fact of my Jewishness would most likely be central to any examination of the paper I was running.

In the time I am writing about, I did not feel the need to constantly check in with my Jewishness. Except when it mattered to others, most of the time it did not matter much to me. I did not lie awake at night wondering whether the fact that I was Jewish meant that I was pushing the paper's coverage of Israel and Palestine in any particular direction. I often did lie awake at night wondering whether the paper was the best it could be — as ethical, fair, and accurate as it could be, and open to criticism and to correcting errors.

During the seven years in which I was editor of the paper, the Camp David peace talks were held, and President Clinton made a final, desperate peace proposal that would have established a viable Palestinian state — not the one that many Palestinians and their supporters thought they deserved by right, but a viable state nevertheless. I was affected by the violence and the killing, and by the hatred in Israel and the occupied territories after the peace plans and the hope of peace collapsed. I was concerned about the safety of my family in Israel, and about the safety of my friend and her son who had made aliyah from Melbourne. Then came the Second Intifada, when many hundreds of Israelis were killed by suicide bombers.

I wondered how my family were living their lives — catching buses, going to nightclubs, eating at pizza cafés — when they could be killed at any time by a young man wearing a suicide vest.

The suicide bombers and the Israeli response, the invasion of the West Bank, helped kill the Israeli peace movement and cripple the Israeli left, including the once great Labour Party of Ben-Gurion and Golda Meir and, later, Yitzhak Rabin, who was murdered by a Jewish terrorist in 1995. The hope that had followed the Oslo Accords, and the Camp David summit and the peace plan that Clinton proposed in the months before he left the presidency, was almost extinguished. It is now, more than twenty years later, barely alive.

On some level, at the level of worrying about family, I was not as emotionally concerned about the Palestinian civilians — yes, men, women, and children — living in terrible danger during the Israeli Defense Force's invasion of the West Bank; about the fierce fighting, often street by street, between Israeli soldiers and Palestinian militia in the refugee camps and cities; and about the two thousand or more Palestinian fighters and civilians who were killed.

But I believed that none of this meant that the suffering of the Palestinians during the Intifada was not heartbreaking, any less of a tragedy, than the suffering of the Israelis. I do not think most people could go back and read *The Age*'s coverage of the Intifada and conclude that the paper was more focused on the suffering of the Israelis than on the suffering of the Palestinians.

Newspapers are not democracies. The editor has the final say about what is reported and how, what prominence the story is given, who writes the stories and takes the photographs, and, ultimately, whether the story is honestly reported. Even things that the editor does not literally decide — because no editor of a big and complex daily paper can be across every story in the paper—is nevertheless the editor's responsibility.

I don't think I struggled much with how I wanted the paper to cover the Israel–Palestinian conflict. I wanted principles of what constituted fair and ethical reporting to guide our coverage, as I hoped it underpinned our reporting of every subject.

Did I ever give in to the demands of people who nowadays are referred to as the Israel Lobby when they contacted me—which they did quite often, sometimes daily, even twice daily, when there was major news coming from Israel or the occupied territories—to complain about some aspect or other of our coverage? I don't believe I ever did.

Sometimes, after listening to these Jews, I thought they had a point, that there had been a lack of context in a particular story, or that there had been a factual error that had slipped through. When that was the case, I would talk to the editors, and sometimes even call our correspondent in Israel to talk about it. I am sure there were occasions when the editors disagreed with me—the correspondent certainly did—but I am pretty sure they did not think I was a captive of the Israel lobby.

I always defended our correspondent, and always defended the editors—mostly, the foreign editor and the op-ed editor (who decided which opinion pieces on the conflict he would run) when they were criticised by both sides of the Israel–Palestinian conflict. I defended them not just because that's what an editor does, but because I believed—and this was confirmed for me in the paper every day—that they were ethical journalists, committed to fairness and accuracy, and to refusing to publish agenda-driven journalism.

Nevertheless, there were instances when the fact that I was a Jew mattered, not so much to me, but to some journalists and readers, and even to some old friends. Sometimes this Jewish thing had nothing directly to do with Israel or the Palestinians. It had to do with a sort of cliché about how Jews should be and act, what should be important to them after all they have suffered.

At a function one evening, a friend who I had not seen for some time greeted me warmly as we walked towards the Great Hall of the Victorian National Gallery. The function was being held not long after the so-called Tampa federal election of 2001, when there was outrage on the left about the Howard government's treatment of people who came to Australia in boats, fleeing persecution and sometimes poverty, and the government's exploitation of the boat arrivals to win an election.

I had always loved Kate Durham's work. When I was editor of *Time Australia* in the early 1990s, I commissioned Kate to design and do the art for a couple of *Time* covers. I think they were brilliant. We became friends who had coffee together. Then we lost touch. When I saw her at the National Gallery, she was with her partner, the well-known barrister Julian Burnside, who had appeared in the Tampa case representing the Victorian Council of Civil Liberties. (Twenty years later, in 2021, Burnside posted a tweet that compared Israel's treatment of the Palestinians to Nazi Germany's treatment of Jews. When there was an outcry, he apologised, but then made a similar claim in an email.)

She did not introduce me to him. Instead, she said how good it was to see me — partly, she said, because, for some time, she had wanted to ask me how I, a Jew, could in all conscience give such scant coverage in *The Age* to the refugees and their plight. A Jew born just after the Holocaust?

Kate made this little speech with Burnside standing beside her, and with journalists and other people I did not know standing with me, listening in to what Durham was saying. I think I tried to say it was nice to see her and that I hoped things were going well for her. I wanted to say that it was not very nice to accuse me of being a bad Jew, not living up to the sort of moral clarity expected of the Jews, given their history of persecution, and especially in my case of having once been a refugee, homeless, the child of Holocaust survivors.

It was not nice because down that path lies the accusation, the libel, that Jews, having suffered the eliminationist racism of the Nazis, are now — sadly, of course — behaving like the Nazis against the persecuted and powerless Palestinian people. Kate Durham had every right to demand that I do my human duty, but not to confront a Jewish editor and demand that he do his Jewish duty.

What was that Jewish duty? I guess it was in some way connected to the idea of Jews being the chosen people. It is this concept, so central to Judaism — that God has chosen the Jews to be a 'light unto the nations' — that has been the cause of both Jewish suffering and Jewish continuity. Enemies of the Jews have interpreted this chosenness as evidence of Jewish claims to superiority over non-Jews. Chosen by God!

It is undeniable that some Jews — many Haredi Jews, for instance — have interpreted chosenness as superiority. But in the main, throughout history, Jews have seen it as both a gift and a burden. A gift because their God has singled them out to be the torchbearers for an inclusive humanity, where the Stranger is welcomed and every life is equally precious. It is a burden because Jews, as a result, are held to higher moral and ethical standards than other people — both by themselves and by non-Jews. Jews are expected to behave better.

I do not believe in Jewish chosenness. I do not believe that suffering and persecution leads Jews to moral clarity, nor even to special empathy. What I have observed is that those who were once persecuted and homeless—Jews included—are no less inclined than other people to treat 'illegal migrants'—refugees—with little compassion or empathy. Suffering and persecution can be morally disfiguring. And singling out Jews, setting higher moral standards for them and demanding greater empathy from them, is troubling, to say the least.

I think that is what the renowned and much-loved cartoonist Michael Leunig was doing when he drew a cartoon for *The Age* in 2002 suggesting that the Jews, far from being purified by their persecution, were on the way to behaving as their persecutors had behaved. In one of the cartoon's two panels, a little man wearing a Star of David and carrying a bundle of clothing on a stick is walking towards Auschwitz. In the second panel, a soldier with a rifle and wearing a Star of David is walking towards a Palestinian refugee camp.

When I decided this cartoon would not be published in *The Age*, I understood that the fact that I was a Jew would be important to some people. But I did not know that it would be the sole prism through which my decision would be widely and often fiercely debated and condemned. I was not prepared for a debate that was almost wholly about the fact that I was a Jew, based on the assumption that the fact that I was a Jew had caused me to spike the cartoon of one of Australia's living treasures.

Michael Leunig and I went back a long way. We were friends. We liked and respected each other. I am sure—because he told me—that he was very hurt by what I had done. But I could not move him from his explanation for what I had done: I had censored him because I was a Jew.

I found it almost impossible to answer those people who wrote to me, and some of my fellow journalists, who were convinced that the Jew in me had decided to censor Leunig. What answer could I give that would have any weight? And I did not have an easy answer, because these things are always hard, especially when you are accused of doing something not because you have thought about it and wrestled with it, but simply because of who you are.

I was psychoanalysed by people who had never met me. A well-known cartoonist in New York, who had seen the cartoon and read about the controversy, emailed me. He said he understood where I was coming from, that I was, like him, a second-generation Holocaust survivor. He understood, he sympathised. But I had to move on, get over the trauma as best I could, and not see everything through the lens of my suffering. Move on from what, I wondered, given that I did not feel like I was suffering from post-Holocaust trauma? And move on to what? I did not respond to this email. Nor did I respond to the hate-filled emails. A sort of theme ran through most of them: I was a powerful Jew doing what Jews have done through the ages, using my power to further the interests of the Jews at the expense of the rest of humanity.

The editor of the opinion pages where the Leunig cartoon would have appeared, and the other senior editors at the paper, agreed with my decision. They agreed that the suggestion that the Israelis had become Nazis, that there was any sort of equivalence between Auschwitz, where close to a million Jews were gassed and burnt in crematoria, their ashes filling the day and night sky, and a Palestinian refugee camp, where, during the Intifada and the subsequent Israeli invasion of the West Bank, there was fierce street-to-street fighting between Israeli soldiers and Palestinian fighters, was at best based on ignorance and at worst was an act of bad faith.

Accusing Israelis of behaving like Nazis is now commonplace

on the left. Far worse cartoons, far more explicit accusations that Jews are the new Nazis, get a run, sometimes in the mainstream media, and social media is full of this sort of stuff. For many people on the left—as well as on the far right, of course—the words 'Jew' and 'Zionist' have become interchangeable and are never a compliment.

I was a Jewish editor, but did that mean anything? What sort of Jew was I? For those people who judged everything I wrote and every decision I made through the lens of my Jewishness, I was a Jew who put the interests of the Jews before the interests of society in general, not to mention Australia's national interests. The Jews had interests that conflicted with the interests of non-Jewish Australians. What else could it mean, the insistence on a public declaration that I was a Jew when I wrote anything that even tangentially involved the Jews? What else could it mean, when I was *The Age* editor and the Israel–Palestinian tragedy was going through yet another violent convulsion?

I was—and not by choice—a public Jew. That was clear after the controversy over the Leunig cartoon. It had been forced on me. Just as it had been forced on Jews through the ages. And just as it had been forced on the journalist Nick Cohen, who was not Jewish but nevertheless was a Jew in the eyes of many on the anti-Zionist left, because of his name and because he was not wholly on board with the ideology that says Zionism is evil and that Israel is an apartheid state. A public Jew was a sort of metaphor. It was an abstraction, a label. It had virtually nothing to do with the Jew I was—to my children and my friends, and even in the Jewish community.

This idea of Jews as metaphors is an ancient one. It goes back to the birth of Christianity, which had been conceived by Jews, but which quickly became Judaism's successor. The Jews

killed their own saviour. They would forever be God-killers. All
of them, from generation to generation, would be a metaphor
for the denial of God and his providence. Anti-Semitism, both
theological and secular, has at its centre a metaphorical evil that
is embodied in metaphorical Jews. Anti-Semites — and not just
anti-Semites — do bring individual Jews into their narrative,
but invariably, like Shylock in *The Merchant of Venice*, they are
stitched together from what are commonly regarded as Jewish
characteristics: a special sort of physical ugliness, a Jewish
greed, a Jewish sort of duplicity, Jewish pitilessness, and Jewish
disloyalty.

In truth, I don't think I spent much time worrying about the
public Jew I had been forced to become. I did not feel set upon,
or under siege. There were tougher things I had to deal with
when I was an editor. The digital train was entering our station,
and the old model that funded our journalism and that made
our papers so profitable, based on those rivers of gold that came
from classified advertisements, was about to be obliterated.

And I did not think much about identity, my identity, which
nowadays defines everything you are, and explains everything
you do and believe. Back then, I did not think too much about
what it meant, for instance, that my wife and I sent our children
to Sholem Aleichem College, a small Jewish primary school
(with around 130 students at the time) that taught Yiddish,
the only secular Yiddish-focused school anywhere in the world.
We had grown up in Yiddish. We were honouring our parents.
Although they were dead, we wanted our children to know a bit
of the language of their ancestors. After primary school, they
went to a state high school. We never seriously contemplated
sending them to a Jewish school.

I did not go to synagogue. I did not observe Shabbes. I did
not — as I once had with my sisters when I was young — go

to shul on Yom Kippur for Yizkor, the prayer session in the morning, on the day of fasting, for dead parents. We celebrated Pesach with a feast of Pesach food — gefilte fish, chopped liver, chicken soup and kneidlach, and roast veal brisket. We set out a plate with the food that helped Jews tell the Pesach story. We told the story with God absent from it.

When I was a boy, we told the story as a universal story of the human struggle for freedom. We did it that way because we were universalist Jews. I still believe it is a universal story, but a particularly Jewish one as well.

# CHAPTER TWELVE

# Where I stand

And so to my views on the conflict between Israel and the Palestinians. I say Palestinians rather than Palestine, because there is no UN state of Palestine, although I hope that one day the state of Palestine, with internationally recognised borders, will be born. The UN General Assembly voted by a large majority in 2012 to recognise the state of Palestine as a non-member observer state in the UN. But the reality, in my view, is that all the things that go to defining statehood—a national government and recognised borders, at the very least—do not exist for the Palestinians.

This all sounds very pompous, I know, as if my views on Israel and the Palestinians have any consequence for a resolution of the conflict. In a sense, they only matter in the context of this book and the Jewish journey I am on. I can offer no 'solution' to the conflict, and I am not sure I have anything interesting and revealing to say that has not been said before, many times. The best I can hope for is that some people reading this will take a little time before putting me in an ideological box—a box marked 'Jew' to begin with, and then these boxes: for or against the Palestinians, Israel, a two-state or one-state solution; and boxes that I have not even considered.

For me to remain out of any box for as long as possible, I

shall try to tell a story, of how I came to some of the things I think and feel about what is for me a tragic conflict — tragic for the Jews, and tragic for the Palestinians. It is a Jewish story, and if that is a disqualifier for some people, too bad. I will start at the beginning, my beginning.

I was eight months old when the United Nations General Assembly, on 29 November 1947, voted for the partition of Mandatory Palestine into two states, an Arab state and a Jewish state. We were living in the displaced persons' camp in Linz, the Austrian city in and around which Hitler had spent his childhood and teenage years. My family had been in the camp for almost two years.

We were still there six months later when, on 14 May 1948, David Ben-Gurion, the executive head of the World Zionist Organization and chairman of the Jewish Agency for Palestine, declared the establishment of the state of Israel. The UN partition plan, which included an economic union between the two states and with Jerusalem an international city, was never implemented. When Ben-Gurion made his declaration of independence, the surrounding Arab states sent armies into Palestine to fight alongside the Palestinian Arabs, who had launched an uprising, triggering a civil war between the Arabs and the Jews, which the British mandatory authorities did nothing to end. The ensuing war between Israel and the Arab-Palestinian armies lasted nine months. By then, I was two years old.

For Israel, from that time onwards — and for most Jews around the world — this was the 1948 War of Independence. For the Palestinians — defeated in the war, along with the Arab armies that had come to support them — this was the *Nakba*, the Catastrophe.

The history of the conflict between Arabs and Jews in Palestine over more than a century is contested. The history of the past seventy-five years, including the wars fought between the Arabs and Israel, is fiercely disputed. I am not a historian and am unable to adjudicate these disputes. Some of the facts — the UN partition vote, the Arab rejection of the partition plan, the civil war that followed, the invasion of Palestine by the Arab armies, the defeat of those armies — are not contested. But the Jews and Palestinians memorialise these momentous events in ways that fit their different national narratives. For the Jews, it was a time of triumph; for the Palestinians, of catastrophe. The contest over history is not only about facts, but about how they are interpreted, which facts are emphasised, and which are ignored. It all depends on where you're coming from.

My family were stateless refugees stuck in a displaced persons' camp. Despite what had just happened — the murder of millions of their people — Jews were in the main denied refuge by most of the West. America, Canada, Australia, and many other countries were reluctant — at best — to accept the refugee Jews. I do not remember ever talking to my family about those months, of the UN partition plan that failed, the Ben-Gurion declaration of independence, and the war that followed it. But I have no doubt that my mother, my father, and my sisters felt deeply connected to the Jews who regarded the declaration of independence and the subsequent victory over the Arabs as miraculous, not just because they came only a few years after the Holocaust, but because the Jews had triumphed in the war against formidable odds.

I doubt that my family — or most Jews — gave any thought to what had happened to the Palestinian Arabs, except as enemies of the Jews. I doubt they knew that around 700,000 Palestinian Arabs had either fled, hoping to return once the fighting ended and the Jews were defeated, or that the Israelis had forced them, sometimes brutally, to leave Palestine during the 1948 war. Had they known, I doubt it would have worried them much. Stateless and unwanted as they were, stuck in a DP camp, having lived through the Holocaust, what mattered to them was that Israel survive, and defeat its surrounding enemies. Most of all, they wanted their relatives in Israel, those who had chosen to go to Palestine from the refugee camp, to be safe, to survive the fighting.

I am pretty sure that they knew, without question, that for millennia the Jewish people had been connected to Eretz Yisrael—the literal meaning of which is 'land of Israel' and refers to the Israel of the bible, long predating political Zionism. This connection was renewed every year at Pesach, when the last prayer of the Haggadah ends with 'next year in Jerusalem'. Even a secular Jew like my father accepted this connection between the Jews and Eretz Yisrael. The time when the long history of Jews and their ancient ties to Israel would be denied by the Palestinian national movement, by many Muslims, and by much of the anti-Zionist left was a long way into the future.

It was in my family that I vaguely, emotionally first became conscious of Israel and its meaning for my mother, father, and sisters, and the Jews I knew, the Jews who were all Holocaust survivors. In this Jewish family, I had no sense of the Arab Palestinians' connection to the place the Jews called Eretz Yisrael. Everything about the Jews and Israel was determined by what they had been through. This was true not only for my Jewish family and for the hundreds of thousands of Jews like them who went to Palestine because they had nowhere else to go, but also for the non-Jews—either those who had been perpetrators of the Holocaust, willing helpers in murder, or those who had been bystanders to the genocide of the Jews of Europe. Guilt and shame, more than anything, determined the Western response to the conflict between Israel and the

Arabs. The fact that the 1948 war made victims of hundreds
of thousands of Palestinians refugees was overshadowed by
Jewish suffering and victimhood, for which the West, to varying
degrees, had been responsible.

For a decade and a half, perhaps two decades, after the
Holocaust, the left—from social democrats to Marxists to
communists—saw the conflict between Israel and the Arabs
from within the shadow and shame of the nearly successful
genocide of Europe's Jews. The Jews were the quintessential
victims, and the left was always for the victims and the
powerless. Zionism was a movement of the left, and the Zionists
who governed Israel after independence, who established the
kibbutzim and the trade union movement, and ran the economy
on socialist principles, were welcomed into the international
socialist movement.

But those years after the Holocaust in which I was raised
turned out to be a singular time. I do not think that leftists
marched in protest outside picture theatres screening *Exodus*,
starring Paul Newman as a Jew looking like an Aryan god,
which was the take of Leon Uris and Hollywood on the 1948
War of Independence—a fantasy of Jews as magnificent
fighters, with the Palestinian Arabs nowhere to be seen, except
as a generalised mass of menace.

While I did not entirely buy this fantasy about Jews and
Arabs and the Holy Land—I was, after all, a child of the Bund
and of Skif—I was a child of a particular Jewish family living at
this unique time. I think my older sisters took me to see *Exodus*
when I was fifteen. I think they might have cried during it, and
while I probably did not, I do remember how much I liked and
admired the soldier—the Jewish Paul Newman, and Eva Marie
Saint, his blonde and beautiful non-Jewish love. I am sure that
many of those young left-wing Zionists we *Skifistn* used to

meet up with mostly bought this fantasy. Among many of these people, disillusionment with Zionism and Israel began when they realised that *Exodus* and its version of the establishment of the state of Israel and the 1948 War of Independence was not exactly historically accurate.

That unique post-Holocaust period is long gone. I don't think *Exodus* could be shown at any theatre in the world today without attracting large and often violent protests. I don't think it could even be shown in Israel, where Arab Israelis would likely react to the screening of this Hollywood fantasy about them in a way that is not hard to imagine.

Israeli filmmakers and writers have never made Israeli versions of *Exodus*. Their work confronts the reality, complexity, and human suffering of the conflict between Israel and the Palestinians in a way that would make Uris turn in his grave.

The Holocaust survivors are almost all dead. Their children, like me, who lived day to day with the reality of what had happened to them, are old. Their grandchildren are approaching middle age. Some still have grandparents who lived through the Holocaust, but its shadow is fading. Israel is a more distant and, for many, a more troubling reality. The children of this middle-aged generation will be the first generation of Jews who have no living connection to the Holocaust. Will Israel be more of a burden for them than the miracle it was for the Holocaust survivors and many of their children?

For the left, Jews are no longer quintessential victims. The change in the way the left sees Jews has evolved over time. It has mirrored the gradual dying-off of Holocaust survivors and the subsequent fading to nothingness of the shame and guilt that was widespread at the way nothing was done in the West—not even the raising of significant protests—while the Germans slaughtered the Jews.

When the Jews won the 1948 war, it was the first war they had fought and won in more than 2,000 years. That world has changed. Israel has since become a significant military power. It has developed a first-world economy. The fact of Israel's existence has changed the way Jews see themselves.

The Palestinians—and the Arab countries that sent their soldiers into Palestine—lost the 1948 War, and the narrative of the Palestinians was shaped by that defeat. It is a narrative of victimhood and powerlessness and grave injustice. In the seventy-five years since Israel was born, the Palestinians have had no victories over the Jews, who were and remain responsible for Palestinian powerlessness and suffering.

In all the wars that Israel won against the Arabs—in 1948, 1967, and the Yom Kippur War in 1973—Jews believed that the Jewish people faced another Holocaust. The threat of annihilation was central to the post-Holocaust Jewish story, even after the establishment of the state of Israel. When Ben-Gurion declared Israeli independence, Jews had been powerless victims of organised violence for thousands of years. That was the Jewish story, and it was unlikely to change for a long time despite the miracle of Israel—without which, after the Holocaust, darkness and despair would have enveloped the Jewish people.

Until recently, the Holocaust was a living reality for survivors and even for their children. The Jews were unwelcome strangers and outcasts, threatened by anti-Semites, alone in the world, with no allies when they were most threatened and when they were being murdered. Despite the wars Israel won, even as it became a powerful and wealthy nation, the darkness in Jewish history—a history of persecution and murderous pogroms—remained at the centre of the Jewish narrative. How could it not, while the Holocaust survivors were still alive, and their children lived with the consequences of their parents' experience?

Yet for young Jews, especially for third- and fourth-generation Americans whose ancestors did not live through the Holocaust or its immediate aftermath, powerlessness, persecution, and even genocide happened a long time ago and in far-off places. It is not part of their experience of being Jews. For many of them, Israel is not a miracle, a Jewish resurrection story. It has always existed; there is no time they can recall when Israel was the fantasy of Zionist dreamers.

So there is no single shared narrative of Israel even among the Jews, let alone among the non-Jews.

Jews are a people of different ethnicities, they are religious and secular, and they live in the diaspora in countries as diverse as Russia and America, with vastly different political systems, cultures, and languages. Within a foreseeable time, more of the world's Jews will live in Israel than anywhere else. Jews can't even decide who is a Jew and who isn't.

The Palestinian people, on the other hand, have a narrative, a shared story. It is not an ancient narrative like the many stories the Jews have told about themselves for millennia. Consciousness of a distinct Palestinian peoplehood is around a century old. Palestinian nationalism—as opposed to pan-Arab nationalism—is entirely based on the belief that the Palestinians, and only the Palestinians, are the indigenous people of what the Jews call Eretz Yisrael. It is a post-colonial narrative, with Zionism as the colonial ideology of the Jews who have driven the Palestinians from their land, oppressed and ethnically cleansed them, rendered them powerless and stateless, and settled Palestine with colonising Jews who had and have no historic connection—let alone a claim—to any part of Palestine.

This Palestinian narrative, Palestinian nationalism, in which Zionism is a racist and colonialist ideology, in which the Jews have virtually no historic or even religious connection to any part of Palestine, including Jerusalem, is now the prism through which much of the left sees the conflict between Israel and the Palestinians.

It is not my prism. I grew up and was educated in the Bund and in Skif about the evils of colonialism and the dangers of chauvinist nationalism. We Jews were the victims of malign nationalism. No Jew like me can dismiss the Palestinian narrative, the reality of Palestinian suffering and defeat, the Palestinian longing for self-determination, for a nation of their own.

This means that I am among those on the left who still believe, as the writers Amos Oz and David Grossman and A.B. Yehoshua did, that the only solution to the conflict between Israel and the Palestinians that does not involve unspeakable violence is a recognition by both sides, the Palestinians and the Israelis, that both have a right to self-determination in what was once Palestine, that both have the right to a state, with all the benefits—and downsides—that statehood confers. It is true that this possibility feels like it is receding, but history is not linear. Most events that change history cannot be predicted.

Writing this brings back a memory of a lecture that the late Tom Uren gave to a group of fourteen- and fifteen-year-old *Skifistn* at a camping ground outside Sydney. It was in 1963, and Uren was a giant of the Labor Party left, later a leader of the anti–Vietnam War movement and a minister in the Whitlam and Hawke governments. We were on our annual two-week summer camp—the highlight of my year and, for a long time, of my life. These camps were no stroll in the park. Each year, we were given an assignment that involved some aspect of leftist thinking and concern. The year Uren came to speak to us, our assignment had to do with challenges in the post-war decolonisation of South-East Asia, which had suffered not just European imperialism, but, most recently, Japanese imperialism, with all its attendant horrors.

Having been a prisoner of war, Uren was qualified to speak of these Japanese imperial horrors. Perhaps he did describe to us some of what he had suffered at the hands of his captors, but that is not what I remember about his captivating lecture. What I recall is Uren's passion and his empathy for the people of South-East Asia who were fighting for and winning their freedom.

He admired Sukarno, Indonesia's first president. He admired Ho Chi Minh and the Vietnamese forces who had driven the French colonialists out of Vietnam before the US imperialists invaded their country. I was mesmerised by this paean of praise and empathy for the victims of colonialism and imperialism, and for the freedom fighters everywhere vanquishing their oppressors.

Over the years, I came to believe that not everything Tom Uren said in that lecture had been incontrovertibly true. But at the time, and later, Uren's understanding of the evils of colonialism and imperialism, of the need to support national liberation movements, was also my understanding. I think it was the understanding of my mentors in the Bund and among these 100 or so *Skifistn* at those glorious and memorable summer camps long ago.

Looking back, it is puzzling that Uren had nothing to say about the post-imperial world of the Middle East, the decolonisation of the Arab states, the rise of Arab nationalism, the UN partition of Palestine, and the way the British colonial power had simply abandoned the place. We were at a camp of young Jews, the youth organisation of the Bund. I am sure Uren knew some of the leading Bundists. I am sure he knew we were anti-Zionists, or at least that we had been until Israel, against our better judgement, was born. We were certainly not Zionists.

The only explanation I can think of is that back then, in the early 1960s, the Palestinian liberation movement had not yet been formed, and Palestinian nationalism was still an infant ideology. The Jews were not yet colonialists, and Israel was not yet deemed to be an 'apartheid state'.

I write of Uren now because what he had to say and how he said it, how he seemed to live what he was saying, still informs how I feel and think when it comes to the Palestinians and their predicament. They are powerless. They have suffered, physically and psychically, because of their powerlessness, the denial of self-determination and national liberation. They are still suffering. The Jews, Israel, have been—and remain—the cause of some of this suffering. Israel is the occupier and ruler of the Palestinians who live in the West Bank, even though the Palestinian Authority nominally runs much of the occupied territories. Israel does not rule Gaza, but Israel decides what comes in and out of Gaza, and when and if Gazans—and how many—can leave the heavily populated strip of land to work in Israel or go to the West Bank, where many have relatives. Some people may contest the assertion that the Jews and Israel have caused and continue to cause Palestinian suffering, but I believe these people are blinkered ideologues unable to empathise with the Other, or they are twisted by hatred.

But many Palestinians—and many of their supporters on the left—have also been twisted by hatred. That hatred has deformed the Palestinian narrative and Palestinian nationalism, and a large section of the left, for whom the Palestinians have become the modern-day Jews, and the Israeli Jews and their diaspora supporters have become the new Nazis, or something close to that.

To transform the Jews into racists, colonialists, and neo-fascists, Jewish history has to be distorted at best; repudiated at worst. The Jews have to be denied any historic connection to any part of Palestine, and Jewish suffering has to be minimised almost out of existence. The fact that the racist colonisers of the Palestinian imagination and of the imaginings of the left were more than 200,000 traumatised Holocaust survivors with nowhere else to go is wilfully forgotten, buried under an avalanche of accusations of Zionist collaboration with the Nazis, and in a growing Holocaust denial among the Palestinian leaders in Gaza and the West Bank.

At the same time, anti-Semitism is being defined out of existence on the basis that the Jews are powerful and that racism is only and always about the powerless—who cannot, by definition, ever be racists or anti-Semites. Yet anti-Semitism, which within the living memory of elderly Jews was the cause of the murder of most of their mothers and fathers and siblings, has infected the Palestinian narrative and the left's version of it.

I am a Jew with a particular Jewish history, one unique to my generation. It is through the prism of my Jewishness and my Jewish history that I respond to the denial of Jewish history by the Palestinians and their supporters: the reduction of Zionism to an evil ideology; the transformation of the Jews from the victims of Nazism to Nazis; and the increasingly horrifying accusations against Jews, Israeli Jews, of being gleeful child-killers and happy slaughterers of Palestinian civilians. It is through the prisms of being a Jew and a journalist that I respond to the conspiracy theory about the Israel Lobby, that there is a group of powerful Jews—agents of influence for Israel—that can and does distort the foreign policies of Britain and most of the EU, as well as the United States, Canada, and Australia, and who stop the editors and journalists working in some of the most powerful media organisations in the world from telling the truth about what Israeli Jews are doing to the Palestinians.

I am a Jew and a journalist, and I regret that I am not able to say anything that comes from contact and conversations with Palestinians. It has been a long time since I was on the ground in the West Bank and in Gaza. I have read articles by Palestinian journalists and academics, but the voices of Palestinians — voices were my speciality when I was a reporter — are missing. I know and have heard Israeli voices in a way I never have the voices of the Palestinians. Because of this, I am more deeply invested in what is happening in Israel, and with Israelis and with Jews in the diaspora and their attitude to Israel, than I am in what is happening to the Palestinians — which I can only try to understand from the outside. And I believe that much of the journalism coming from Western foreign correspondents is flawed, not so much biased as shallow.

I am fearful, at a visceral level, about the growing strength in Israel of the far right — the racist, fascist right. They are fellow Jews. I fear the growing strength and influence of religious fundamentalists, in Israel and in the diaspora, who say that it would be sacrilege to give up even an inch of Eretz Israel, which for them includes the West Bank, and which they call by its biblical names, Judea and Samaria, because the land was given to the Jews by God. Together with the Islamists of Hamas, they are transforming the conflict between Israel and the Palestinians into a God-based conflict, each side with their holy text, a war in which no compromise can ever be possible. As a result, the two-state solution, the basis for the Oslo Accords process in the 1990s, for which Yitzhak Rabin was assassinated, is becoming—I fear it might have already become—a pipedream.

But there is no good alternative that I can see to a two-state solution. Even now, given what is happening in Israel, a poll taken in May 2023 by *Arab News*, in conjunction with the YouGov research company, found that a majority of Palestinians—a narrow majority, it is true—living in the West Bank and Gaza support a two-state solution. Just 21 per cent supported the creation of a single Israeli-Palestinian secular state. And on 11 May 2023, a group of former senior Israeli security officials, just days after three days of violence between members of Palestinian Islamic Jihad and Israeli forces, wrote in *The Times of Israel* that only a two-state solution would deliver peace to Israelis and Palestinians, and guarantee Israel's security.

This, despite the growing convergence between, on the one hand, the Zionist right in Israel and in the diaspora—especially the ultra-nationalist religious right—and, on the other hand, the anti-Zionist left supporters of Palestinian fundamentalism, the ideology that erases the Jews from Palestine. Both believe that inevitably there will end up being one state. 'Palestine will be free from the river to the sea' is the slogan of the anti-Zionists, but the slogan could easily be chanted by the ultra-nationalist, religious Zionists—just substitute 'Eretz Yisrael' for 'Palestine'.

I think Jewish anti-Zionists might say that what grieves them most, of all the wrongs in the world, are the wrongs done by their fellow Jews—Israeli Jews in particular. I suspect that they, like Hannah Arendt, are more deeply affected by these wrongs done by the Jews of Israel than by the violence done to Jews in the diaspora by people who call themselves anti-Zionist supporters of the Palestinians.

I am thinking of Louise Adler, in particular. From time

to time, while I was writing this book, sitting in a room with photographs on the bookshelves—one being a photo taken long ago of me and Louise at a dinner that she had organised for her authors—I have wondered about the events that led to this journey of mine and became the first chapter of this book. Our friendship has not been repaired. We have not spoken to each other for two years, since the publication of the John Lyons booklet, *Dateline Jerusalem*, which claimed that a powerful group of Jews had intimidated editors and journalists into telling lies—by omission—about the terrible things Israel was doing to the Palestinians. She also signed a petition that urged what amounted to a silencing of not only those people whom Lyons had accused of intimidating editors and journalists, but of journalists and writers and commentators who do not accept that Palestinians are simply the victims of Israeli oppression, powerless and with no agency.

In line with that petition's demands, for her first program as director of Adelaide Writers' Week in 2023, Louise invited the Palestinian American novelist Susan Abulhawa and the Palestinian poet Mohammed el-Kurd. I have not read their work. Perhaps they are great writers who deserve to be invited to one of Australia's oldest and most prestigious writers' festivals. But I have read some of their Twitter commentary on Israel and the Palestinians. Both Jewish and Ukrainian organisations complained to the Adelaide Festival organisers about the invitation to these two writers, because what they have tweeted—in many tweets over a long time—about the war in Ukraine, in Abulhawa's case, and about the Jewish president of Ukraine in particular, and about the Israel–Palestinian conflict from both El-Kurd and Albulhawa.

Here is what Abulhawa has had to say, among other things, about Volodymyr Zelenskyy: 'This man is no hero. He's mad and far more dangerous than Putin.' In another tweet, she described Zelenskyy as a 'depraved Zionist trying to ignite World War III'.

In his tweets, El-Kurd described Israel as a 'demonic entity' and a 'death cult', and compared Israel to the Nazis. Abulhawa often compared Israelis to Nazis. I suppose all this, like Abulhawa's characterisation of Zelenskyy as a 'depraved Zionist', could be regarded as extreme but a matter of opinion. But El-Kurd has also accused Zionists of harvesting the organs of Palestinians to feed to Israeli soldiers. This is a question of fact: Zionists either harvest the organs of Palestinians so that Israeli soldiers can feed on them, or they do not. If they do not — and neither El-Kurd nor those who have made similar accusations have ever come up with any evidence that Israelis eat Palestinian organs — then it's not an opinion, but a lie. It is blatantly anti-Semitic, and an incitement to violence against Jews.

And Abulhawa's views on Zelenskyy — if they were simply that he, rather than Putin, is the villain in the war in Ukraine — could be regarded as extreme but legitimate commentary. But to suggest that Zelenskyy is a 'depraved Zionist' whose goal is to take the world into another world war is really to say that he is a Jew acting for malign international Jewish interests that threaten to engulf the world in a cataclysm. It is an expression of Jew-hatred. In light of these revelations, the Labor premier of South Australia, Peter Malinauskas, said he would not be attending the sessions of Writers' Week in which these Palestinian writers were participating. He 'completely abhorred the comments that had been made ... they don't accord with South Australia's value system'.

Louise was not concerned about any of this. Responding to a letter from the Executive Council of Australian Jewry to the

Adelaide Festival's CEO, she said that 'neither myself nor the Adelaide Festival have any interest in debate that is bigoted, stereotyping people or inciting violence or hatred. We should encourage a diversity of opinion and create a brave space, a courageous space ...' She said she would not be a party to anything that had to do with cancel culture.

Then the CEO, Kath Mainland, weighed in: 'Louise Adler, director of the Adelaide Writers' Week, as a daughter of Holocaust survivors, is intimately aware and very well educated about the Holocaust and as such is well placed to curate such a discussion.'

What discussion was Mainland referring to? As far as could be established from the program that had been released, there were no Israeli writers invited, and certainly no Jewish writers who could in any way be described as pro-Israel. But her reference to the Holocaust and Louise's Jewish and Holocaust bona fides was, well ... how should I put it politely ... ridiculous. It illustrated two things: the belief on the left that Jews, especially the children of Holocaust survivors, could never support or promote writers who are prone to using anti-Semitic tropes and peddling Zionist world conspiracies; and, implicitly, that other Jews cry anti-Semitism and invoke the Holocaust at the drop of a hat in order to shut down criticism of Israel and Zionism, and therefore their complaints should not be addressed or debated but ignored.

The well-known journalism researcher and journalism ethicist Denis Muller from Melbourne University's Centre for Advancing Journalism addressed the controversy in a piece for *The Conversation*. Muller, whom I worked with when I was director of the centre, essentially argued that while Susan Abulhawa's comments about Ukraine might have upset some people in the Ukrainian community, they represented a legitimate view about the war, and some people being upset was not a good reason to disinvite her. He pointedly ignored her charge that Zelenskyy is a 'depraved Zionist' who wants to start World War III. Was this legitimate commentary about the war in Ukraine? Characterising Zelenskyy, who is Jewish, as a 'depraved Zionist'?

Muller went on to describe El-Kurd's tweets as 'grossly offensive', and to state that any speech that 'creates any equivalence with the Holocaust' is a problem. In the end, though, he reckoned that the tweets were extreme but acceptable commentary and opinion on the Israel–Palestinian conflict:

> However, are they [El-Kurd's tweets] anti-Semitic? The Anti-Defamation League says they are, and the League's point of view must be respected.
>
> But a counterview is that El-Kurd's comments are directed at Zionists and at the State of Israel specifically rather than at Jews as a people, and that therefore they are political in nature rather than racist.

So it seems that Muller believed that, as long as Zionists and not Jews were being accused of eating Palestinian organs, there was no anti-Semitism involved. Implied was the canard that the Jews are once again using the charge of anti-Semitism to stifle debate, to silence Palestinians and their supporters. What's more, Muller was suggesting that the charge that Israelis eat Palestinian organs is a matter of opinion and not of verifiable fact. Since it is common knowledge that Jews were accused for centuries of killing and using the blood of Christian babies to bake the unleavened bread for Passover, is it so hard to see that these tweets are using anti-Semitic tropes? It was hard for Muller, apparently. And for Louise.

For Adelaide Writers' Week, Louise invited eight Palestinian writers. They were part of what she described as the truth-telling part of the program. Each of them told the same truth — that Israel is a brutal occupier and oppressor of the Palestinians, an apartheid state, a colonialist enterprise from its birth. I did not support disinviting any of these writers. But if Louise had truly been interested in truth-telling, would she not have invited at least one Jewish Israeli writer — someone like the renowned novelist David Grossman, who has long spoken and written about Israel's cruel and often brutal occupation of the West Bank? But she did not invite a single Israeli writer. She did not do so because she had long believed — with a growing passion and certainty — that the truth-telling she was promoting was the truth of the Palestinian writers she had invited to Writers' Week, a version of the truth that she shared. And to which she was committed.

As I wrote this book, Louise was hardly ever present, except when I looked at the photograph on my bookshelf. Then came this controversy about her choice of writers for Writers' Week. As the end of this book approaches, I understand that, for me, the end of our friendship was about much more than the John Lyons booklet and the open letter she signed. For years, we had talked about a book about the Jews and the left that she wanted to read and that, as only Louise could do, she urged me to write. It would have been a partly personal story — hers and mine, really — about the long and consequential history of the relationship between Jews of the left like us and the various iterations of socialism, from Marxism to social democracy.

I never did write that book. I think I felt that it would not be the book she had in mind. She wanted a book that would honour the history and participation of Jews like us and like our parents in the left's project of justice and equality and freedom for all people. The book I would write, however, would be about how the relationship between Jews like me and the left was becoming more fraught. My thought was vague, but I knew it had to do with my feelings and views about Israel, which were changing from what I had felt and believed while growing up in the Bund and Skif.

We are different Jews, Louise and I, and, as I write, I realise that I am writing a version of *The Jews and the Left* that Louise might have published, but with which she would have certainly been disappointed. In a *Guardian* article that defended Lyons, Louise wrote of her experience of Israel when she first went there as a seventeen-year-old idealistic young Jew and Zionist:

> I was met by Ashkenazi Jews stamping my passport, Sephardi Jews sweeping the floors and Palestinians cleaning the toilets. It was a depressing introduction to a society mired in race and class divisions.

Nowhere in the piece does she say that this first charact-erisation of Israel when she was seventeen years old has changed over subsequent decades. Israel remains a sort of failed state for many Jews of the left like Louise — a tragic mistake, at best, and, at worst, the product of a colonialist and racist ideology. Given where this Jewish journey has taken me, I think that, sooner or later, our friendship would have ended. The differences between us are too great.

The thing is, I have a special affection for Israel — this place where Jews, for the first time in a long history, can exercise self-determination. More than that, I believe that Israel's achievements are dazzling. If its creation felt miraculous to many Jews, its achievements feel miraculous to me. Even for non-believers, there is something mystical in the transformation of Hebrew from a language of prayer and Torah to a national language with its literature and music and theatre.

And there is cause for humble celebration in the ingathering of millions of threatened Jews from the Arab countries and North Africa after 1948, the aliyah of a million or more Jews from the Soviet Union who had been denied any expression of their Jewishness, and of the thousands of Ethiopian Jews who for millennia had dreamed of a return to their Holy Land.

It is a cliché, I know, that the Israelis of the kibbutzim and moshavim — these mostly urban, middle-class European Jews with no experience in agriculture — made the Negev desert bloom, but they did. Often at great cost, as Amos Oz's autobiography, *A Tale of Love and Darkness*, showed so powerfully. In seventy-five years, Israel has transformed itself from a struggling third-world economy into an economic powerhouse, and a leader in new technology and scientific and medical research.

Israel remains a democracy, albeit one with serious failings and contradictions, a fragile and partial democracy because of the occupation, in a part of the world where there are no democracies, and where ethnic and religiously based civil wars have repeatedly destroyed nations and rendered millions of people stateless refugees. For all its democratic failings, Israel remains an open society. I think all this is incontrovertible. I also think it is astounding.

Even so, I believe that the Zionist dream that the Jews would become a nation like all others — normalised, in other words — after their ingathering into Eretz Yisrael has not come to pass. Herzl was wrong when he argued that only the establishment of a state for the Jews would defeat anti-Semitism and make the Jews safe.

But even if Herzl got it wrong, even if it is true that

nationalism can be malign with disastrous consequences — and there is a growing malign nationalism in Israel — and even though Israel is morally challenged and coarsened by the decades-long occupation of the West Bank and its treatment of Gaza, none of this even begins to justify support for Israel's elimination. None of Israel's failings, none of the unfulfilled promises of Zionism, can be made right by eliminating Israel and replacing it with one state from the river to the sea. Such a development, along with the right of return of millions of Palestinian refugees of the 1948 War, and their children and grandchildren and great-grandchildren, would mean a majority-Arab state.

When Jewish supporters of one state in Palestine, such as the American academic and writer Peter Beinart, describe the state they envision that will replace and consume Israel, I do wonder how they can believe this can be achieved peacefully, with Israel agreeing to give up statehood? The state they say they envisage would be multi-ethnic, democratic, with equal rights for all its citizens, no matter their religion or ethnicity — a majority-Arab state with large ethnic and religious minorities. Such a state has never existed in the Middle East, nor does the emergence of one look even remotely possible in the foreseeable future. The closest to it, by far, is Israel. It is hard for me to understand how this is not obvious to people such as Beinart, a writer and academic of distinction who may well have studied the history of the conflict between Israel and the Palestinians, including the history of Zionism, far more closely than I have. What world do they live in, these Jewish dreamers of a liberal, democratic Palestinian state, where the Jews would be a minority, but would be safe and free?

Those who describe Beinart as a Radical Zionist — what do they mean? In the first half of the twentieth century, there was a Zionist faction—always a small minority in the movement—that believed the Jews should have a homeland in Eretz Yisrael that wasn't a state, because with statehood inevitably came chauvinist nationalism. Among these anti-nationalists were Albert Einstein, Martin Buber, and Gershom Scholem. Theirs was an impossible dream, too, because decades of enmity and violence between the Arabs and Jews rendered impossible any sort of homeland for the Jews where their safety and freedom depended on the goodwill of people who hated or feared them.

By the time Ben-Gurion declared Israel's independence, this tiny anti-state faction of Zionists had long since lost the ideological battle against mainstream Zionism, which saw itself as a national liberation movement: without a state, the Jews would never be safe.

Beinart is a Radical Zionist of a different type. He is not opposed to a state in Palestine—not at all. Indeed, he is a supporter of Palestinian nationalism and the Palestinian aspiration for a state of their own. He is opposed to a Jewish majority state. He has come to reject Jewish sovereignty and self-determination. The state of Palestine that he envisages is an American dream of a state like the United States where the Jews of Palestine, like America's Jews, would be equal citizens, a respected and happy minority. I doubt that his dream is shared by any but a tiny minority of Palestinians and Israelis.

I do not share it, to say the least. It is an impossible dream. I am a Jew of the left, but some dreams of the left I do not share. I have concluded that the attempt to make dreams like Beinart's a reality—against the wishes of the Palestinians and the Israelis—always end badly. Impossible dreams become bad dreams with terrible consequences. They become nightmares. But Israel is not the consequence of a bad dream. It is not a nightmare. In many ways, I believe, Israel is a Jewish dream come true. It has taken me a long time to come to this position, but here I am. I cannot imagine a Jewish world without Israel.

Sometimes I respond with despair and anger and fear about what the future holds for the Jews. There is increasingly no common ground, no shared facts or shared truth, between people like me and much of the left about Israel and the Palestinians. The conflict is a tragedy for the Palestinians, and a tragedy for Israel and the Jews of the diaspora. Even what I once assumed was uncontested by much of the left is now contested: increasingly for the left, there is only one tragedy in this conflict, and that is the tragedy of what has been done and is still being done to the Palestinians by Israel, with the support of Jews in the diaspora.

This is not a left to which my father belonged — a factory worker who supported the Labor Party all his life in Australia — nor is it the left of my mentors in the Bund. It is not the left in which I grew up, where at every meeting of the Bund and Skif we sang 'Di Shvue' ('The Oath'). We sang it in Yiddish, but here are several verses in English:

> Brothers and sisters of work and need
> All who are scattered like far-flung seed —
> Together! Together! The flag is high,
> Straining with anger, red with blood,
> So swear together to live or die!
> We swear to strive for freedom and right
> Against the tyrant and his knave,
> To best the forces of the night,
> Or fall in battle, proud and brave.
> So swear together to live or die!

To wage the holy war we vow,
Until right triumphs over wrong.
No Midas, master, noble now —
The humble equal to the strong.
So swear together to live or die!
To the Bund, our hope and faith, we swear
Devotedly to set men free.
Its flag, bright scarlet, waves up there,
Sustaining us in loyalty.
So swear together to live or die!

We did not sing every verse, I am sure — I can recite only the first and last verse. But each time we sang it, it felt like a vow and a prayer, and a commitment to freedom and justice and an end to capitalist exploitation of the working class. Most of all, what I found thrilling was the vow to fight and, if necessary, die for freedom and justice and the liberation of the working class. That's what I call an inspiring socialist vow, even if the lyrics — and the tune, I have to say — have some of the characteristics of communist agitprop in the first decades after the 1917 Russian Revolution. I think 'The Oath' is still sung at meetings of the Bund, and were I to attend one such meeting, I would happily and proudly sing, with as much gusto as I could summon. It might be a century old and over the top, but in it is the core of what it once meant to be a Jew of the left.

But I do not believe that the Jewishness of Jews like my father, my mentors, and my teachers in the Bund and Skif — secular, socialist Jews who were steeped in cultural Jewishness and lived so much of their lives in Yiddish — can any longer be passed down from generation to generation. Not in countries like Australia, where Jews are, thank goodness, free to assimilate and, if they wish, cease to be Jews in any meaningful way.

Neither can an attachment to Israel, a love of the country and an affinity with its people, be passed on from generation to generation. Each generation of American secular Jews — and this will eventually be true, I think, for Australian Jews — has less of an attachment to Israel, a love of the place, than do their parents and certainly their grandparents.

I believe that Israel is vital for Jewish continuity, but I do not live my life in Israel. In some ways, it is as alien to me as, say, France or Italy. I do not speak French or Italian; I do not speak Hebrew, to my regret. I do not live in Israel's day-to-day realities. I can read Israeli writers only in English. I do not listen to much Israeli Hebrew music. When I was reporting from Israel, I was always aware that there was a limit to what I could know and understand. I was not, am not, Israeli.

I do not accept that my lack of enthusiasm for anti-Zionism, for some parts of the Palestinian narrative, and for the erasure of parts of Jewish history in any way disqualifies me from membership of the left. The notion that it does so is obscene. I can understand that some people have disavowed their membership of the left before they could be officially — on Twitter, that is — cancelled. Not all of them, like David Mamet, have moved away from the left at such a speed that they couldn't stop until they fell into the arms of authoritarian populists such as Donald Trump.

Still, on Israel and in the conflict between Israel and the Palestinians, these newly minted right-wing Jews have concluded that there is no left-wing position that has any genuine and consequential commitment to Israel's survival as a Jewish majority state. The left, they say, has at best no love for the Jews.

There is evidence to support this position. In September 2022, the Palestinian American US congresswoman Rashida Tlaib said what many progressives believe: one cannot be a progressive and support the 'apartheid government of Israel'.

In October 2021, the Washington, DC, branch of the US Sunrise movement, a youth movement primarily advocating political action on climate change, withdrew from a voting-rights rally because three other organisations it said supported the 'colonial project' of Zionism and Israel were to take part. The three organisations collectively represent millions of American Jews.

After protests, the national Sunrise movement's leaders issued a statement condemning the position taken by its Washington affiliate, albeit on narrow grounds. 'To be clear, Sunrise DC's statement and actions are not in line with our values,' the Sunrise Movement said in a tweet. 'Singling out Jewish organizations for removal from a coalition, despite others holding similar views, is antisemitic and unacceptable.' The national movement's tweet did not address the DC branch's position on Zionism and Israel.

Similarly, a Jewish feminist involved in running the Women's Marches held annually for three years from 2017 to protest against the election of Trump reported that two other organisers had made anti-Semitic comments at an early planning meeting. The numbers at the 2019 march plummeted after this, and other allegations of anti-Semitic and anti-Zionist comments by some organisers surfaced.

At American, British, and Australian university campuses, student and academic bodies have taken positions that amount to a call for the boycott of 'Zionist' guest speakers at all events, even if the subject matter has nothing to do with Israel and the Palestinians. They demand a boycott of Israeli academics and, increasingly, the expulsion of 'Zionist' student organisations from all universities.

At the same time, there is incontrovertible evidence that anti-Semitism in Europe, the US, and even in Australia is on the rise, including assaults and threats of violence, and mountains of Jew-hatred on social media. And yet many on the left refuse to even acknowledge any of this. Instead, Jews who call out left-wing anti-Semitism are accused of being Zionist shills, defenders of apartheid and colonialist Israel. This is particularly painful and disempowering when much of the left is committed to allowing the victims of racism to say what is and what is not racist about how they are treated. None of this applies to Jews and anti-Semitism. Jews who say they have been the victims of anti-Semitism are often accused of having ulterior motives—of deflecting criticism of Israel, or trying to deny their 'white privilege'.

I do not wish to imply that the whole left has embraced the idea that Zionism is evil and that Israel is an apartheid state. For example, many members of the Australian Labor Party and the federal Labor government—including cabinet ministers, Foreign Minister Penny Wong, and Prime Minister Anthony Albanese—support Israel as a Jewish state, and advocate for a just peace between Israel and the Palestinians that recognises the legitimate national aspirations of both peoples. But the trend on the left, even in the Labor Party, is towards anti-Zionism.

Nor do I want to suggest that I am some sort of lone and embattled left-wing Jew who is prepared to declare a love for Israel and its importance for Jews everywhere. I know Jews on the left who, like me, openly embrace Israel. Philip Mendes, a professor of social work at Monash University, has published numerous academic papers on Israel and the Palestinians critical of anti-Zionism and the BDS movement. Mendes is a self-described Jew of the left and a long-time supporter of a two-state solution to the conflict—a position that, for a long time, was treated with some hostility by some of the Jewish community leadership. He is the author of *Jews and the Left*, published in 2014, which traces the history of the connections between Jews and the left, and includes a critical analysis of left-wing anti-Zionism. In 2015, with Nick Dyrenfurth, the executive director of the John Curtin Research Centre, he wrote *Boycotting Israel is Wrong*. Mendes and Dyrenfurth are part of the dwindling numbers of left-wing Zionists who are prepared to suffer being cast out of the left for their Zionism.

I also know leftist Jews like Mendes who are critical of the occupation, and of Netanyahu and the far-right extremists who are now ministers in an Israeli government, but who, for the most part, feel unable to forthrightly express their support and love for Israel. I am talking about journalists in particular, but not just journalists. And there are Jews on the left who are not anti-Zionists and feel connected to Israel, who even have some affection for the place, who feel unable to publicly say anything like this because the risk of being dismissed from the left in general and from every activist campaign on the left—groups advocating for everything from climate change to LGBTQ rights—is real and growing. I feel that these left-wing Jews who support Israel but find it hard to offer that support in an unqualified fashion are anxious Jews, universalist Jews, who dread reading about any new political or military horror in Israel, because such horrors will make their already near-impossible task of defending Israel's right to exist truly impossible. Perhaps I once shared these concerns and this dread. No longer.

Or so I thought. In the Israeli elections of November 2022, a right-wing coalition of four parties led by Benjamin

Netanyahu won sixty-four seats in the Knesset, giving this coalition a comfortable majority of four seats. Two of the four parties in the coalition are Haredi parties: Shas of the Haredi Sephardi population, and United Torah Judaism of the Haredi Ashkenazis. Both parties have a narrow political goal to ensure that the state supports their religious institutions so that their men can devote themselves to Torah study and remain exempt from military service. These parties are not nationalist or even Zionist. At different times, they have been part of coalitions of the left. The fact that they are part of a right-wing coalition government is not some sort of earthquake in Israeli politics.

But there has been an earthquake all the same. The Religious Zionists, a coalition of two far-right ultra-nationalist parties, won fourteen seats in the November election, making it the third-largest party in the Knesset, behind Benjamin Netanyahu's Likud and the left-of-centre Yesh Atid, whose leader, Yair Lapid, was the outgoing prime minister. Although they received only 10 per cent of the vote, the religious Zionists achieved what had long seemed impossible: political power. Without them, Netanyahu could not have formed a government.

So it was that the Religious Zionist leaders, Bezalel Smotrich and Itamar Ben-Gvir, became senior ministers in Netanyahu's new government. Both are authoritarians at best, racists, and Jewish chauvinists. Ben-Gvir has a history of racist incitement against both Israeli Palestinians and the Palestinians in the occupied West Bank. For a long time, he championed the Israeli terrorist Baruch Goldstein—a member of the extremist Kach movement, banned from participating in Israeli elections—who massacred 29 Muslim worshipers outside a mosque in Hebron in February 1994. Until he concluded that lauding Goldstein might be a step too far, even for some of his supporters, Ben-Gvir, a fellow member of Kach, even had a portrait of Goldstein hanging in his living room. It is astounding, unthinkable, unbearable that these two racists and Jewish chauvinists, who at various times have advocated the expulsion of Palestinians from the God-given 'land of Israel', sit at the heart of an Israeli government.

Where the aftershocks of this earthquake will lead is unknowable. With Smotrich and Ben-Gvir as senior members of the Netanyahu government, what will be the consequences for Israeli Palestinians and Palestinians in the West Back and East Jerusalem? What will be the consequences for Israeli democracy? Will the coalition government survive when there are members of Likud—most of them, admittedly, not in the parliamentary party—who do not support Smotrich and Ben-Gvir? Is Netanyahu prepared to sacrifice Israeli democracy to stay in power, as his support for the stripping of the Supreme Court's powers indicates? Will the continued demonstrations by hundreds of thousands of Israelis against the government's plan to do so have any effect? Will the Biden administration draw red lines that the Netanyahu government may cross, and put at risk America's almost unqualified support for Israel? Will the leaders of diaspora Jewish organisations call out and reject the racists and authoritarians—if not fascists—who are now senior members of an Israeli government? And if they do, what will be the consequences?

It is hard to be optimistic about the future. But did I revert to being an anxious Jew after the 2022 Israeli election? Did I dread reading and hearing about what was happening in Israel because it would make it hard for me to continue to support Israel publicly as a majority Jewish state? Did I, like some left-wing Jews, want to 'wash my hands of Israel'?

No, I did not. I do not believe that the election of this far-right government—it received around 34,000 more votes than the opposition parties in an election in which nearly 4.8 million people voted—signals the end of Israeli democracy. Or that the election outcome and the presence of Smotrich and Ben-Gvir in Netanyahu's cabinet means that Israel's right to exist is more open to question than it ever was, and that the anti-Zionists have been right all along. Washing your hands of Israel means washing your hands of the millions of Israelis who voted against this government, and the hundreds of thousands who have gone to demonstrations, week after week for months on end, to express their opposition to its so-called legal reforms. In the end, it remains a terrible thing for me that the election by a slim margin of a far-right Israeli government should lead to serious questioning by some left-wing Jews of Israel's right to exist.

That is not where I am.

# CHAPTER THIRTEEN
# Coming home

My wife and I shared a childhood. We met at Skif when we were children. My mother was not a Bundist, but my father, while not a card-carrying member, was a Bundist fellow traveller. My wife's parents, on the other hand, were Bundist royalty.

In 1936, my wife's mother was one of the stars in a film made in a summer camp run by the Bund for working-class Jewish children on the outskirts of Warsaw. In a most affecting scene from the black-and-white and faded film, *Mir Kumen On* (*We Are Arriving*), she is singing a classic Yiddish lullaby for the children, who are looking at her with rapt attention. As she sings in her pure and haunting voice — a voice that my wife and children inherited and that I have always loved — the camera pans over the rapt faces of the children sitting in that circle.

These children are perhaps twelve years old. When the Germans invaded three years later, these children would have been around fifteen years old. It is impossible for me to watch the film without being aware that most of these children would not have survived the war. Those who did survive would have endured years of incarceration in concentration camps — like the little girl singing that heartbreaking lullaby in that pure voice of hers, my wife's mother, who survived Auschwitz.

Some of these survivors ended up in Australia, in Melbourne, Bundists still, despite what had happened to the hundreds of thousands of Bundists in Poland. And that is where we met, two children of Bundists and Bundist sympathisers, those lovers of Yiddish and its culture, secularists and democratic socialists, and that's what we were when we got married in 1974 in the registry office in Melbourne — to the dismay of my two eldest sisters, who reckoned our mother would be turning in her grave knowing we had not married in a synagogue.

Were we anti-Zionists? We were not Zionists — in the way we had always understood what it meant to be a Zionist — but I don't remember talking about the Bund's anti-Zionist history. I do know that when we got married, neither of us had been to Israel or had ever contemplated living there. It is true that I had gone to the Zionist headquarters in Melbourne just before the war in June 1967 to volunteer my service to Israel in any way that might be needed, because I believed the Jews of Israel were threatened with annihilation. But, then again, I was a twenty-year-old looking to get out of university, which I hated, and looking for adventure.

I do not know how long it was after my daughter was born, in September 1975, that I started to think about Jewish continuity. My Jewish continuity. In the eyes of my eldest sisters — and I am sure in the eyes of my mother and even my secularist father, had they lived to see it — even though I had been married in a registry office, I had at least not committed the much bigger transgression of 'marrying out', of marrying someone who was not Jewish.

In *Fiddler on the Roof*, the long-running Broadway musical that in recent times has been staged in Yiddish, Tevye, the main character, has five daughters. Each one causes him grief. One, for instance, marries a socialist revolutionary; another refuses to marry the rich suitor he has triumphantly lined up. After much talking and arguing with God, Tevye forgives his daughters for their rejection of traditional shtetl values and norms.

When his third daughter, Chava, comes to tell him she wants to marry a young man who is not Jewish, Tevye forbids her to meet him again. When the couple then elope, and Chava comes back to explain, Tevye sends her away, determined never to see her again. He says Kaddish — the prayer for the dead — over her. But he can't erase her. He loves her. She is his daughter. Later, when the family are about to leave the shtetl and begin their long journey to America, Chava returns with her husband to ask for Tevye's blessing. Chava and her husband are leaving for Krakow to start a new life. Tortured and heartbroken, Tevye nevertheless acknowledges his daughter and her husband, and wishes them well. In the midst of great sadness at the thought of being driven out of the shtetl because of rising anti-Semitism in the Pale of Settlement, there is still room for the triumph of love and even hope. So the musical has a happy ending. All great Broadway musicals have happy endings. It's the American way. *Fiddler on the Roof* is a quintessential American musical of the middle of the twentieth century.

And this particular happy ending was essential, because by the time *Fiddler on the Roof* was staged, more than one-third of America's Jews were marrying out. The figure is now well over 50 per cent, and rising fast. A father rejecting his daughter, saying Kaddish for her because she married out, would not have gone down well with most American Jews, to say the least.

*Fiddler on the Roof* is based on a sequence of stories written by Sholem Aleichem, one of the key figures in the emergence of modern Yiddish literature, and featuring the character Tevye the Milkman. In the stories, initially published in serial form in Yiddish newspapers, Tevye has seven daughters — two more than in the Broadway musical. He does have to come to terms with their movement away from shtetl norms, with its traditions and Torah-based restrictions, into a tentative embrace of modernity. But there is a limit to what Tevye can accept.

There was no happy ending in Sholem Aleichem's stories. As Dara Horn wrote in *People Love Dead Jews*, there is hardly ever a happy ending in Yiddish literature. When Tevye learns of his daughter Chava's determination to marry the non-Jewish boy she loves, he is devastated and in no doubt about what he will do. He will cast her out, never see her again. He will say Kaddish for her, as if she no longer exists for him except in memories. In the stories, Chava does return, but alone, without her husband. She asks to be taken back into the family. She has abandoned her husband because she has found she cannot live in a world of vicious anti-Semitism and pogroms. I imagine that the Jews of the nineteenth and early-twentieth centuries in Eastern Europe and even in America who read about Tevye the Milkman's troubles would have entirely supported Tevye's rejection of Chava. Marrying out was exceedingly rare, and represented a rejection of Judaism and even of God himself.

I do not think my father saw *Fiddler on the Roof*, but I am sure he read the Tevye the Milkman stories, and I think he might have read a book of the collated stories with me when I was studying it at Sunday school. Had he seen the Broadway show, he might have enjoyed it — he loved some American musicals, such as *The Jazz Singer*, with Al Jolson — but I doubt he would have found Tevye forgiving his daughter for marrying out as anything but a bit of American schmaltz.

Sholem Aleichem's Tevye could never forgive his daughter. That's how it was in the shtetl. Jews did not marry non-Jews. They lived Jewish lives. Their family, their friends, were all Jews. Their daily lives were ruled by the commands and rituals of

Judaism, in which they were born and lived and died. Marrying out meant just that: removing oneself from the Jewish people. It was regarded as a death in the family and in the community.

This is the world into which my mother and father were born, and where they lived as children and young adults. My mother stayed in that world long after it had vanished, physically, in the Holocaust. Even in Australia, it was the only world she ever knew, and Yiddish was the only language she could speak. My father had left that world when he was still a teenager, enthralled by the promise of the wider world, captured by the dream of socialism, in love with the great writers of Yiddish literature.

Ever since my daughter was born, I have asked myself this question: how would my parents have reacted if I had married a non-Jew? My mother would have been devastated. Destroyed. Would she have cast me out? Probably. My father? I think he would have been disappointed. He had long before left Judaism behind, but he was steeped in Jewishness. He knew what he had rejected: he had grown up in Judaism, and in some way, as a sort of muscle memory, Judaism still lived within him. He was concerned about Jewish continuity. He wanted Yiddish to live, and he wanted Yiddish culture to live on, and he wanted to pass his love and commitment to his children and grandchildren. He wanted the Jewish people to live on. Perhaps he would have been more than disappointed in me.

And the Bundist royalty who became my family? I think they would also have been disappointed if their daughter had married a non-Jew, because they, too, believed in and prayed for—in a non-religious way, of course—Jewish continuity. They believed they were part of the Jewish people, nearly destroyed in the Holocaust, but still there. Hitler had been thwarted. The Jewish people lived!

Perhaps our marriage was no accident. We had known each other since childhood. I often thought we were destined somehow to be together. Being Jewish had nothing to do with it.

Then we had our daughter. Sometime after she was born, perhaps a month or two later, it struck me that I was a Jewish father, just like my father had been, and that I had a Jewish daughter. I wondered what that meant to me. I wondered why at times it felt thrilling, and at other times like a burden. I did wish that my father and mother had been alive to see their Jewish granddaughter. I felt something vague but deep when my eldest sister sang to my daughter in Yiddish.

The Bundist royals, my wife's mother and father, especially her mother, the girl singing in that heartbreak of a film, sang that lullaby to their granddaughter forty years later. My wife would sometimes sing along, harmonising with her mother. What the Bundists called *di goldene keyt* (the golden chain) tied us, sometimes against our will, to the Jewish past and present. But the Jewish future? Back then, almost a half-century ago, I started, haltingly, tentatively, in an unfocused way, to think about my Jewish future and, especially, the Jewish future of my daughter.

I had no ties to the Jewish community. I was not a member of the Bund. I was not a member of any synagogue congregation and had no connection with any Zionist organisation. We did not even have the money box with a Star of David on its front in our home. The boxes were ubiquitous in Jewish homes. Zionist organisations distributed them, children filled them with coins, and I think volunteers would come and empty them when they were full. And so Jewish children grew up putting coins into boxes, money they knew would go to help build Eretz Yisrael. I think my sisters all had such boxes, but we did not.

And yet, when I looked at my daughter, something in me was stirred by long-forgotten memories of reading with my father, of my mother and sisters and me scrubbing dishes and pots and utensils in the mud to make them kosher for Passover, or of my favourite Sunday school teacher who admired the poems I wrote in Yiddish class. What stirred was a sense of loss. What dawned on me was that I was not the sort of Jew that my mother and father and Yiddish teacher and Bundist mentors had been.

By then I had lost touch with most of my childhood friends from Skif. Some had gone on to be active members of the Bund and had, like me, married people they had known from childhood, from their time at Skif. Many had married out. Slowly, I had come to believe that there was no Jewish future for Jews like me, let alone for my children. I had grown up with secular, universalist Jews who were nevertheless encased in their Jewishness, in their deep love and knowledge of Yiddish and its culture and in their Jewish history, and even in the secularised celebrations of Judaism's festivals. That sort of Jewishness was unique to a particular time and place — Eastern Europe, mainly — and only for the first half of the twentieth century, when my father's generation of Jews, which had grown up in orthodox Judaism — the boys having been educated in cheders, few of them attending secular schools — rejected this sort of Judaism and became secular Jews, still living a rich Jewish life but engaged with the world.

This rich Jewish life could not be passed on in its fullness to the next generation, to people like me, not in places like Australia or the US, where assimilation had no barriers, only attractions. A Jewishness based on living part-time, at best, in a Yiddish world was unsustainable. I had become a hugely watered-down version of the Jew my parents and mentors had been. For my daughter, that sort of Jewishness would be watered down even more—to a Jewish nothingness, I feared. Sooner or later, for Jews like me, *di goldene keyt* that bound us Jews together over generations would be broken.

Did this matter? Was I really concerned that the Jewish people should live forever—because they had lived, almost miraculously, for such a long time? Did I really believe that this was important to me because I had a Jewish daughter and I wanted her to be a Jew who, like me, would be interested in Jewish continuity, would want her children to be Jews?

I do not remember the first time I raised the idea of moving to Israel. Perhaps it was after I had read something by the Israeli writer A.B. Yehoshua, a great writer even in English translation, who argued that there was no Jewish future for the Jews of the diaspora, and that only in Israel was Jewish continuity guaranteed.

Perhaps he had a point. Yes, in some ways, it was a classical Zionist position, one I had always rejected, but the evidence suggested that Yehoshua might be onto something. We talked about moving to Israel, but in a perfunctory way. I do not think my wife considered living in Israel. And so it did not happen.

Instead, we moved to London in 1977. The Jewish thing was not big in our lives. Our visit to Israel in 1981 was a life-changing experience, but the changes took decades to fully manifest themselves. We did not really contemplate the idea of moving to Israel even when we came to believe that at the centre of the Jewish story in the twentieth century was the Holocaust and the birth of Israel, both in different ways singular events in millennia of Jewish history. This meant different things to my wife. Although Israel became precious to her, migration there was not an option. For me, a dangerous thought dawned from time to time: to be a diaspora Jew was to live on the periphery of modern Jewish history, and not at the place where Jewish continuity and the Jewish future would ultimately be determined. As best I could, I dismissed that thought.

But it did not die. From time to time—when our son was born, when our children started school, and when my wife's parents died—I would raise the idea of living in Israel, at least for a while, to see how it went, to stay or to go home, as we chose. We talked about it, but we did not go. We had several reasons: we had ageing families; we were too old to learn a new language; our kids would have to serve in the army.

In April 2007, I was about to leave Washington and full-time journalism to move on from Fairfax and *The Age*, where I had worked on and off for more than 35 years. I had managed to choose my time of leaving. Some doors had closed for me. Some I had closed. Doors close as you grow old. Possibilities become impossibilities, or so I thought.

My wife and I had loved Washington and America. I had written a book about my time as the Washington correspondent for *The Age* and *The Sydney Morning Herald*. The book, *An American Notebook: a personal and political journey*, was a sort of love letter to the America of my dreams—culturally and politically—when I was a young man. We were getting ready to go home. I had an offer from Melbourne University to set up a centre for journalism and to develop a master's degree. Along with other elite Australian universities, Melbourne had not offered degrees in journalism. Journalism had been considered a trade, not suitable for a degree at an elite university.

Then I got a call from the editorial director of Fairfax. Would I consider going to Israel as the correspondent for the Fairfax papers? The Middle East correspondent had resigned. If I wanted to go for a couple of years, he said he would try to make it happen.

I was surprised. I thought the editor of *The Age*, who had not wanted me to cover the Israeli elections the year before because I was Jewish, would not have loved having me as the Middle East correspondent. And I was about to leave full-time journalism, with no regrets. But when the tentative offer came, I saw it as a chance to keep doing the reporting work I loved — in Jerusalem, of all places!

For several days, we debated our choices. We wanted to be close to our children back in Melbourne, even if that was not necessarily what they wanted. We hoped to be there when they had children. We wanted to be grandparents, and to spend time with close relatives, some of them elderly. I had a sister who was close to eighty. Whenever I called, she told me it was time for us to come home.

But our talk was less about the present than about time passing and time past, and how, before we had gone to Israel with our two small children and had spent our days dazzled by this ancient place full of Jews of every conceivable ethnicity, neither of us had thought seriously about living there. My wife certainly had not. For most of our lives, neither of us had felt the pull of Eretz Yisrael, as my mother called it, often with tears in her eyes, because her sisters and her brother were there, and she knew she would not see them again.

But the offer of a posting to Israel had come too late. I knew that although I had loved journalism and being a reporter, I no longer had the heart and drive for it, not even in Jerusalem, in Israel. My wife and I stopped talking about living there. The time for doing that had well and truly passed.

What we both really wanted was to go home to Australia. But we had been changed, both of us, by living in Washington, with New York a train ride away. I can't wholly explain it, but there was something confronting and at times thrilling about living in the world's most powerful country, which happens to be home to half the world's Jews and in which Jews are prominent, sometimes singularly prominent — those Jewish intellectuals and writers, Jews in Hollywood, in music, and Jews who wrote some of the classics of American popular song.

Back in Australia, I went to work at the university. I wrote a column for the Fairfax papers. Each morning, I went for a walk with my dog along the beach near where we lived, and I wrote a daily blog about our walks that was published on the *Crikey* news website. Louise Adler, who was CEO of Melbourne University Publishing by this time, published a collection of my blog posts as a book. Its title was *Rocky and Gawenda: the story of a man and his mutt.* When I think about it now, it was a sort of memoir, but it was not the memoir of a Jew.

# CHAPTER FOURTEEN

# The long road to coming out

For a long time, I was sure that assimilation from generation to generation of we secular Jews would inexorably be linear. Each succeeding generation's inheritance would be a diluted sort of Jewishness, with the latest generation a pale imitation of Jews like their grandparents, who were secular but who were immersed in Jewish life, in its traditions, history, and language.

I was wrong. Nothing about history is inevitable. My children showed me the errors of my thinking. Over time, they concluded that their limited Jewish education had shut them off from any deep engagement with Judaism or with Israel, and they were not prepared to accept that being watered-down Jews was inevitable. They wanted more.

A decade or more ago, my daughter, my son, and my nephew formed a band, The Bashevis Singers, and recorded an album of classic Yiddish folk songs, ones they had learnt as small children. Their grandmothers and mothers had sung these songs to them. My daughter, son, and nephew kept their essence and made them into modern folk songs.

Then my son started studying Torah and Jewish mysticism. I listened to him, and I wondered whether I could travel part of the way with him. I thought I could. Nathan Wolski, his teacher, who lives in Melbourne, is one of the world's leading authorities on the Zohar, the primary text of Kabbalah — Jewish mysticism. Wolski loves Yiddish, and it was a love of Yiddish that first brought them together.

The Reb, as my children call him — short for Rebbe, the name the Hasidim give their revered rabbi — comes from a secular Bundist family. He loved the songs on the first Bashevis Singers album. He wanted to take them somewhere else with their music.

And so my children's Jewish journey has taken a new direction. Their grandparents were secular leftist Jews with a profound love of Yiddish and Yiddish secular culture. Their grandfathers — but not their grandmothers — had rejected Judaism. They were secular, democratic socialists. They opposed the rule of the rabbis in Jewish life, its obscurantism, and the passivity it created among the Jews, as if their suffering was God-ordained. These men were the children of the Jewish Enlightenment — the Haskalah — which began in the late eighteenth century in Germany and started to gain some traction in Eastern European Jewish society from the middle of the nineteenth century.

The Haskalah had two aims: to preserve the Jews as a separate, unique collective, and at the same time to integrate them into the wider communities and cultures in which they lived. One of the slogans of the early proponents of the Haskalah was 'A Jew at home, a German on the street'. In Germany, and in Western Europe generally, the Haskalah largely failed in its mission. There, it led to radical cultural assimilation and, frequently, to conversion. But in most of Eastern Europe, where the movement towards secularisation came later and was often expressed in the embrace of utopian political movements such as socialism, communism, and Zionism in place of religion, attachment to the idea of a distinct Jewish identity proved more tenacious. Nonetheless, preserving Jews as a unique group while at the same time freeing them from both forced and self-imposed isolation was a challenge wherever Jews lived.

What would they make of their grandchildren working with one of the world's leading authorities on the Jewish school of mysticism that had been a formative influence on Hasidism when it emerged in the eighteenth century? Apart from the Zohar, the Reb also teaches them about the Torah and the Talmud, because without studying these texts, the Zohar is inexplicable.

The Bashevis Singers have recorded two more albums. The first is a song cycle, a Holocaust liturgy based on the poems of a Yiddish poet, now little known, of the first half of the twentieth century. These songs are indescribably powerful, the music and melodies heartbreakingly beautiful. The poems, slightly edited to fit the structure of the songs, are a cycle of meditations and accusations about God and his absence while his people are being annihilated. The last song, though, describes a reconciliation between the poet, the accuser, and God. They are songs about life and death and faith, and about God's presence or absence in the world. It is in a Yiddish I never knew and that I am only slowly learning to understand. Rich with Hebrew and references to the Torah and the Kabbalah, it is difficult for someone like me, raised on the secularised Yiddish of the Bund. It was difficult for my children and nephew, too, but they are mastering it. The poems echo the dialogues and arguments between Jews and their God in the Talmud, and in some of the classics of Hebrew and Yiddish literature. The Bashevis Singers are reclaiming Yiddish as a sacred language for Jews who are neither Hasidim nor secular, left-wing non-Zionists.

The second album is a song cycle linking the major Jewish festivals. It is based on a popular guide to Judaism written in 1727 by the son of a rabbi in Frankfurt. The first edition of the guide had no music. In the second, the author included some rudimentary notations for melodies to go with the text. These are the earliest notations for any Yiddish music.

The Reb and The Bashevis Singers transformed these 300-year-old Yiddish texts into songs. They called the work *Soul Joy 1727*, the English translation of *Simkhes ha-Nefesh*, the Yiddish name for these texts. The music is modern, but the tunes are ancient. What is timeless about them is that the songs, based on the ancient texts, are an unchangeable guide to living a Jewish life, to the rituals, and to the meaning of the religious holidays, the holiness of Shabbes, and life and death in Judaism's teachings.

The early Modern Western Yiddish is almost impossible to understand at first—like Middle English—but the Reb has modernised the texts without losing their ancient resonances. The music echoes the singing of the Torah portions in the synagogue on Shabbes. It is not a secularised version of Judaism's most profound festivals. Instead, it reminds me of those afternoons sixty or more years ago when my father sat me down on Sunday afternoons to read the Tanach—the Hebrew Bible—in Yiddish with him.

The Reb had projects he had long wanted to do, and when he found The Bashevis Singers, he knew that he wanted them to work on these projects with him. He had the support of his university, and he had raised some money for recording. Through this work, the Reb introduced my children not just to the world of Jewish mysticism and Judaism, but to a Yiddish they had not heard or read before—to a non-secular Yiddish, to Yiddish as a holy language. Yiddish, the day-to-day language of the ultra-Orthodox, was also—and had always been—a holy language.

Israel looms larger in the lives of my children than it once did for me. My son went there, loved the place, went back, and went back again. His feeling deepened as his friendships and personal connections grew stronger. He is in Israel now, and I believe that at some stage he might live there for a while. My daughter has been just once. She will go again with her family, but in the meantime she has developed a regard for Israel that is a bit like mine. She has come to regard Israel as a vital part of the Jewish world.

At times, in the past, I had half-wished that my children would go to Israel and find their Jewish soulmates. They seemed not to be able to find them in Australia. But why the need for Jewish soulmates? It was and remains a mystery to me that I felt this way. Why did it matter? I was not my father and definitely not my mother, not the sort of Jew who had a soul-deep belief in the need for Jewish continuity. Close to half of Australian Jews who were not Orthodox — secular Jews, both Zionists and non-Zionists — had married out, and the rate of intermarriage was accelerating among Jews like me.

My daughter is in that near-half of non-Orthodox Jews who have non-Jewish partners. She and her partner, David, got together nine years ago. I call him by his name because I do not know how else to describe him — 'my daughter's partner' is a clumsy and distanced way of describing him, and we are not distanced. They are not married and, anyway, 'son-in-law' is too cold and legalistic a description for how I regard him. He is like a son to me.

David is not Jewish. I think that before he met my daughter he had known no Jews — not at school, or at university, or at work. When my daughter first told us that she loved this guy called David and that she thought he was the one, I felt overwhelmingly, wholeheartedly happy. No thought of my mother or father, even fleetingly, crossed my mind. The statistics about the accelerating rate of intermarriage never for a moment entered my head.

Later, I did think about my mother and father, and felt that I had probably been right when I had said that if we really wanted our kids to marry Jews, we had to go to live in Israel. But after a very short time, on the rare occasions when I thought about these things, it felt as if these once urgent questions were irrelevant. My daughter and David were together, and, as far as I could tell, happy together. David is my grandson's dad and, as a result, David and I, no matter what might happen, are forever connected. We are family.

And this rendered almost meaningless every question, doubt, or feeling of trepidation I once had about my children having non-Jewish partners. But it was meaningful as well, because there was a Jewish problem. Some of this is trivial: our family is rather loud, and we tend to talk over each other and anyone else who might be in the vicinity. I am not saying this is invariably a Jewish thing, but it is undeniable that such behaviour is common in Jewish families. David has learnt to speak louder than he used to, but he is a quietly spoken person, and I do not believe he will ever acquire the loudness of voice he needs to match us. I can't be sure, but he seems relaxed about this. Sometimes I look at him, and he is smiling — enjoying himself, I think.

My daughter and David say that they have worked out what the Jewish problem means for them. My daughter is more deeply immersed in Jewishness than I once was. She is a Zionist. She does not consider herself secular; rather, she is travelling down a road alongside Judaism, and one day, perhaps, Judaism might be even closer to her in her travels than it is now. David is there with her. They are not on the same road, but they are travelling together.

David's son is a Jew, according to Halacha, Jewish law, because his mother is Jewish. David has agreed that his son will be raised a Jew. And David knows, because we have talked about this from time to time, that in Jewish history, even recent history, and even now, being a Jew brings consequences, not all of them pleasant. His son had a bris—he was circumcised—eight days after he was born, and he will have a bar mitzvah, when he will be called to the Torah and will recite his Torah portion.

My grandson goes to Sholem Aleichem primary school in Melbourne, just as his mother and uncle did. He loves Yiddish and Hebrew. On Friday mornings, the school has a secular Shabbes ceremony, with challah (braided egg loaf eaten on the Sabbath), and candles, and Shabbes songs in Yiddish. In the evening, we also have challah and candles, and my son and daughter and grandson say the Shabbes prayers. In recent times, David has said one of the prayers.

This may sound like secular Jews doing a kitsch performance of the rituals of Judaism—pop Judaism, all surface and not much substance. I accept there is some truth in this, but it is not the whole story. David has been reading what I am writing here, chapter by chapter, as have my wife and children. I wanted them to come with me because they are part of it, and I did not want them to be surprised and shocked—or, worse, dismayed—by my Jewish story, in which they play such a large part. And, frankly, it is a way for me to overcome fear, which, if a writer gives in to, renders the work seriously flawed because the writing has an empty centre, with punches being pulled, and difficult and painful things avoided. Often, this fear is about hurting and even betraying people you love.

A few days ago, we all met to talk about what I had written about them. I wanted to know how each of them felt, but it was David who I was most worried about, because I thought what

I was writing might feel to him like a forced 'coming out'. But that was not how he felt. He told me that he and my daughter had long wanted to get married, but that they wanted to get married under a chuppah (a Jewish wedding canopy) with a rabbi officiating, and they understood that this might not be possible. Then he said that he felt part of the Jewish family, of our Jewish family. He wanted to learn more Yiddish, and to learn about Judaism. He said he was not a religious person, but if he had to convert to Judaism in order to marry my daughter under a chuppah, he would consider it. After all, he felt Jewish.

Who is a Jew? This question has become personal for me. It is personal because David is asking it, and because my son might one day have a non-Jewish partner, and therefore, according to some Jews—and non-Jews, for that matter—he will have non-Jewish children. This matters to him. It matters to me, too.

Who is a Jew? There is no single, universally agreed answer to this question. For millennia, it has been a question that anti-Semites, including eliminationist anti-Semites, have thought it vital to answer. The business of non-Jews deciding who is and is not a Jew has a long and often violent history. Over centuries, anti-Semites have answered the question of who is a Jew in various ways, none of them good for the Jews.

The Jews were the people who rejected Christ as the Son of God and murdered him. They were Christ killers, and later they were said to be ritual slaughterers of children as well. They were God-forsaken, because they had forsaken God. That was the agreed definition for centuries. In the nineteenth century, when race theories were considered a promising development in science, Jews were suddenly a race—simultaneously an inferior and superior race. This 'scientific thesis' was eagerly embraced by anti-Semites in Europe and even in the United States, and we know what that led to in the twentieth century.

The anti-Semites of the revolutionary left, from the nineteenth century and into the twentieth century, defined Jews as quintessentially capitalist oppressors of the working class. Marx was the first to offer up this answer to who is a Jew, and he has had a long list of successors, as you would expect. Theological and race-based anti-Semitism existed side by side, and they are still relatively common.

It is not only anti-Semites who are in the business of deciding who is and is not a Jew. Increasingly, anti-Zionists—some of them Jews—have taken on the role of deciding just what an 'authentic' Jew might be. According to anti-Zionists, authentic Jews do not feel part of the Jewish people, or believe the Jews are a nation. They do not believe that the Jews have deep and long connections to the land of Israel—not just biblical connections, but historical connections established by historians and archaeologists. And they do not feel that their identity as Jews inextricably involves a special regard for and connection to Israel.

Taken together, this list means that, according to most anti-Zionists, the vast majority of the world's Jews are not authentic Jews at all. They have 'invented' their history: they have created the fiction of Jewish nationhood or peoplehood, and they have constructed for themselves an identity based on a falsehood that Jews have a long and deep connection with Eretz Yisrael. I am not suggesting that all anti-Zionists who buy this are anti-Semites, or even fellow travellers with anti-Semites. But the possibility of anti-Semitism in this anti-Zionist definition of authentic Jews is surely there.

And how do Jews define themselves? Before the Jewish Enlightenment and the subsequent rise of Jewish secularism and nationalism, the rabbis, interpreting Halacha, decided who was a Jew. There was no controversy: a Jew was someone who had a Jewish mother. The Orthodox and ultra-Orthodox have not wavered from this belief: a child born of a Jewish mother is a Jew. And who is a Jewish mother? Answer: a woman whose mother is Jewish. So what does being Jewish mean in this context for Orthodox Jews? It means that the child's mother was born of a woman who the Orthodox considered Jewish, or of a woman who went through an Orthodox conversion. It all sounds tautological, a sort of closed circle, and so it is.

For ultra-Orthodox and most mainstream Orthodox Jews, Progressive Judaism is not Judaism at all. They do not recognise Progressive marriage ceremonies or Progressive-ordained rabbis, or any convert to Judaism who has gone through a conversion process supervised by a Progressive rabbi. The trouble is that the majority of the world's Jews — most of all in America and Israel — are not ultra-Orthodox or Orthodox, and do not accept the old — in many ways, pre-Enlightenment — definition of Jewishness. Most Jews in Israel are secular. In America, most Jews are either secular or adherents of Reform/Progressive Judaism.

Who is a Jew under Israel's Law of Return, which gives Jews who make aliyah the automatic right to citizenship? The Law of Return is in many ways central to Zionism and Israel's raison d'être as both a safe haven for Jews fleeing persecution and as the only place on Earth that grants not only entry but citizenship to all Jews who want to live in the Jewish nation-state.

The answer to who is a Jew under the Law of Return has evolved since Israel was established in 1948, but the answer has never been based on the rulings of the ultra-Orthodox and the Orthodox rabbis. At different times and for different reasons, the Law of Return has had to redefine who was a Jew in order to recognise the realities of the worlds from which Jews came to Israel.

For example, it was impossible to use the traditional Orthodox definition of Jewishness when it came to the great mass migration to Israel in the 1980s and 1990s from the Soviet Union. The million or so Jews who made aliyah were highly assimilated, an assimilation that the Soviet Union basically forced on them. They had no proof of their Jewish ancestry, no knowledge of Judaism, no sense of themselves as Jews. The Law of Return was adjusted so that those Soviet Jews who had one Jewish grandparent could make aliyah. If they did not have documentary proof of their Jewish antecedents, they were taken at their word. They were Jews. That definition of who is a Jew—a person having one Jewish grandparent—applies to everyone wishing to make aliyah, as it must.

But once in, you will discover that, while you are a Jew under the Law of Return, you are no Jew at all according to the Orthodox rabbinate. In a state where there is no civil marriage or divorce, Jews who are not accepted as Jews cannot marry in Israel, according to the rabbis. Many thousands of Soviet Jews have gone to Cyprus to get married. While the rabbis do not recognise these marriages, the state does, as it must under international law. The suffering caused by this contradiction is immense, and has continued from generation to generation. The rift between America's Reform/Progressive Jews and the Orthodox rabbinates in America and Israel grows ever deeper and more bitter. We Jews, I sometimes feel, don't know who we are.

David, it seems to me, does know who he is. He feels Jewish, part of the Jewish family and of a particular Jewish family. These feelings are based on the realities of his life and his embrace of us, and on the fact that he has a Jewish child. He might well go through a conversion, although if he thinks that will make him a Jew for all Jews, he will be disappointed.

For me, David has embraced the Jewish people and he is,

as a result, part of the Jewish people. He has taken to Yiddish, and he has embraced the Shabbes prayers and songs we perform each week. His son is not just halachically Jewish but goes to a Jewish school, and David, inevitably, has developed relationships with some of the parents. He feels part of the school community—a community mainly of Jews. Where he might go in future, I of course don't know, nor do I have a say in it. What I do know is that David is like a son to me, and I am a Jewish father.

That is not the end of this question of what it means to be a Jew, because neither the enemies of the Jews nor the Jews themselves can say with one voice who they regard as real Jews and imposter Jews. It is not the end of it for me. For a long time, like the Tunisian-born writer and intellectual Albert Memmi, I believed that being a Jew was my fate; I had not chosen to be a Jew. That is less and less the case for many Jews who are choosing to be Jews, either through converting to Judaism, or, like David, feeling that they belong to the Jewish people. In time, both for the enemies of the Jews and for most non-Orthodox Jews, this sense of belonging to the Jewish people might be enough to make someone like David a Jew.

But what does a sense of belonging mean? To be a Jew must mean taking on the burdens of being a Jew—burdens that so many Jews have rejected over the centuries by converting to Christianity, or by hiding their Jewishness from the people among whom they lived and from their own children. It must entail a sense of connection with Jewish history because, in many ways, Jews have always lived their history as if the past is always present. Perhaps controversially, it must mean a desire to somehow connect with Judaism, although I am not at all sure what form that may take. David will decide what form it takes for him.

So it is not an easy path that David is moving down. In a sense, I am travelling with him, but I do not have answers to the questions I am asking myself. Why, for instance, given that I reject the Orthodox definition of who is a Jew—a person with a halachically Jewish mother—do I hope that my son marries a Jewish woman, not a woman who feels Jewish, but a woman who was born Jewish or has converted? Is it because there would be no question that their children would be Jews? Unlike my daughter, my son would not, in the eyes of many Jews, have Jewish children if he married a non-Jewish woman.

This raises the question of why I want Jewish grandchildren at all. Why does it matter to me that my grandchildren are Jews in the eyes of non-Jews and Jews alike? I have no easy answer, but I can try a rational answer, which begins with the fact that I am a child of Holocaust survivors. Many survivors determined that it was best to essentially stop being Jews—the pain they had suffered for being Jews was too great to bear. For example, the late Madeleine Albright, the former US secretary of state, did not discover that she was a Jew until very late in life. Her parents had hidden it from her, pretended they were not Jews. Most of her family, she discovered, had been murdered in the Holocaust. This practice of Jews being forced to relinquish their Jewishness, or voluntarily relinquishing it, is as old as Jewish history. Some of the major thinkers on the left—from Marx onwards—advocated for the end of Jewish particularity. Jewish intellectuals such as Arthur Koestler, the author of *Darkness at Noon*, predicted and hoped that, in time, the Jews of the diaspora would disappear and that the only Jews left would be the Jews in Israel.

My parents went the other way. They were passionately determined not to give Hitler the victory over the Jews that he had not quite achieved through mass murder and attempted genocide. We Jews lived! We Jews had survived! It was our duty to ensure that our children and grandchildren would be Jews, and that there were no weak links in *di goldene keyt*, the golden chain that bound Jews together over time and space. That's what my parents lived and believed and yearned for. It is part of who I am.

But even that does not wholly explain why Jewish continuity matters to me, for my children and grandchildren. Even after all this time, I have only vague answers to these questions. I think the Jews are an extraordinary people. Their longevity, their survival and flourishing, despite the discrimination and murderous violence they have suffered, their determination not to be victims, their outsized contribution—for they are a tiny piece of humanity—to every facet of human life feels to me like a burden and a cause for celebration. I do not want *di goldene keyt* to be broken. I do not want the Jewish people to disappear. I want my grandchildren to know and to sing the Yiddish songs that my parents sang to me and that I sang to my children. These are more than songs. They are our history singing. I want my grandchildren to be Jews, with all the burdens and gifts that being Jews will confer on them.

I feel all this, even though we live in a time of confusion about who is a Jew. It is obvious and true that the Orthodox definition of a Jew is unsustainable, yet it remains powerful because, amid all the confusion, there is no argument—from Jews or non-Jews—that a child with a Jewish mother is Jewish. There is no other agreed definition. I believe that will change in time. It is already changing.

In old age, I am a Jew in transition. For most of my life, the question of who is a Jew, how that is decided, and by whom did not concern me much. It concerns me now because it matters to my children, and it matters to David, my halachically non-

Jewish son, and it will matter to his son when he grows up, and it will matter to my grandchildren and the children that my son might have.

It is true that, from time to time, I had been forced to ask myself what it meant, in my public life as a writer and editor, to be a Jew. Mostly, this was because, every now and then, as I've written above, non-Jews attributed Jewish motives to my reporting on anything that involved Jews — ranging from business to the conflict between Israel and the Palestinians, and the coverage of these Jewish-related issues when I was the editor of *The Age*. I do not wish to overstate this. It did not happen often, and most of the time it did not cause me much concern. It certainly did not cause me to think much about these things I am thinking about now — about my Jewish history, about Jewish continuity and why it matters to me, about Israel's meaning for Jews like me, and about how I can reconcile the fact that I am a Jew of the left with what I see as the growing hostility among many of my fellow leftists to Jews.

There is a question some Jewish friends ask me. How can I remain a left-wing Jew when my comrades — well, many of them, anyway — would denounce me and call me a traitor to all the good things the left stands for if they knew how I felt about Israel?

Some add that, sooner or later, I will see that my leftism, if I am honest about the sort of Jew I am, is unsustainable; to them, I am headed, inevitably, to formally declaring my apostasy and joining the growing number of Jews who were once of the left but are now unequivocally of the right. What this means, I think, is that they have had some sort of 'awakening', where they have come to believe that if the left is, at the very least, hostile to Jews, if not anti-Semitic, then the left must be wrong about everything else it has advocated for. People like this, such as David Mamet, may even become supporters of Donald Trump. I think this move to the right by formerly left-leaning Jews is more common in America than it is in Australia.

There is force to their argument; but, in essence, it is an argument that is grounded in identity politics: we vote our identity. Identity politics maintains that what defines you, what makes you who you are, is your ethnicity or gender or race, and whether your identity group is a victim or oppressor. Identity politics is the antithesis of those values and beliefs that I was taught and mainly still believe, which define what it means to be on the left.

I do not believe I will join the right-leaning army of formerly leftist Jews. I have lived my public and my private life with values and an understanding of the world that I first learned from my father when I was a child, and at Skif, where my mentors, more than my school and university teachers, taught me to think, and connected me to the human condition. Those values and that connection with the world remains. In that sense, I remain a universalist Jew. I am immersed in Australian culture, involved in its politics and in its intellectual life. I am an Australian journalist and writer.

But I am also on a Jewish journey. I am searching through my past, and the past of the Jews, for things that might explain how I have ended up here and where I might be going. When I interviewed Noel Pearson, the Indigenous leader and activist, for *The Powerbroker*, he said that he believed Indigenous people could learn from the way that Jews have managed to be wholly involved in the community, in Australian life, across politics and culture and the law, and, at the same time, inhabit their Jewishness, live a Jewish life, and work for Jewish continuity. That is what he wants for Indigenous Australians.

I think Pearson is on to something. I believe there is such

a thing as universal values. I believe in our shared humanity. I am, like Pearson, fully involved in Australian life. I am an Australian. But in this era of identity politics, where ethnicity, gender, and race have become the key determinants of who we are, this search of mine for the Jew I am and might become could be misconstrued. I do not believe that being a Jew will ever encompass all that I am and all that I believe. Identity politics represents a denial of our shared humanity, of what human beings have in common. No matter where this journey leads, it will not be to a place where being a Jew explains all my beliefs and values. It can never wholly—or even mostly—define who I am.

# CHAPTER FIFTEEN
# A Jew in full

I am not sure when I began asking myself, 'What kind of Jew am I?' Was it a decade ago, when anti-Semitism was once again leading to the murder of Jews in Europe? When Jews were being killed by Islamists who were not called out by the left for their anti-Semitism—in particular because this racist violence was being carried out by people who were not white, who were themselves 'victims of colonialism and of Islamophobia'? Did the question become more urgent and time-consuming when the evidence was overwhelming that anti-Semitism was on the rise, not just in Europe, but in America, Canada, and Australia—and not just neo-Nazi and extreme-right anti-Semitism, but anti-Semitism on the left, which concerned me most because I was a left-wing Jew? Did this journey become inevitable when the idea that Zionism was evil and that Israel was its racist, colonialist, apartheid child became the agreed ideology of significant sections of the left?

All these questions took me down the path I am on and prompted me to write this book. But, looking back, I can see that I was in search of Jewish meaning before I asked myself any of these questions. I think I started down this path when my daughter was born, and I came to realise that I had very little to pass on to my children about being a Jew. What connected me with the Jewish people? What would connect my daughter to the Jewish people, and would she even want that connection? My parents and my wife's parents never needed to ask these questions. They would pass on to us their kind of Jewishness, deeply connected to the Jewish people through Yiddish language and culture, and a knowledge of Jewish history, even of Judaism. They wanted their children and grandchildren to be Jews and to play their part in ensuring Jewish continuity.

They could pass on the rich and living Jewishness that they had brought with them to Australia from Poland. But Jews in Australia did not live in separate streets and neighbourhoods from non-Jews while they grew up with Yiddish as their primary language. My mother, born and raised in Lodz, could not speak Polish. My father could speak Polish, but Yiddish was his first language, and he lived in Yiddish literature and culture. It was only possible to be the sort of Jews they were in a place where they did not feel like — and were not regarded as — 'true' Poles. They were a singular generation of secular Jews, but their Jewishness was not, could not be, passed on to their children in Australia. I was not a Jew like my parents, and it dawned on me that my daughter would be even further removed from the sort of Jews her grandparents had been.

For a long time, I had thought that only in Israel could our children live a substantial Jewish life. Only in Israel was it almost certain that they would marry Jews, fulfilling the wishes of their grandparents that they play their part in fostering Jewish continuity. That never happened.

Instead, we sent our children to Sholem Aleichem College, where our grandson is now a student. My wife and I had been students at Sholem Aleichem when it was a Sunday school. Our connection to the place goes back seventy years or so. Through school and through their grandparents and my wife, our children developed a love of Yiddish and particularly of Yiddish song. They are professional musicians, and so this love of Yiddish and Yiddish music was a gateway to a sense of themselves as Jews that transcended what they had received from us.

To some extent, they took me on their journey. One day in July 2012, I was sitting in front of my computer. I was not 'busy'. For the first time in many decades, I could sit in an armchair in the afternoon and read a book, and then I would stop reading and let my mind wander in daydreams.

Suddenly, I started to write something in transliterated Yiddish. One sentence came and another, and soon I had what appeared to be a poem. I was puzzled and surprised. I saw that my Yiddish, which I had not spoken or read for decades, was pretty good. There were words in these lines I did not recall ever knowing. I had been possessed, I realised, by some long-dead Yiddish poet, or by a *dybbuk*—a good one, not the bad dybbuk of classic Yiddish literature.

In the months that followed, I wrote more Yiddish poems. Or, rather, that dead Yiddish poet seemed to be writing them. Some were published in a Yiddish magazine in America.

In the middle of all this, by sheer coincidence, I was asked to be part of a theatre production that involved four writers writing a piece that had a dybbuk in it. My long-dead poet! My dybbuk! Here is what I wrote. A lot of it actually happened to me:

### The Poet on the Windowsill

It is not a dream.

Sometimes at night, I do dream, and on rare occasions, I remember my dreams. My mother and father are not in these dreams. I do not much dream in the past.

It is late afternoon, and I have already had those fifteen

minutes or so when the book I am reading falls against my chest and, drifting, my eyes half open, I travel through endless, gently swirling space.

The sun has dispersed the clouds, and through the venetian blinds come thin rectangles of light. Rocky lies on the couch next to my desk. He is always there when I write. He is at peace with the world as long as he hears my voice from time to time and the tapping of my fingers on the keyboard.

For a while, I have been trying to write something, but I am not sure what it is. I try to sit with the writing an hour at a time, but I do not always succeed, and when I get up too abruptly, Rocky growls as if he is admonishing me. When I ignore him and go down the stairs, he howls as if I have abandoned him and all our hopes.

I go downstairs on this late afternoon and make myself another cup of tea. When I come back, Rocky is sitting beside the desk, as if he is volunteering to take over the writing from me. I often wonder whether he understands what I am saying, sitting there trying out sentences, words, different punctuation. I conclude that he understands everything.

It has been a reasonable day. I have written two hundred words, and I still have two hours to go. If I could stay there for another two hours, I will get to five hundred words, my daily quota.

My fingers become more emphatic. This sentence is good. It consists of three clauses that flow into each other, as if they had always been joined. One of my shortcomings is that there are too many sentences with the same rhythm and structure — short sentences of no more than two clauses. I was a journalist for too long. For too long, clarity had been everything.

It is not a dream.

The sun is beginning to go down behind the block of flats across the road. The light has not yet begun to fade. In the park, a woman comes along the gravel path. When the sun had started its descent, I had pulled open the blind on the window that overlooked the park.

The woman is coming towards me. I see that she is old. Her dull grey hair falls around her shoulders as if dragged down by gravity. She has a thin face. She wears a floral-patterned, shapeless light-blue dress, and she has on a pair of black sandals. Her toes are familiar. They are a mother's toes. As she comes closer, I see that inside the string bag she is carrying, a live chicken is flapping its wings in anguish. She has been to the market to buy a chicken that will be slaughtered for the Sabbath meal tonight.

When I look away from her for a moment, I see that the words on my screen have vanished. The good sentence, the one of three well-connected clauses, is gone.

The screen is blank. The cursor sits at the top, flashing on and off, proclaiming its innocence. I look back towards the park, to the gravely path. She, too, has vanished, the old woman with the thin face. Gone. There is no sign of her, or of her anguished chicken.

The sun is now hidden behind the roof of the flats. The thin rectangles of light have merged into each other and have become a shapeless softening glow.

Words suddenly appear on the screen, the cursor moving with certainty, words not in sentences but in short lines, the word of each new line capitalised, though there is no full stop anywhere, nor a comma, for that matter, short lines — sometimes just a word or two to a line hanging there, alone, brave, forthright, in no need of comfort or wordy companionship.

In the formless light, the poet sits outside my window on the narrow window ledge, so close that I can see the shape of the tear in his left eye, a round and shining translucent tear, like a bubble that floated out of the bubble-maker I had when I was a boy.

He has hold of the anguished chicken in his right hand, but now the bird is calm, its wings folded neatly in on either side of its body, its head resting on the shoulder of the poet's white, collarless shirt. This is a shirt that was much in favour in the 1960s and thirty years earlier, in Poland and Russia, in the Pale of Settlement. Shirts like his, made of rough woven cotton, were worn by Yiddish poets and musicians and the great Yiddish novelists.

The poet has a crown of white feathers on his tightly curled black hair, and he is holding a battered guitar. For a moment, I think that he looks more 1960s Nimbin than 1930s Warsaw. But there is something about him, the tear in his left eye, his trembling lips, the chicken resting its head on his shoulder, and, above all, the notebook that he holds in his left hand with its grey food-stained cover and yellowed pages, that dispel the thought that he is from the north coast of New South Wales.

On the yellowed page that he holds up to me, pressing it against the window, words are written in black ink, in lines of identical length, the words arranged from right to left. It is a poem. A poem, I see, written in letters, as old as any memory, so ancient that I cannot read a single word.

Then the tear floats from his eye and, taken by the wind, I suppose, drifts towards the flats, up over the roof and then down it goes towards the setting sun. He looks at me for a moment. The sadness leaves his face. The letters on the page that he holds pressed against the window escape from the page and drift upwards. Upwards go the letters, in formation, the lines intact, up towards the darkening sky. I watch them disappear into space.

When I look back at the window ledge, he is gone. On the window ledge, there are now four grey-and-white feathers, and beside the feathers a pigeon squats in arrogant indifference.

It is a gentile pigeon. I see that it is T.S. Eliot. The pigeon recites these lines in a thin, unemotional voice:

> And the Jew squats on the windowsill, the owner,
> Spawned in some estaminet of Antwerp,
> Blistered in Brussels, patched and peeled in London.

These lines destroyed me when I was still young. He had thrilled me, the poet, filled me. But when I read those lines, I gave up poetry. I became a journalist.

And the Jew squats ... But the poet is gone from my windowsill. No trace of him but the four feathers remains. The feathers lie still beside the oblivious pigeon. Nor on the pane of glass is there any sign left of the page of the notebook that the Yiddish poet had pressed against it.

I see the words on the computer screen. The lines are even, like the ones that floated away from the yellowing page of his notebook. The words are in English letters, but this is not English.

Rocky leaps into my lap. His head is cocked to the side in puzzlement. The meaning of the words come to me in a rush. I recite them out loud. These words, these lines, have the rhythm of a forgotten prayer.

The Yiddish poet never did return to my window ledge. The beautiful Yiddish letters that had drifted off the yellowing page of his notebook into distant space did not return.

But every morning in the days and weeks that followed, uneven lines of Yiddish words written in English letters appeared on the computer screen. They were the poet's words. They were words and lines he had left unfinished when he went to his death.

Sometimes, when the words appear on the screen, I see his face in the windowpane, smiling and dancing, singing in the sunlight of early morning. I can hear our song.

When I performed this piece in the theatre, my son had by then put one of my poems to music. He sang it when I finished reading. When he wrote the music to my poem and played it for me, it felt as if some sort of bond had formed between us — me, the Jewish poet possessed by that dead Yiddish poet, and him, the Jewish composer, possessed by Yiddish songwriters and composers, and by his Yiddish ancestry. He said that the music wrote itself in a matter of minutes, without any conscious effort by him. Here are the lyrics, which, alone without the music, do not do justice to the song:

**A Song For You**
A song for you, my father dear
In Yiddish long gone for me.
But in my heart you are there,
In Yiddish.
A song from my memory,
With you in my childhood years.

And you, my mother dear,
Lonely and alone in the past,
Long gone.

When I had only one word in Yiddish,
One word,
*Mumele, mumele, mumele*
That was enough for me,
That was enough for you,
My mother dear.

For both of you, my father and my mother,
A song in Yiddish
About an ache without words,
In an orphaned language.
A song about grief,
A song about wonder,
A song about childhood years
Long gone.
In broken words, in Yiddish,
My heart melts with longing

Father dear and mother dear,
Listen.
The children are singing your song.
Your children,
My children.
The children are singing
With joy for all
I thought was gone.

For you a song, my father dear.
For you a word, my mother dear.
The children sing,
The children sing,
The children sing

About all that disappeared
And yet somehow remained.

Most of my poems were limited by the relative poverty of my Yiddish, which had been my first language but which I had not spoken for decades. The song my son performed in the theatre, *Far Dir A Lid (A Song For You)*, and another of my poems that he put to music, are on the first Bashevis Singers album. My children's grandparents would have loved these songs. They are in the tradition of old Yiddish folk songs — they are about a time that has vanished, about memory, and about family.

I am not the Jew my parents were. I am not a Bundist, and I do not believe that some knowledge of Yiddish language and Yiddish literature will be at the centre of any sort of Jewish life in places like Australia. I do not believe that an attachment to Israel, no matter how deeply felt, will be a path to Jewish continuity or to any sort of substantial Jewish life in the diaspora. Haredi Jews do not wrestle with these questions. Nor do modern Orthodox Jews. But I will not become a Haredi Jew, nor am I likely to join the modern Orthodox. And I find the Progressive Jews too much a sort of washed-out, pale, even Christianised sort of Judaism, although this may be no more than a prejudice passed on to me by my parents.

But in some mysterious, inexplicable way — inexplicable to me, anyway — Judaism beckons me, summons me. I think of Avram Zeleznikow, the Bundist leader who was a partisan during the war and who was my Jewish history teacher at Sholem Aleichem Sunday school. Avram ran the Scheherazade café in bayside St Kilda for three decades, from the 1950s to the 1980s, by which time it was the go-to place for people who wanted authentic Eastern European Jewish food. In its heyday, it was a meeting place for Yiddish-speaking Holocaust survivors who gathered on Sunday mornings. Their arguments in Yiddish could be heard along the length and breadth of Acland Street, which was full of delicatessens and cake shops and cafés catering to the post-war Yiddish-speaking Jews, many of them Holocaust survivors, who had managed to be given papers to come to Australia.

A few years before he died in 2013, Avram would take his twelve-year-old grandson every Shabbes morning to a synagogue. His grandson was preparing for his bar mitzvah, and sat in the front pews. Avram would sit in the back pews and listen in silence to the service. The son of a Bundist leader in Lithuania before the war, Avram had never had a bar mitzvah, and had hardly any knowledge or experience of Judaism. He had hardly ever been in a synagogue. What was he thinking, sitting there in the back pews every Shabbes morning in silence? He never spoke about it to me, but he told a friend of mine—a friend who had taken him to the synagogue when Avram first decided to go with his grandson—that he felt a connection to the Jewish people there that he had not felt before and that he could not describe in words.

A path into Judaism. I have been thinking of reading the Tanach in Yiddish with my wife's help, because her Yiddish is much better than mine. Perhaps I will, with her guidance, read some of the classics of Yiddish literature, the novels and poetry our parents loved. Perhaps I will, one day, sitting at my desk, be again possessed by that dead Yiddish poet and write poetry in Yiddish again, in that orphaned language—orphaned because millions who spoke it and wrote in it and lived in it were murdered by the Nazis—the language that my children have adopted.

In the past, I never counted the days and months according to the Hebrew calendar, but now I do every now and then.

Today is the last day of winter: the fourth Day of Elul, 5782, according to the Jewish calendar. The High Holidays are just weeks away. On Rosh Hashanah, the Jewish new year, the synagogue where my mother sent me after school to learn to recite the prayers more than sixty years ago, will be packed with worshippers. A week or so later, the synagogue will be packed again for Kol Nidre, the prayer that is sung before the evening service that ushers in Yom Kippur, the Day of Atonement. My father the atheist loved Kol Nidre. He had recordings of several versions of it, sung by his favourite cantors.

The next morning, there will be the Yizkor service, when dead parents are honoured and remembered. In the Orthodox tradition, only orphans can attend this service. I am eligible.

I have not been in a synagogue for Rosh Hashanah or Yom Kippur for a very long time. I might go this year for Kol Nidre and for the Yizkor service. Perhaps I will fast on Yom Kippur, because how could I go to Yizkor without having fasted? But which synagogue will I go to?

I remember my mother, and how determinedly she sent me to after-school classes at the Caulfield synagogue, the shul my sisters took me to for the Yizkor service after my mother died. Every day, my eldest sister walked me to the kindergarten at the shul in the first weeks after we arrived in Australia. I may find it impossible, given how long it has been, to reconnect with the place. Perhaps the whole idea is fanciful, a sort of fever dream. But that's where I'll go. I will just listen and sit with other Jews who will mostly be strangers to me. Perhaps my mother will come and sit beside me. Perhaps, some way or other, she will be there with me.

# Acknowledgements

When I started this book, I wondered whether it would ever be published. It is a challenging book. It was challenging to write, and I am pretty sure it will be challenging for some people to read. When I sent the draft manuscript to Henry Rosenbloom, Scribe's founder and publisher, he got back to me within a couple of days to say he would publish the book. Through the months of editing and rewriting, he has been forthright, committed, encouraging, and supportive. Henry treated my manuscript with such great care and attention to detail. Working with him — and I have been a writer and editor for a long time — was a great learning experience about editing and about how a good editor can immeasurably improve a piece of writing. I am deeply grateful.

My friend James Button, a fellow toiler in journalism, and a very fine editor and writer, was there for me from the beginning, when I first conceived this book. He talked me through the problems I had, and helped shape the narrative form the book would take. He edited early drafts, suggested changes, and encouraged me to keep going when I felt downhearted. I do not believe this book would have happened without him.

My family were with me on this journey. My children read drafts, they suggested changes, and were always supportive.

My wife, Anne, read and edited every draft. She is a tough editor. She has put up with a lot of grumbling from me as a result.

There were friends—journalists and writers—whom I talked to and listened to during the time it took me to write this book. They were always up for listening, and always honest with their responses.

I should add that there are a number of translations from the German of the letters between Gershom Scholem and Hannah Arendt quoted in this book. The translations I have used accord most closely with the original German, which is in the collection of the Arendt papers at the Library of Congress in Washington, DC.

# Index